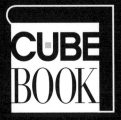

# THE INCREDIBLE

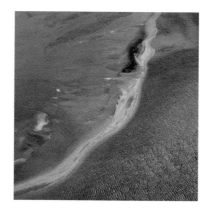

# EARTH

D&C
David and Charles

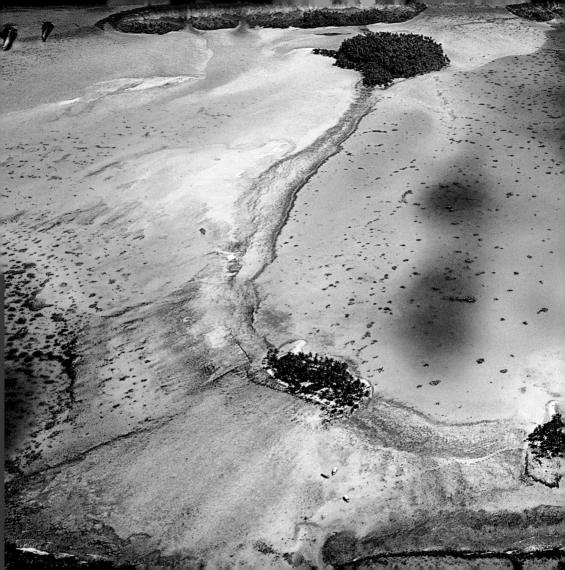

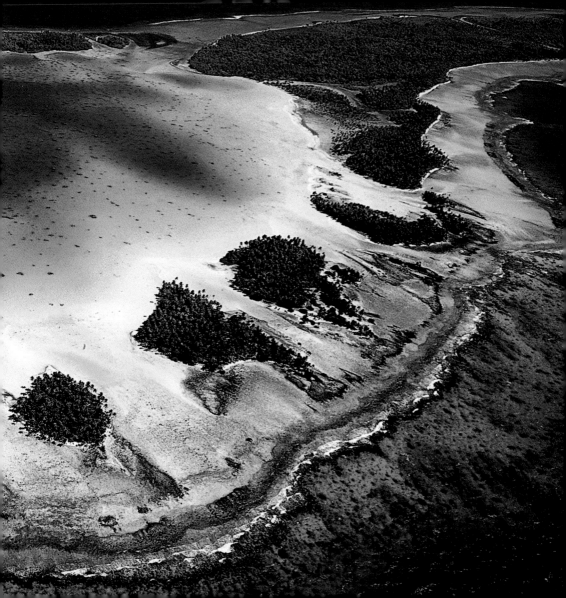

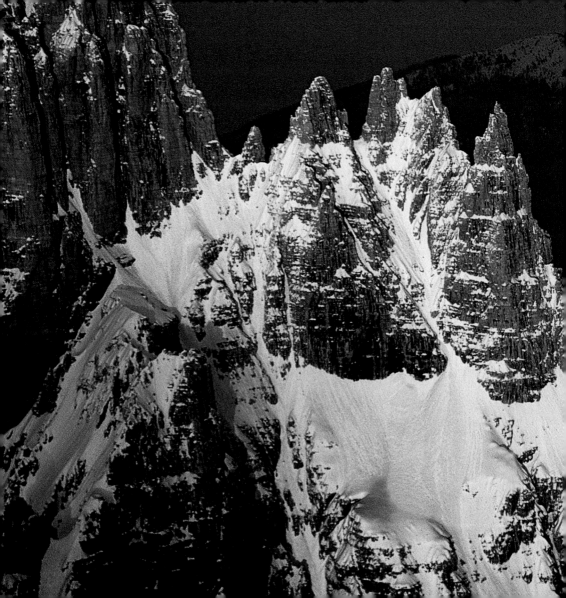

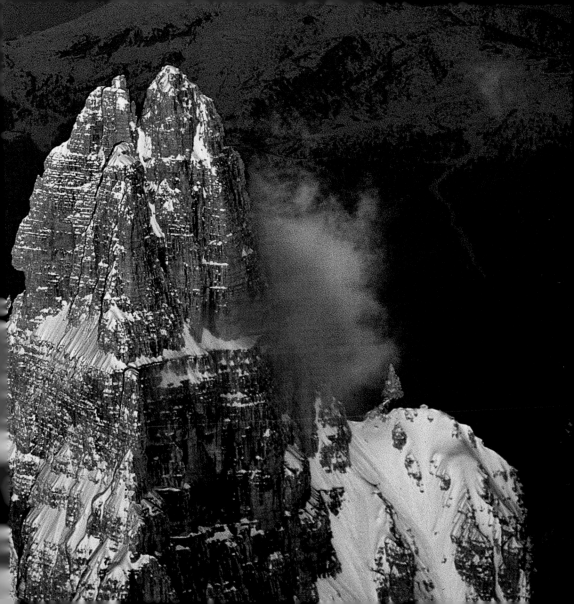

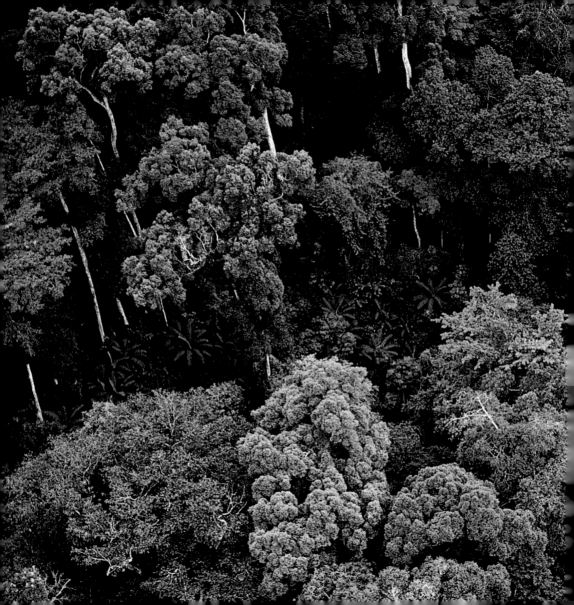

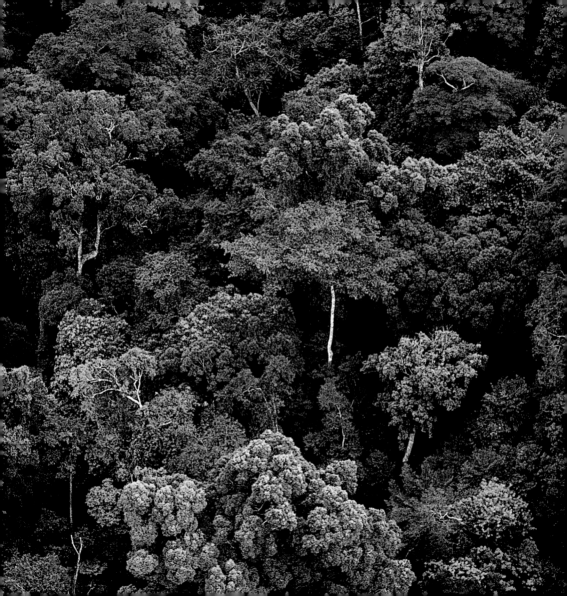

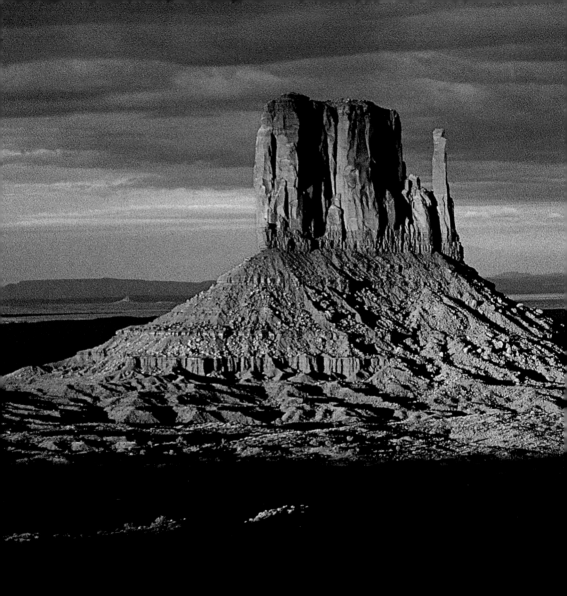

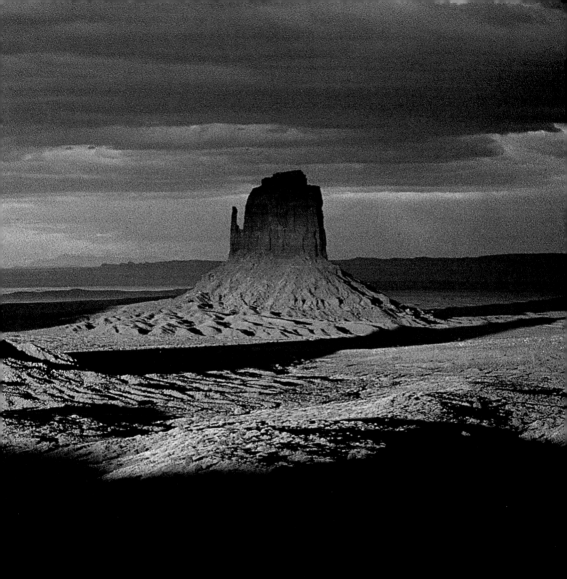

**EDITED BY**

VALERIA MANFERTO DE FABIANIS

**text by**

ALBERTO BERTOLAZZI

**graphic design**

CLARA ZANOTTI

**graphic layout**

MARIA CUCCHI

**translation**

text: RICHARD PIERCE

captions: TIMOTHY STROUD

**A DAVID & CHARLES BOOK**
F&W Media International LTD 2011

David & Charles is an imprint of F&W Media International, LTD
Brunel House, Forde Close, Newton Abbot, TQ12 4PU, UK

F&W Media International, LTD is a subsidiary of F+W Media,
Inc., 4700 East Galbraith Road, Cincinnati OH45236, USA

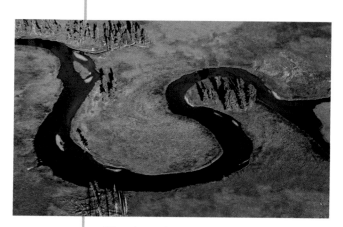

● Wyoming (USA) - Yellowstone National Park.

© White Star Publishers,
Via Candido Sassone, 24
13100 Vercelli, Italia
www.whitestar.it

First published in the UK in 2011

Text and illustrations copyright © White Star
Publishers, except those listed on page 501

ISBN-13: 978-1-4463-0156-2
ISBN-10: 1-4463-0156-7

Printed in China for:
F&W Media International, LTD
Brunel House, Forde Close, Newton Abbot,
TQ12 4PU, UK

10 9 8 7 6 5 4 3 2 1

F+W Media publishes high quality books on a
wide range of subjects
For more great book ideas visit
www.rubooks.co.uk

# CONTENTS

1 ● Red Sea (Egypt) – Ras Gharib.

2–3 ● Rangiroa (French Polynesia) – Blue Lagoon.

4–5 ● Trentino Alto Adige (Italy) – Brenta Dolomites.

6–7 ● Congo – Mayombe Forest.

8–9 ● Utah-Arizona (USA) – Monument Valley.

13 ● Alaska (USA) – Copper River Valley.

14–15 ● Tanzania – Lake Natron.

16–17 ● Kenya – Lake Nakuru.

PREFACE ............................... page 18

INTRODUCTION ....................... page 20

THE PILLARS OF THE SKY ......... page 30

THE BLUE DEPTHS ................... page 92

SILENT PLANET ....................... page 138

ROOTS OF THE WORLD ............ page 174

A SENSE OF WATER ................. page 212

THE MIRRORS OF THE SKY ........ page 258

THE GODS OF FIRE .................. page 296

THE ICE KINGDOM ................... page 316

THE WORLD OF STONE ............. page 340

THE WORLD IN BETWEEN .......... page 380

INVISIBLE BOUNDARIES ............ page 404

ROLLING HILLS ....................... page 422

BETWEEN LAND AND WATER ..... page 442

THE RAINBOW PLANET ............. page 470

BIOGRAPHY, INDEX, CREDITS .... page 498

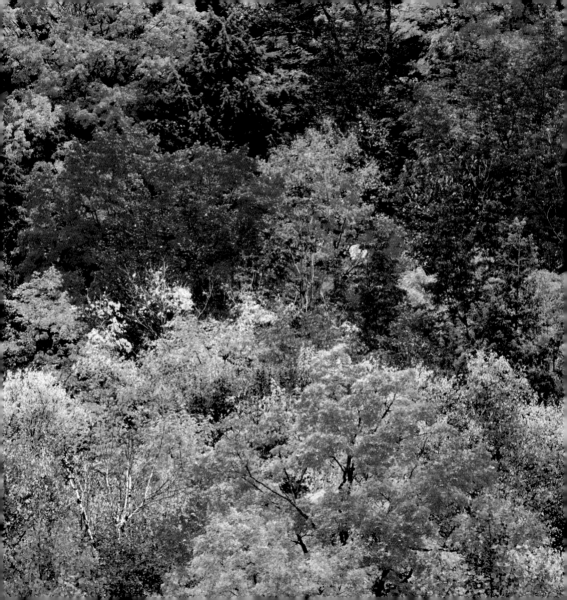

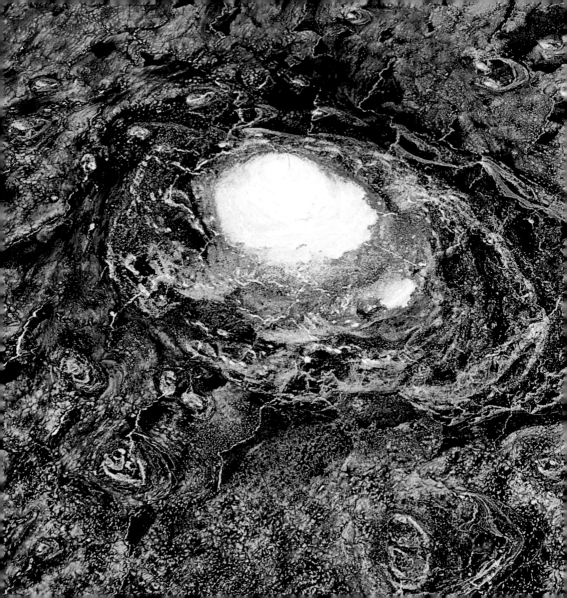

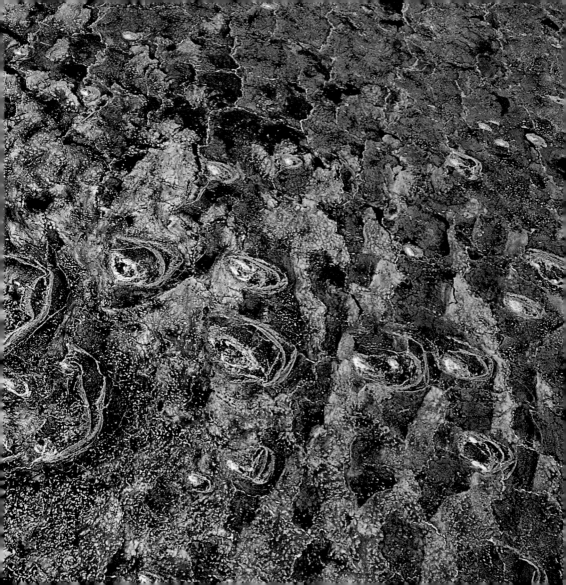

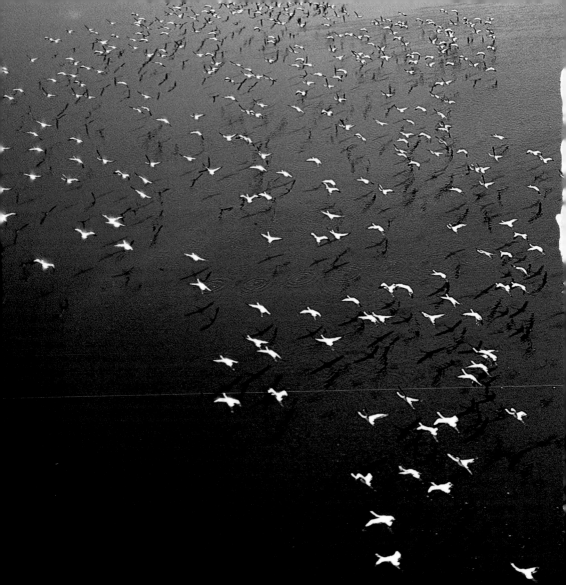

# Preface

THERE IS THE LAND CREATED BY MAN, A LITTLE NEGLECTED BUT LOVED, AND THERE IS THE NATURAL WORLD OF PHYSICAL FORCES AND ENVIRONMENTAL BALANCES. THE FIRST HAS BEEN MOLDED TO BECOME THE UNIQUE EXPRESSION OF THE MOST EVOLVED FORM OF LIFE, THE SECOND IS A SUBLIME MECHANISM, A SYMPHONY IN PERFECT HARMONY, A SCALE IN PERFECT EQUILIBRIUM. THIS BOOK DESCRIBES THE WORLD IN WHICH MAN IS NOT THE CENTRAL CHARACTER BUT SIMPLY AN OBSERVER: NO ROADS, CITIES OR MONUMENTS, BUT WOODS, MOUNTAINS, SEAS, DESERTS AND MUCH MORE. ENCHANTING PORTRAITS OF A WORLD WHERE WE ARE THE GUESTS, NOT THE HOSTS.

Nepal - Ama Dablam.

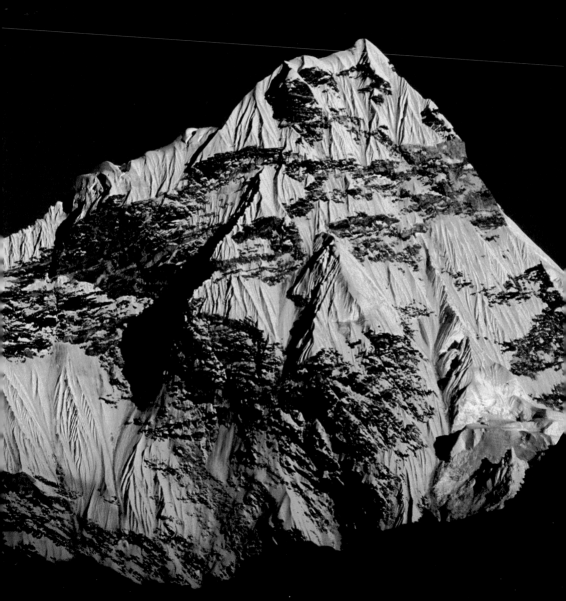

# Introduction

THE ANCIENT AND CONTEMPORARY WORLDS ARE SEPARATED BY A CULTURAL AND TEMPORAL GAP THAT IS NOT EASY TO COMPREHEND. IN THE CLASSICAL AGE THE EARTH WAS A MYSTERIOUS AND UNTOUCHABLE DIVINITY, WHILE NOW, AT THE DAWN OR THE THIRD MILLENNIUM A.D., IT IS BEING STUDIED AND EXPLOITED EVER MORE INTENSIVELY. DURING THE COURSE OF HISTORY, MAN HAS LEARNED TO FORCE OPEN THE "SECRET VAULTS" OF THE PLANET; CONSEQUENTLY, NEVER BEFORE HAS A SPECIES HAD SUCH POWER AND ACHIEVED SUCH A LEVEL OF KNOWLEDGE. BETWEEN THE MIDDLE AGES AND THE MODERN ERA MAN DISCOVERED THE WORLD – SOMETIMES BY INVENTING IT – FIRST THANKS TO FANTASTIC

● Wyoming (USA) - Yellowstone National Park.

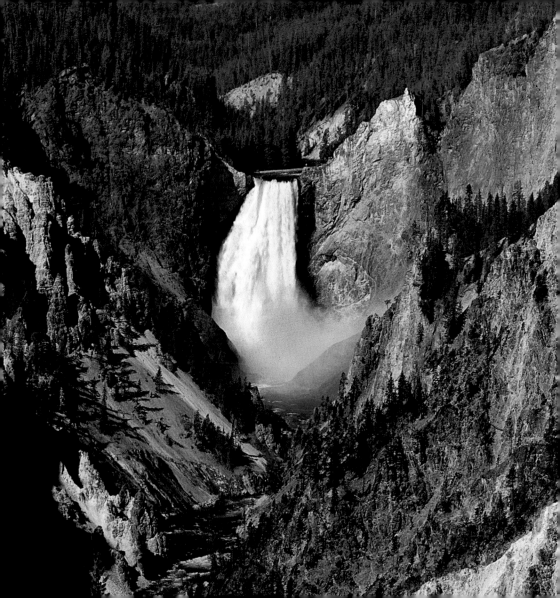

## Introduction

TALES OF JOURNEYS, THEN THROUGH DIRECT EXPERI-
ENCE AND READING, AND LASTLY BY MEANS OF RAPID
TRANSPORT AND COMMUNICATION. TRAVELERS HAVE
SEEN EVERYTHING THERE IS TO BE SEEN ON THE EARTH,
HAVE TRAVERSED ALL ITS OCEANS, CLIMBED ALL ITS
MOUNTAINS, AND VISITED ALL ITS VILLAGES, DISCOVER-
ING THE STRANGEST AND MOST FASCINATING THINGS,
WHICH THEY HAVE DESCRIBED IN TRAVEL JOURNALS
AND NOVELS. THIS IMMENSE STORE OF ACCOUNTS,
ENHANCED OVER THE CENTURIES BY ALL KINDS OF ILLUS-
TRATIONS, HAS GIVEN RISE TO A DIFFERENT CONSCIOUS-
NESS. THE EARTH, OUR WORLD, HAS ACQUIRED DEPTH,
COLOR AND TASTE, WHILE AT THE SAME TIME SHEDDING
ITS EVERY MYSTERY. THE TREASURES OF NATURE, THE

# Introduction

WORKS OF MAN, THE VERY SENSE OF EXISTENCE ON THIS PLANET HAVE ALL BECOME A UNIVERSAL HERITAGE. THIS REVOLUTION, WHICH HAS INFLUENCED HUMAN PERCEPTION AS MUCH AS THE COPERNICAN REVOLUTION, HAS GENERATED THE MODERN URGE TO "TRAVEL WITH OUR EYES WIDE OPEN." WE ARE NO LONGER THE SLAVES, BUT THE MASTERS OF TRAVEL, AND GO AROUND THE WORLD WITH THE SOLE AIM OF INCREASING OUR STORE OF KNOWLEDGE: THE MOST SURPRISING EXPRESSIONS OF LIFE AND NATURE AWAIT US IN PLACES THAT WERE ONCE REMOTE BUT ARE NOW PERHAPS ONLY EXOTIC.... KNOWLEDGE COMES THROUGH OBSERVATION, THAT IS TO SAY, BY STORING IN OUR MEMORY AND THEN REFLECTING AND COMPARING. BY TRAVEL-

# Introduction

ING AND OBSERVING, MAN EXAMINES HIMSELF, HE RE-
ELABORATES HIS VISION OF THE WORLD BY TAKING IN NEW
ASPECTS, EVER MORE REFINED NUANCES. OBSERVATION
ESTABLISHES A RELATION WITH THE OBJECT OBSERVED,
AND IF THAT OBJECT IS NATURE, THAT MIRACLE OF MIRA-
CLES IN THE WORLD, ONE CANNOT BUT BE SPELLBOUND
BY IT. THERE ARE IMAGES, ESPECIALLY THE ONES IN THIS
BOOK, THAT HELP US TO UNDERSTAND, KNOW AND HENCE
LOVE THE ENVIRONMENT IN WHICH WE LIVE: THE MOUN-
TAINS, DESERTS, VOLCANOES AND SEAS THAT RELATE TO
US THE HISTORY AND FUTURE OF A CELESTIAL BODY AND
OF THE FORTUNATE CREATURES THAT LIVE IN IT.

25 ● Fezzan (Libya) - Sahara Desert.

26-27 ● Paranà (Brazil) - Iguazú Falls.

28-29 ● Sichuan (China) - Huanglong Nature Park.

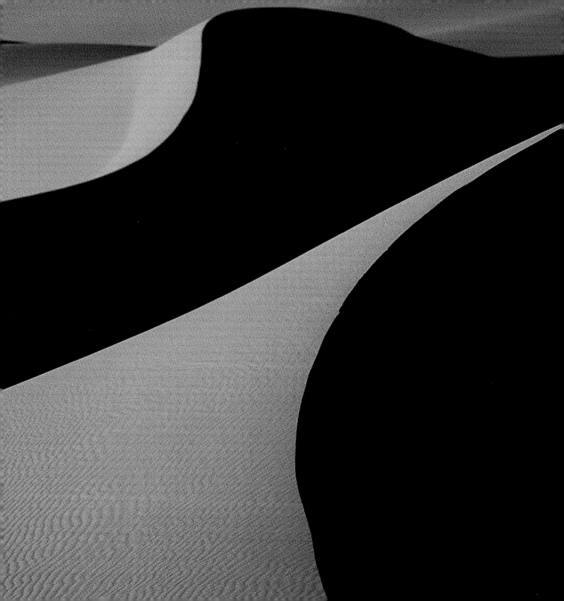

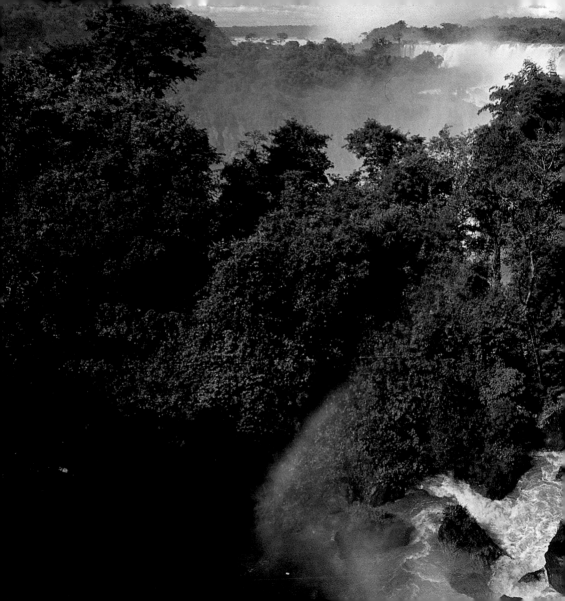

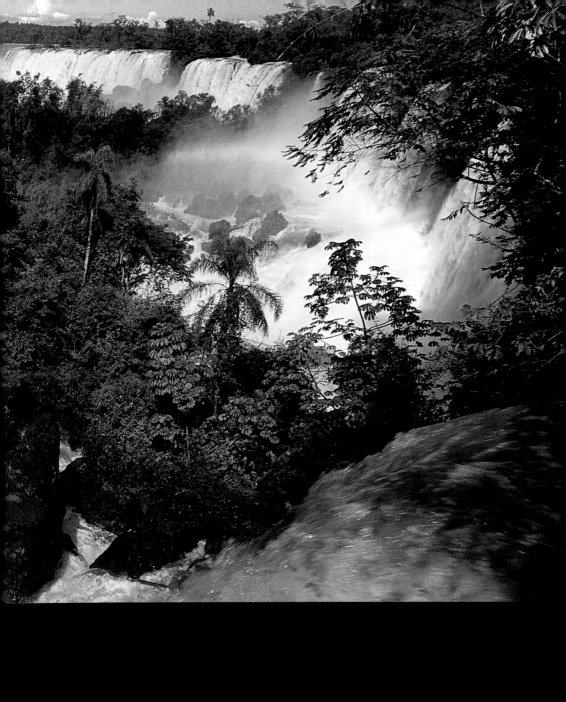

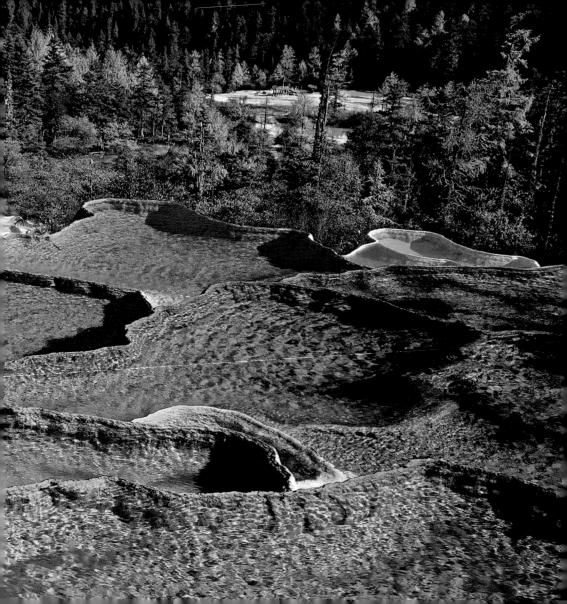

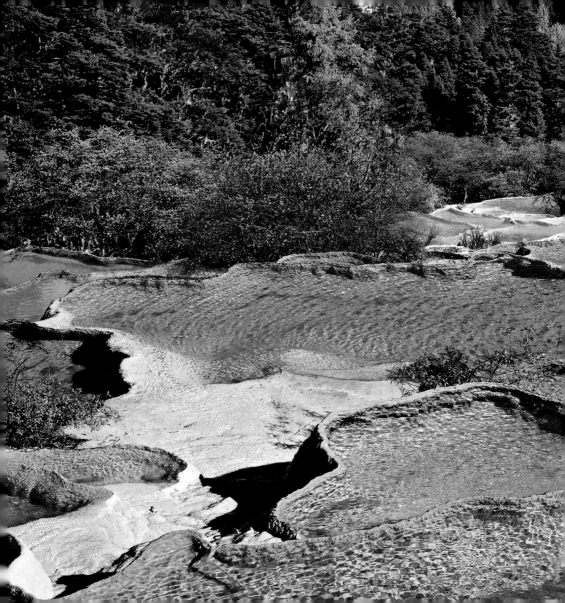

# The PILLARS of the SKY

• Karakorum (Pakistan) - K2.

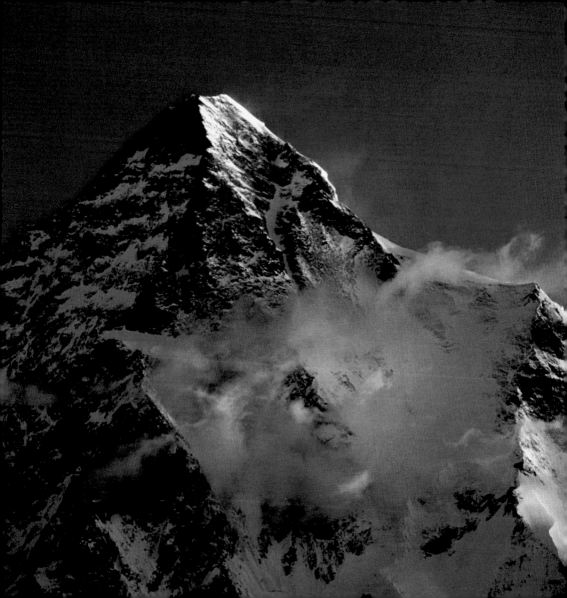

## INTRODUCTION The Pillars of the Sky

A MOUNTAIN CANNOT BE EXPLAINED. IT IS NOT A MERE "IRREGULARITY" OF THE EARTH, BUT A DRAMATIC SYMBOL OF AN ASPIRATION THAT ONLY THE TRUE ENTHUSIAST HAS BEEN ABLE TO DESCRIBE. THE SURVIVORS OF THE MOST DIFFICULT CLIMBS, THOSE WHO WENT BEYOND THE CONFINES OF DEATH, SPEAK OF THEIR BEWILDERMENT BEFORE THE DIVINITY OF STONE AND GLACIERS, HUGE STRETCHES LIKE WHITE DESERTS POPULATED BY DEMONS OF THE IMAGINATION. THESE GIANTS OF THE EARTH HAVE ERECTED FORMIDABLE BARRIERS IN FRONT OF THE FEAR OR ARROGANCE OF THE MANY PERSONS WHO HAVE TRIED TO SCALE THEM, DEMANDING A HUGE TRIBUTE OF BLOOD. ACCORDING TO THE SHERPA, AT TIMES THE MOUNTAINS HAVE EVEN SPOKEN. THIS

## INTRODUCTION The Pillars of the Sky

POPULATION IN NEPAL LIVES IN SYMBIOSIS WITH MOUNTAINS, TREATING THEM LIKE DIAMONDS IN THE ROUGH, LIKE SEEDS FROM WHICH ANY FLOWER MIGHT SPRING FORTH, LIKE AN IRASCIBLE AND BEAUTIFUL GOD THAT IS TO BE DEVOUTLY WORSHIPPED. THERE ARE RANGES WHOSE IDENTITY LIES IN THEIR ALTITUDE. THE HIMALAYAS, THE ROOF OF THE EARTH, ARE THE QUINTESSENCE OF THE HIGH MOUNTAIN. THE ANDES, BUFFETED BY THE MOST UNPREDICTABLE BAD WEATHER, SEEM TO MIRROR THE HARSHNESS AND GRANDIOSITY OF THE SOUTH AMERICAN LANDSCAPE. THE ANTARCTIC MOUNTAINS ARE FRAGMENTS OF OTHER WORLDS TOSSED ONTO OUR PLANET FROM ON HIGH; THEY HOST STORMS THAT MAY LAST FOR MONTHS, THEY ARE BATTERED BY CYCLOPEAN

# The Pillars of the Sky

Introduction

WINDS, THEY TOWER OVER DESOLATE AREAS THAT LOOK LIKE EXTRATERRESTRIAL DESERTS. THE MOUNTAINS OF NORTHERN CALIFORNIA ARE MONUMENTS CARVED OUT OF ANCIENT ROCK, WITH THE MOST INCONCEIVABLE COLORS – RED, YELLOW, ORANGE, OCHER – STANDING SHEER OVER EXPANSES OF WASTELAND.

MOUNTAINS ARE TRUE SPECTACLE. THOSE WHO CLIMB THEM AFTER HAVING OBSERVED THEM FROM AFAR, EXPERIENCE AT EVERY STEP THAT SUBTLE TINGLE THAT EVERY PERSON FEELS WHEN ENCOUNTERING UNEX-PLORED REGIONS. EVERY CORNER HAS ITS OWN THRILLING SECRET, EVERY PATH CONTAINS THE JOY OF DISCOVERING A BIT OF STILL UNKNOWN NATURE.

*35* • Trentino Alto Adige (Italy) - Brenta Group, Dolomites.

*36-37* • Trentino Alto Adige (Italy) - Catinaccio Group, Dolomites.

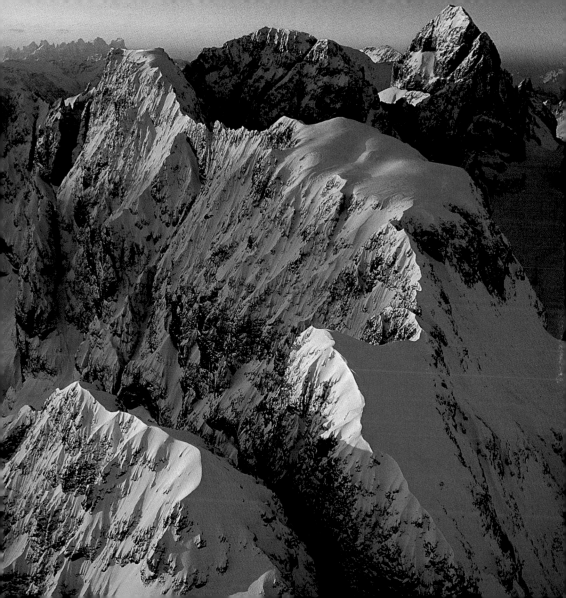

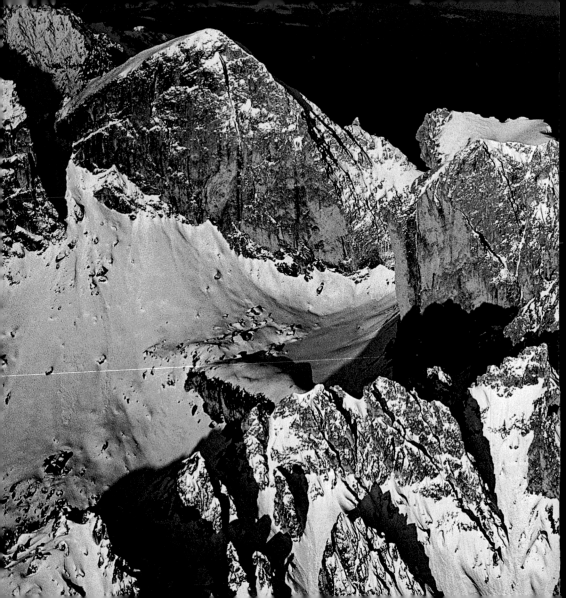

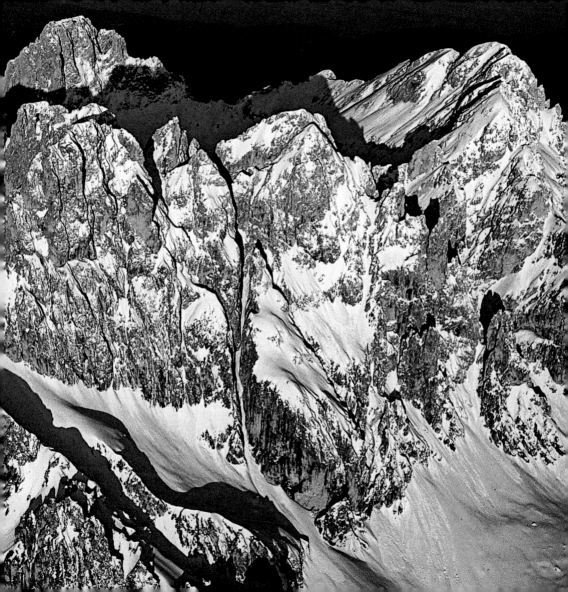

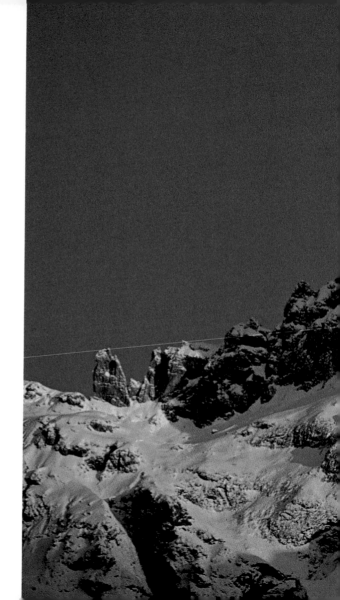

- Alto Adige (Italy) - Sass Maor and Cima Madonna, Dolomites.

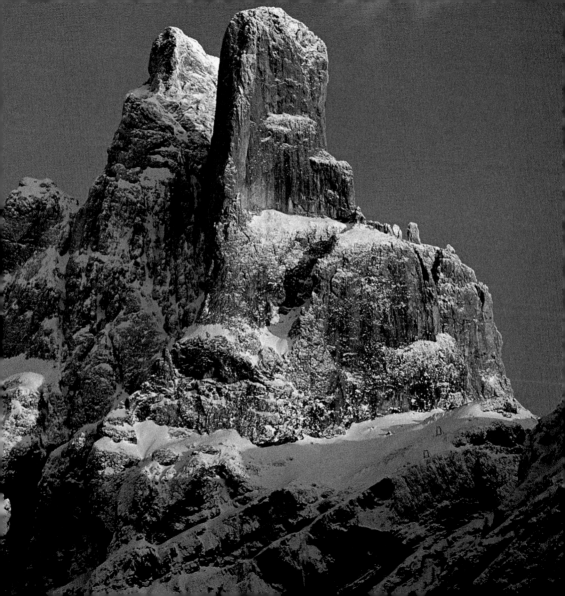

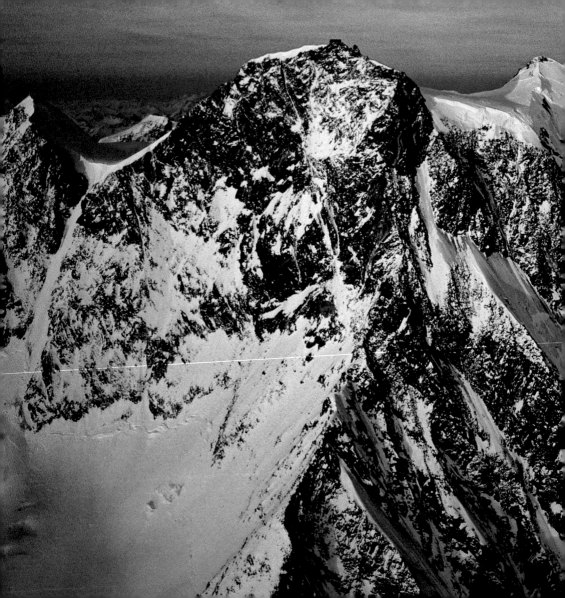

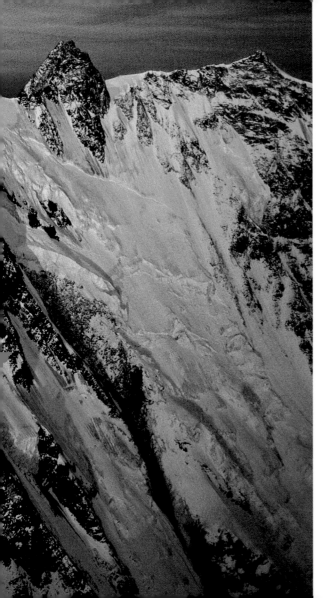

40-41 ● Piedmont (Italy)
- Monte Rosa.

42-43 ● Valle d'Aosta
(Italy) - The Matterhorn.

44-45 ● Valle d'Aosta
(Italy) - The Giant's Tooth,
Mont Blanc massif.

46-47 ● Haut Savoie
(France) - Mont Blanc
massif.

48-49 ● Haut Savoie
(France) - Mont Blanc.

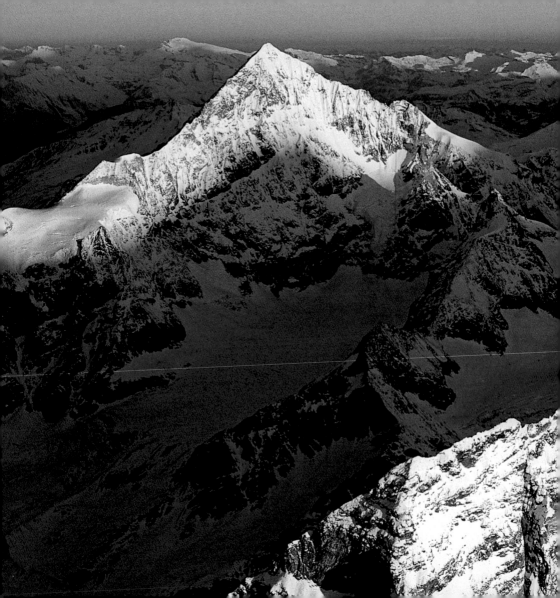

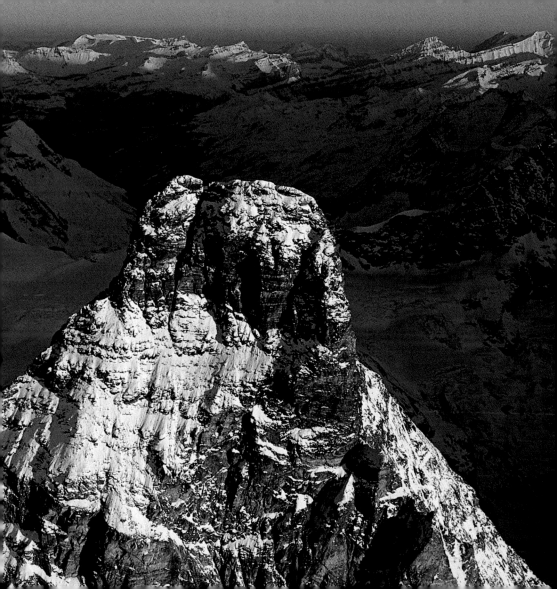

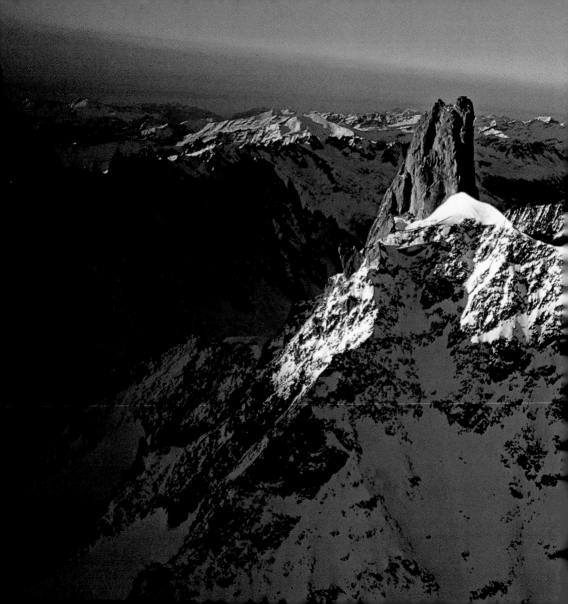

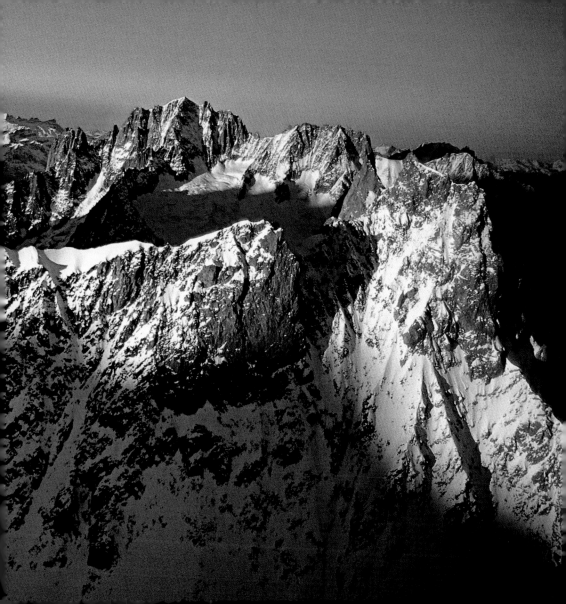

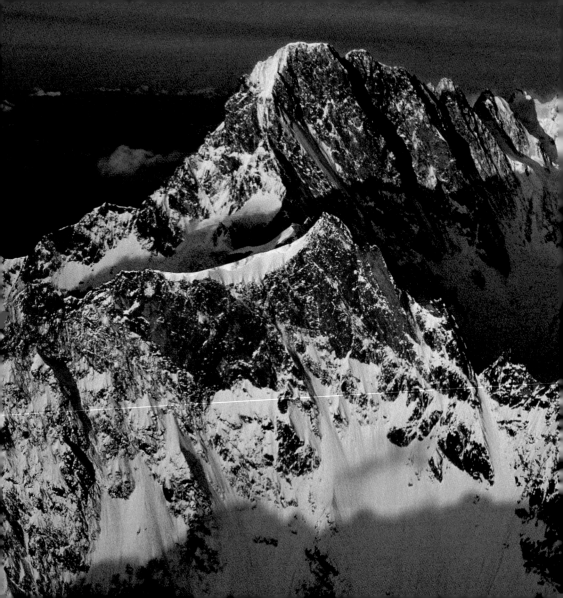

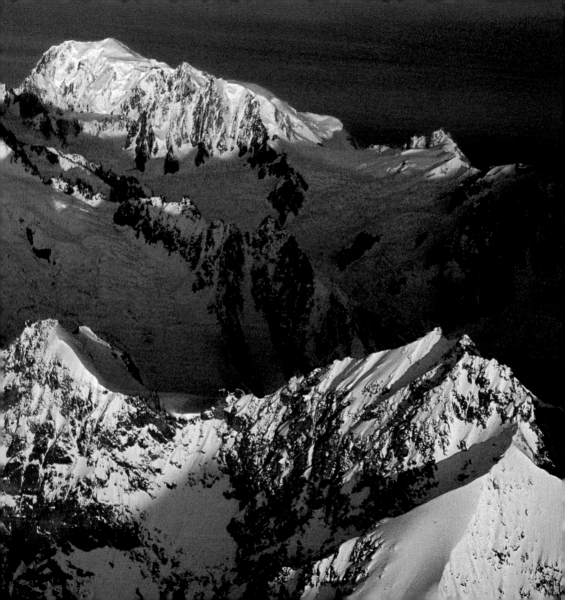

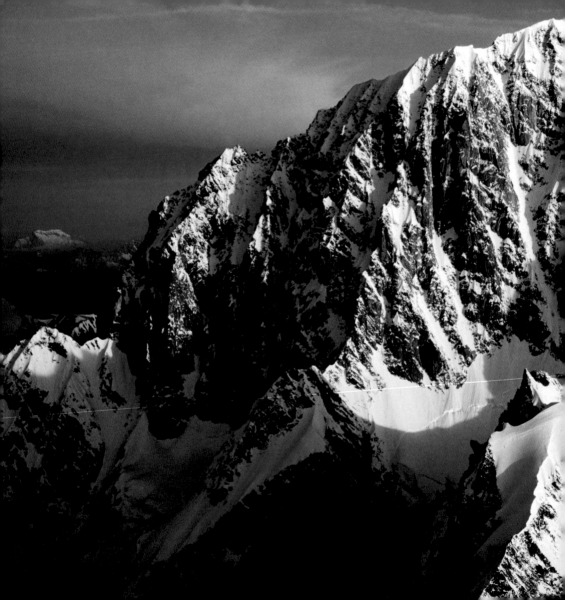

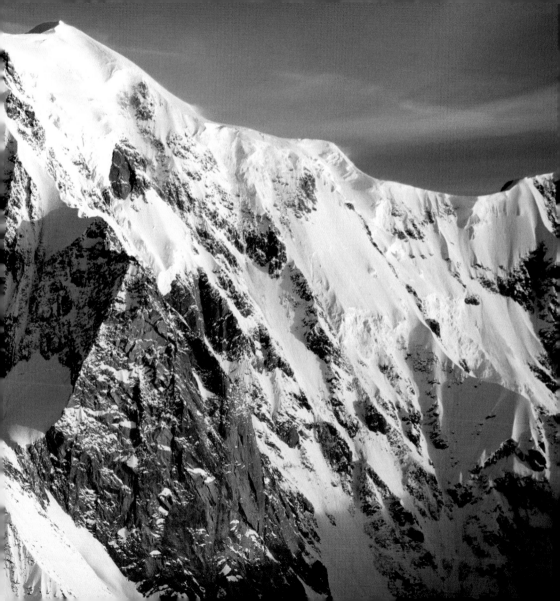

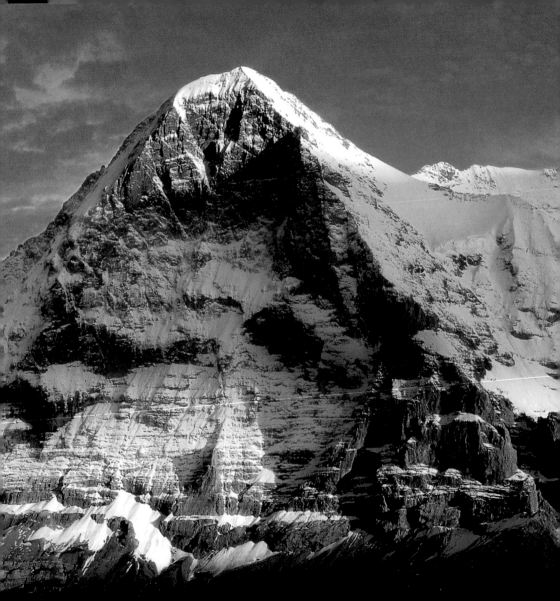

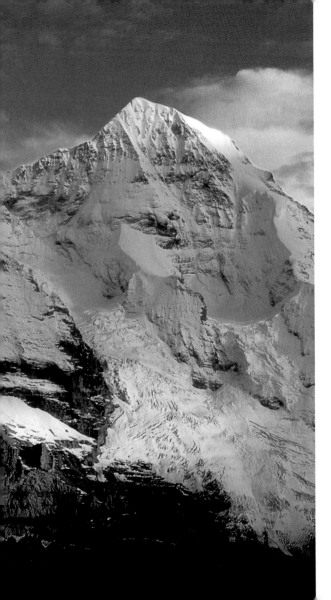

50-51 ● Bernese Oberland (Switzerland) - The Eiger, Jungfrau and Mönch.

52-53 ● Bavaria (Germany) - Watzmann (right) and Little Watzmann, Bavarian Alps.

54-55 ● Sichuan (China) - Siguniang.

56-57 ● Tibet (China) - Mt. Everest.

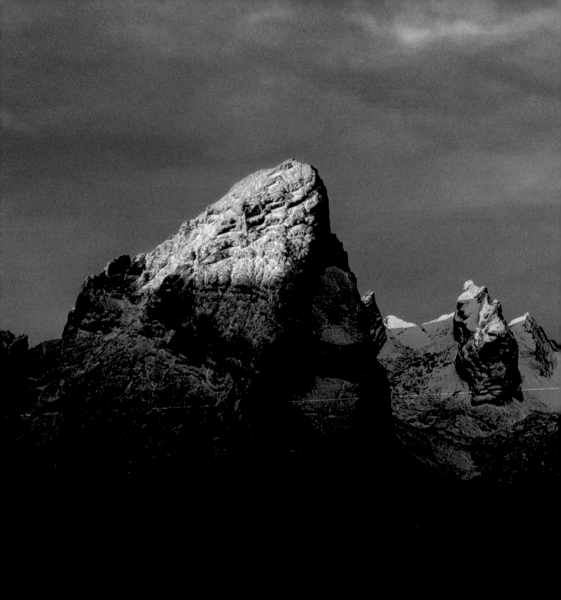

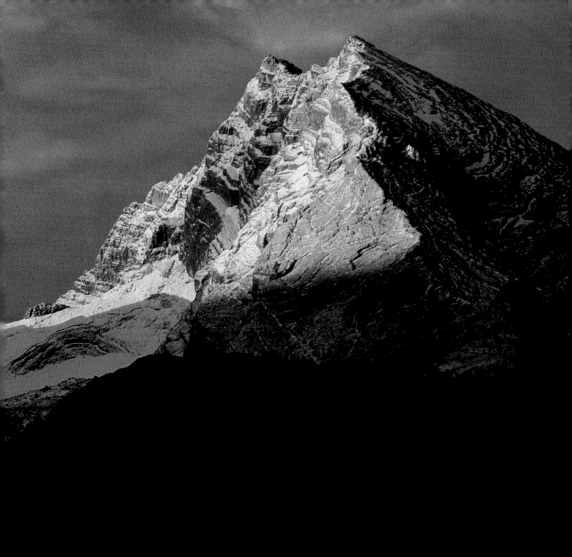

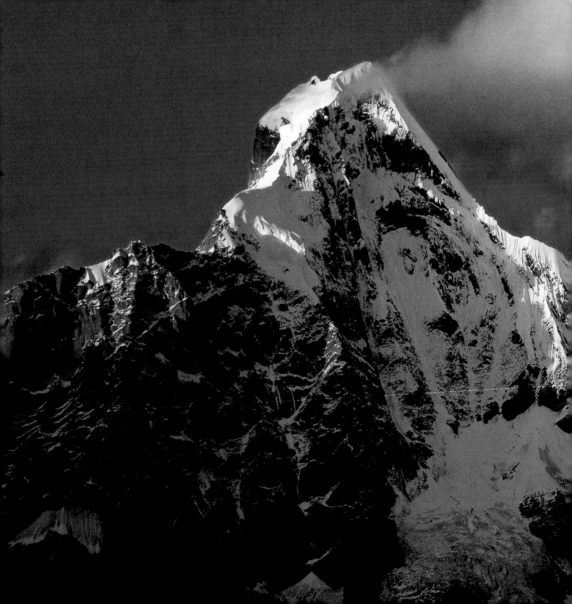

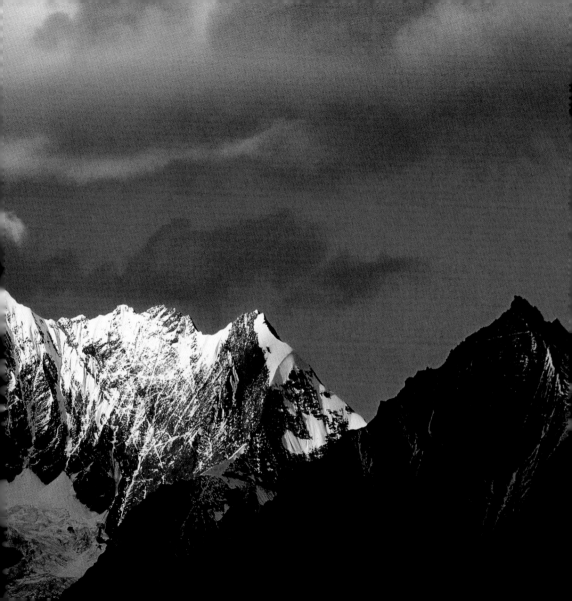

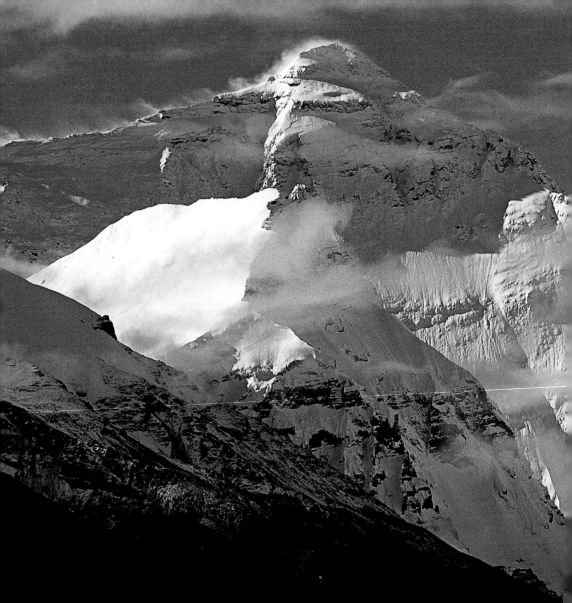

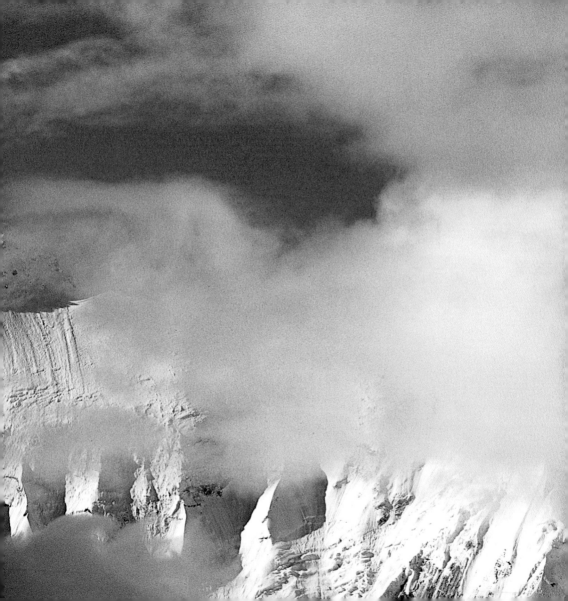

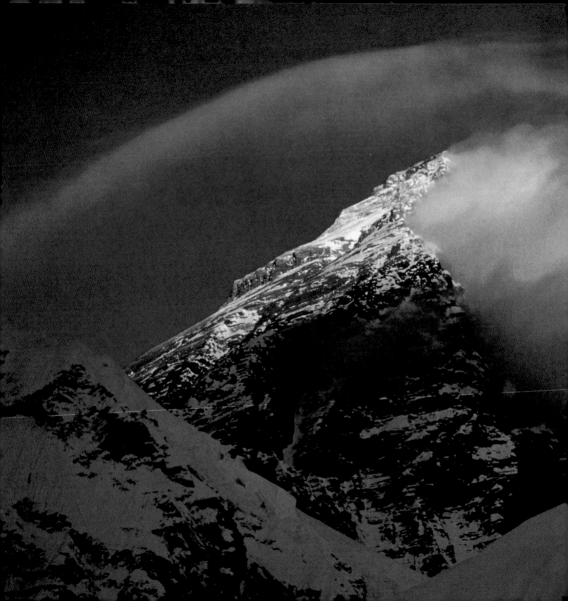

Khumbu (Nepal) - Mt. Everest.

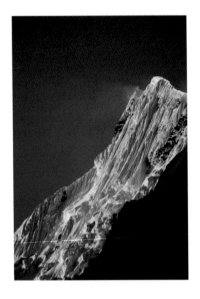

60 ● Nepal - Gangapurna.

61 ● Tibet (China) - Kailash.

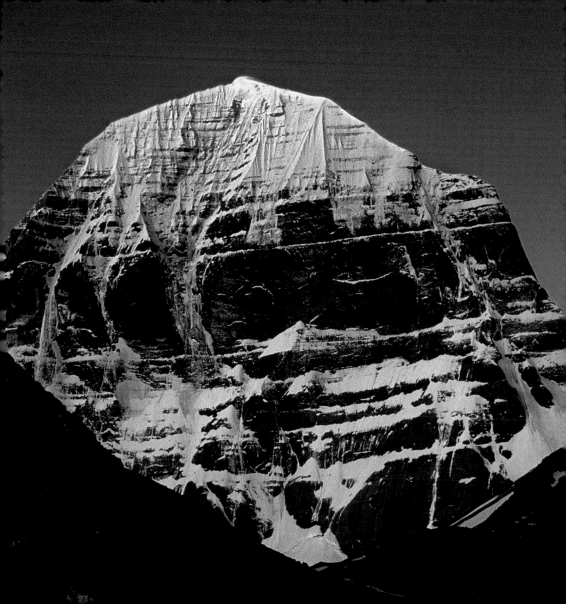

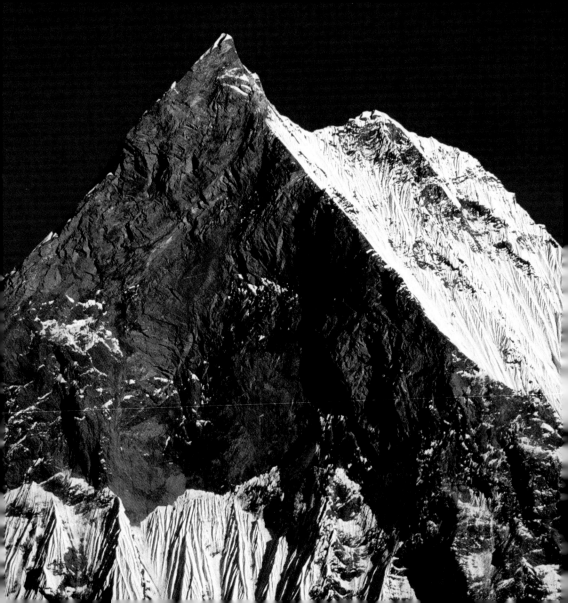

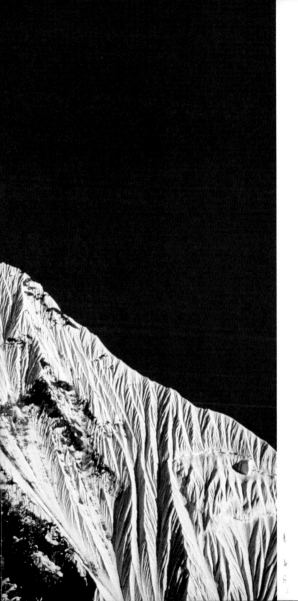

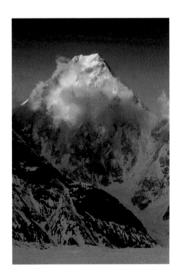

62-63 ● Nepal - Machapuchare,
Annapurna Sanctuary.

63 ● Karakorum (Pakistan) -
Gasherbrun IV.

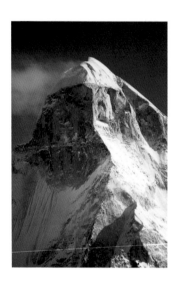

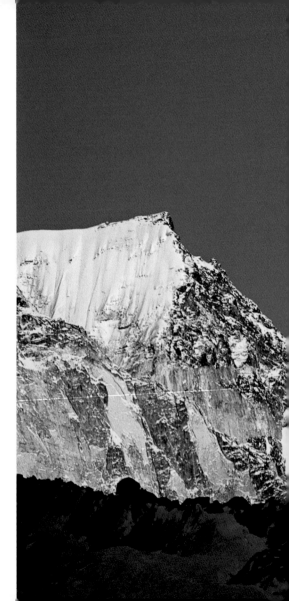

*64* ● Uttar Pradesh (India) - Shivling Peak.

*64-65* ● Uttar Pradesh (India) - Bagirathi
Peaks.

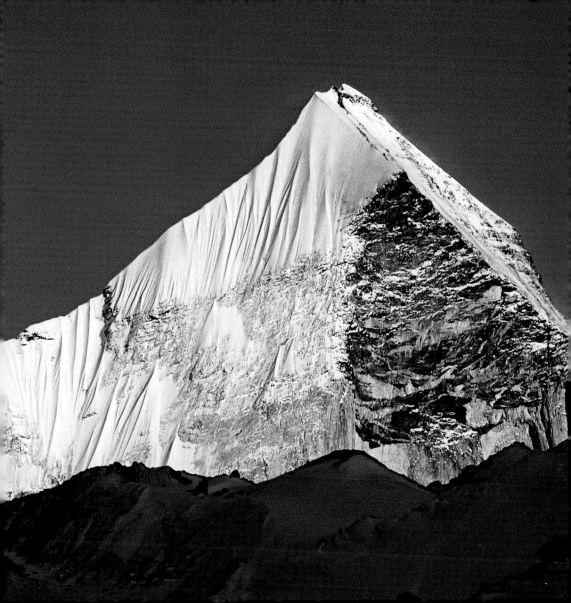

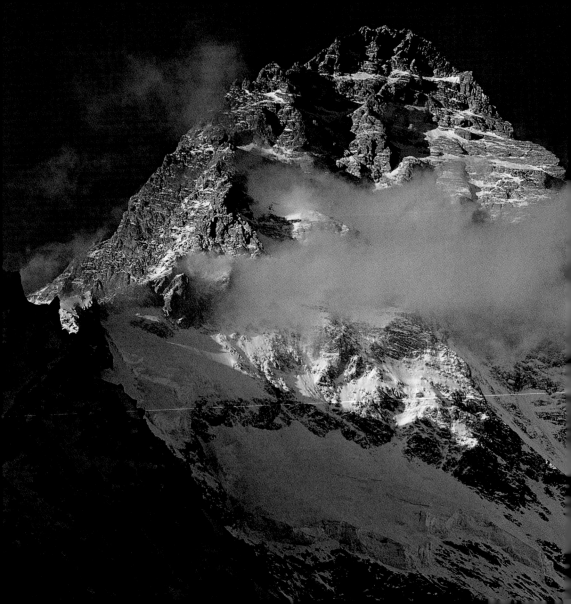

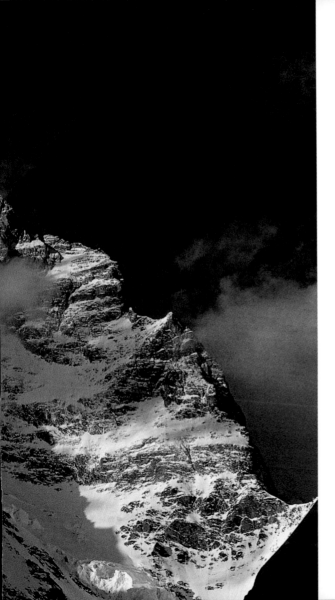

*66-67* ● Karakorum (Pakistan) - West face of K2.

*68-69* ● Yukon Territory (Canada) - St. Elias Mountains.

*70-71* ● Alaska (USA) - Alaska Range.

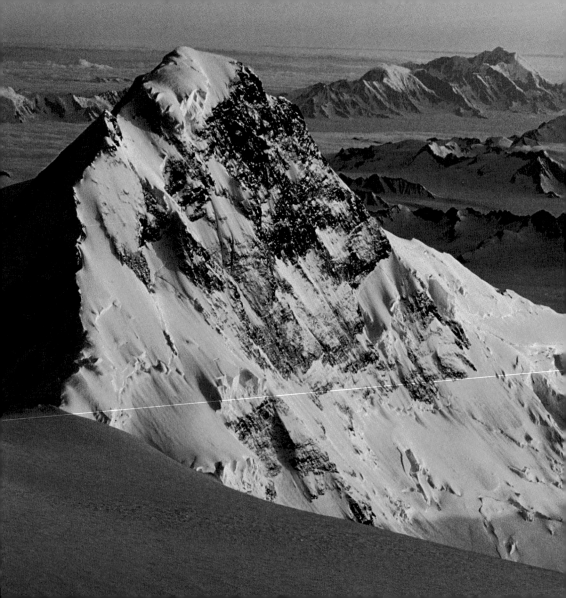

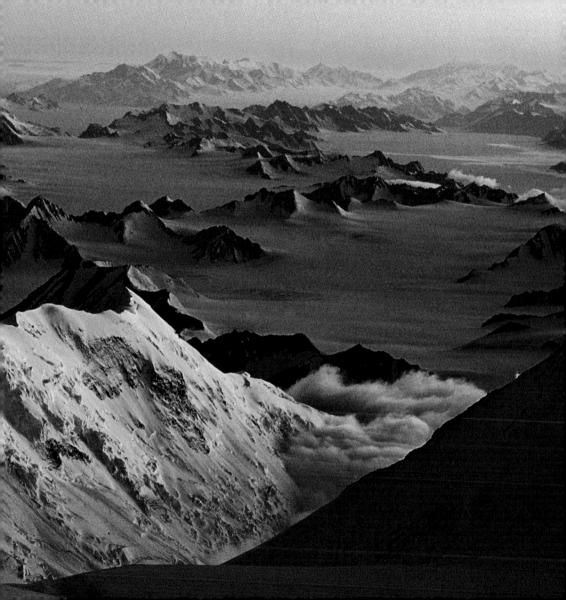

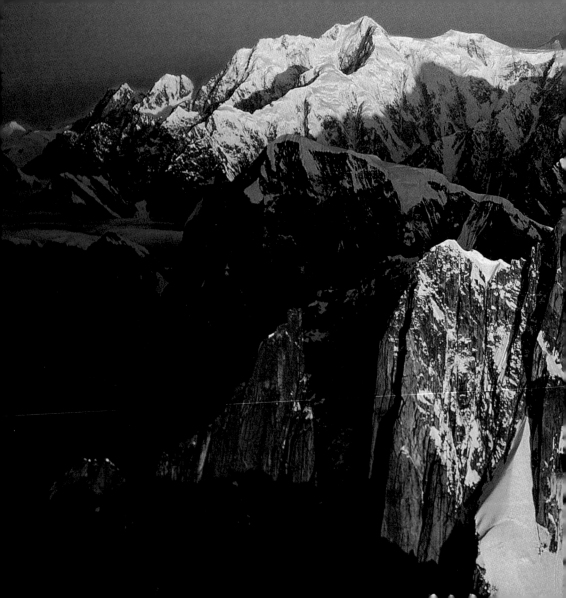

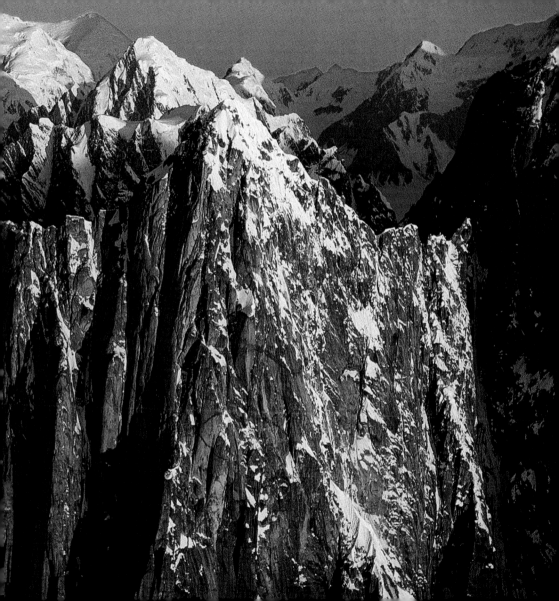

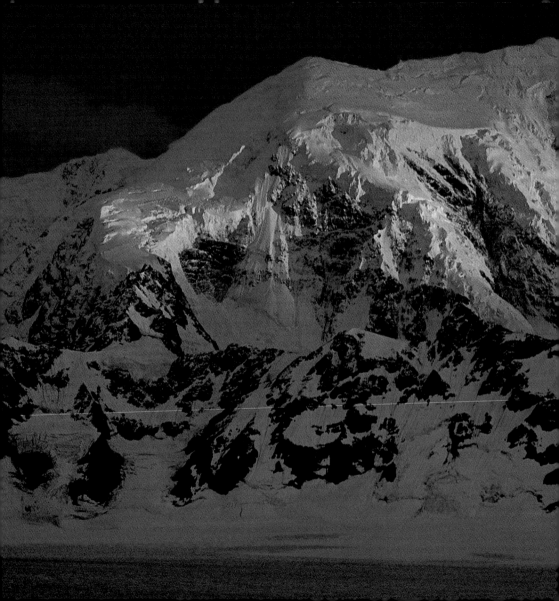

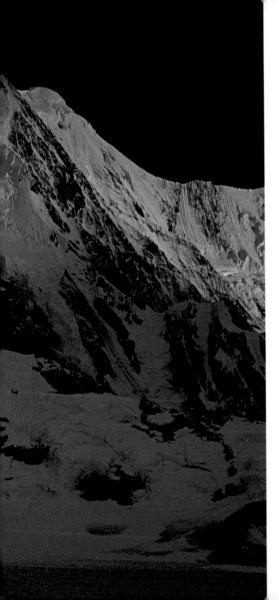

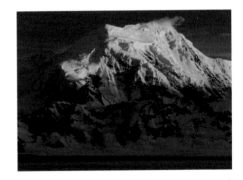

*72-73 and 73* ● Alaska (USA) -
Wrangell-St. Elias National Park.

*74-75* ● Alberta (Canada) - Rampart Range
Peaks, Jasper National Park.

*76-77* ● Alberta (Canada) - Canadian
Rockies, Banff National Park.

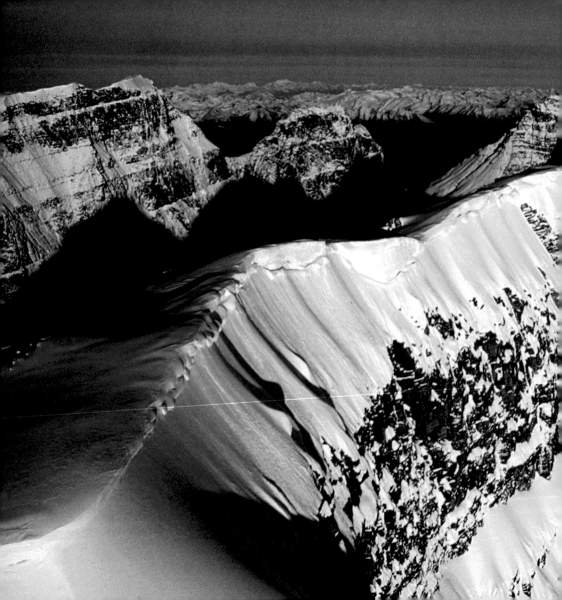

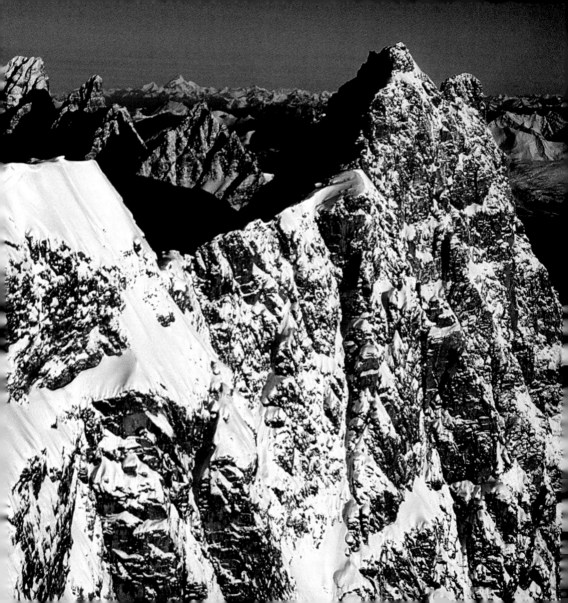

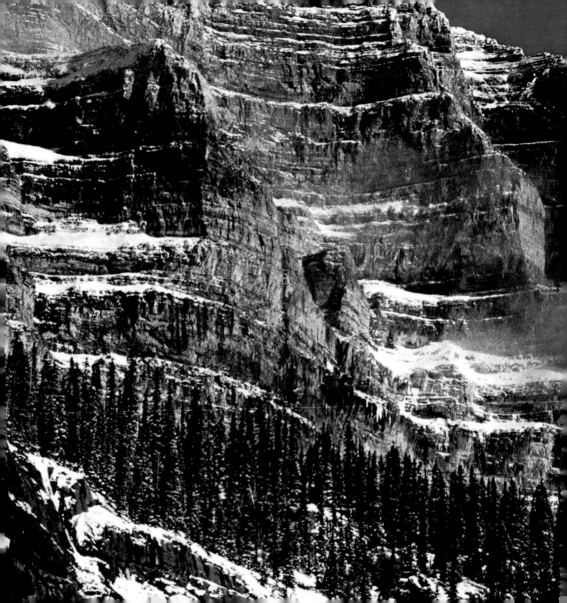

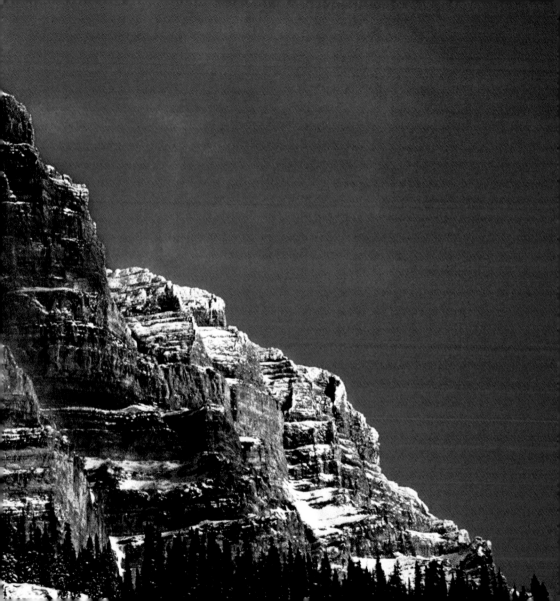

" THE SPIRIT OF A MOUNTAIN LIES IN ITS SNOWFIELDS AND CREVASSES, BEYOND THE LAST ROCK THAT EXTENDS TOWARDS THE SKY. ITS WORDS ARE WRITTEN IN THE CLOUDS THAT SHROUD THE SUMMIT AND ARE HEARD WHEN THE WIND HOWLS DOWN ITS PATHS, RECOUNTING THE STORIES OF THE MEN WHO HAVE TRUDGED THEM. "

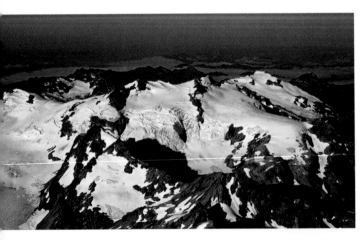

78 ● Washington (USA) - Mt. Mount Olympus, Olympic National Park.

79 ● Washington (USA) - Mt. Mount Rainier.

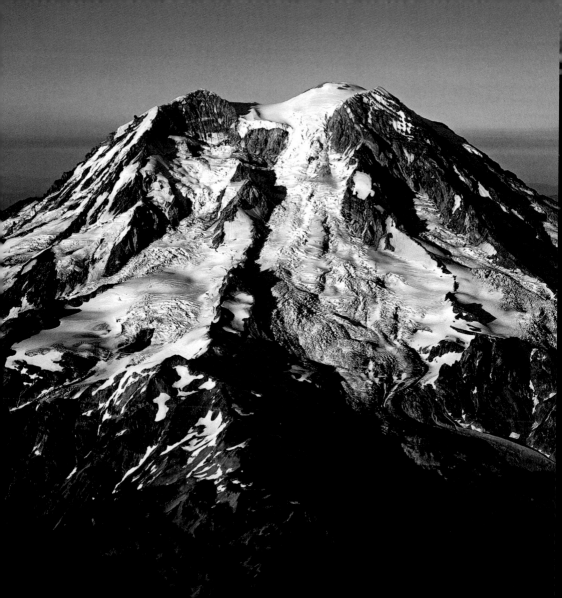

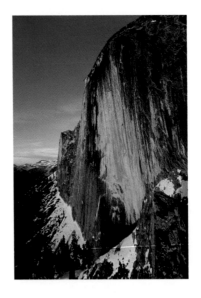

*80 and 81* ● California (USA) - Half Dome, Yosemite National Park.

*82-83* ● Patagonia (Chile) - Torres del Paine.

*84-85* ● Patagonia (Argentina) - The Fitz Roy Group, Parque Nacional los Glaciares.

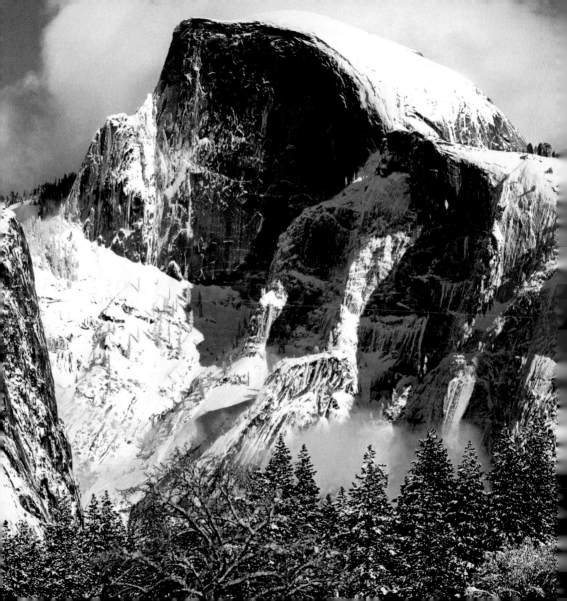

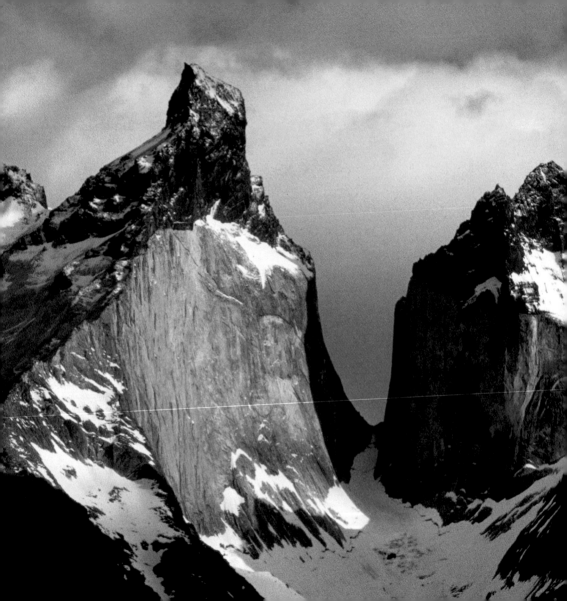

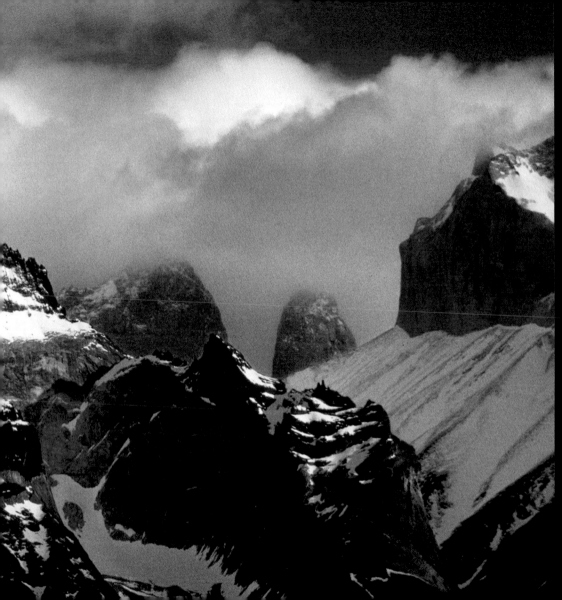

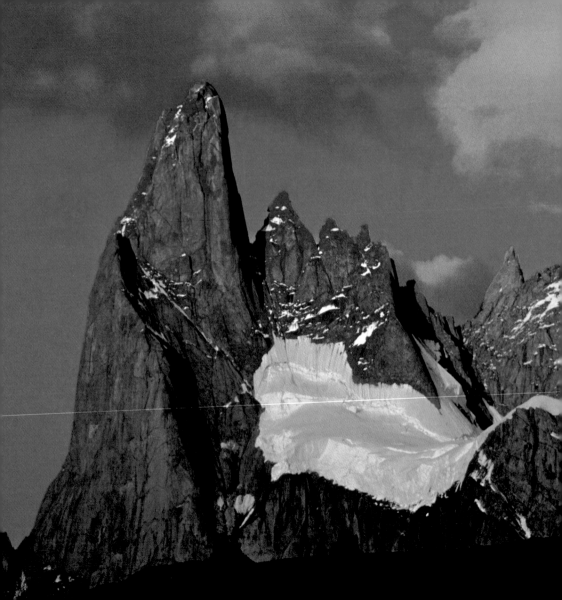

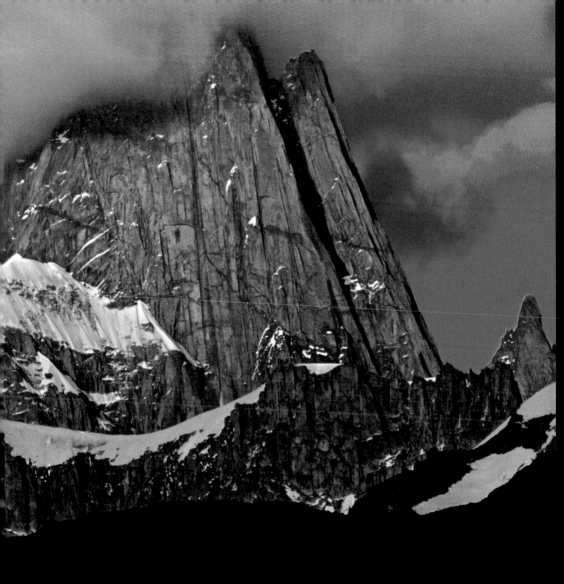

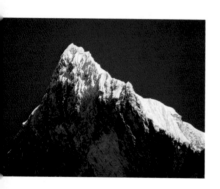

86 • Peru - Huandoy.

86-87 • Peru - Huascaran,
Cordillera Blanca.

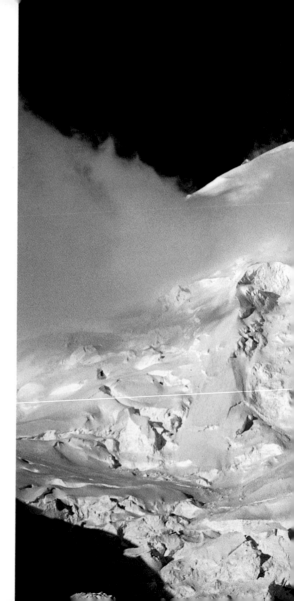

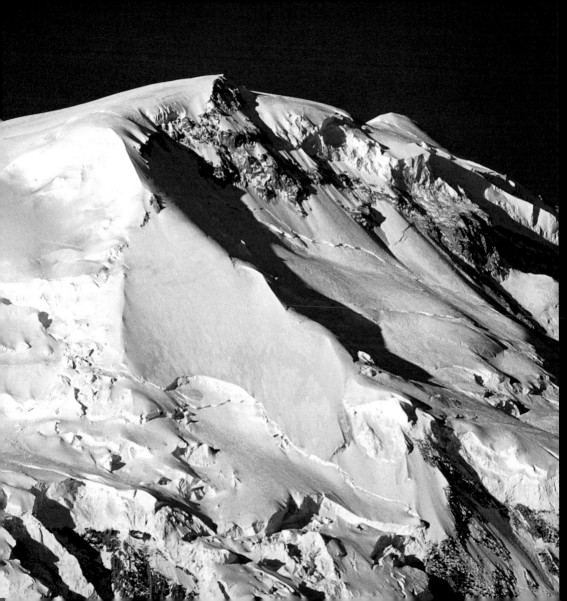

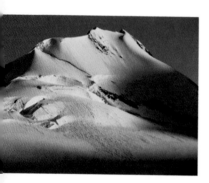

88 *and* 88-89 ● Antarctica - Fief Mountains, Wiencke Island.

*90-91* ● South Island (New Zealand) - Mount Cook.

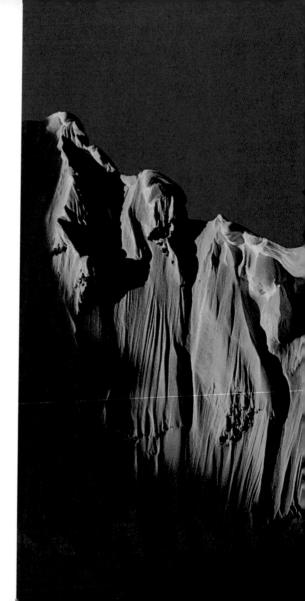

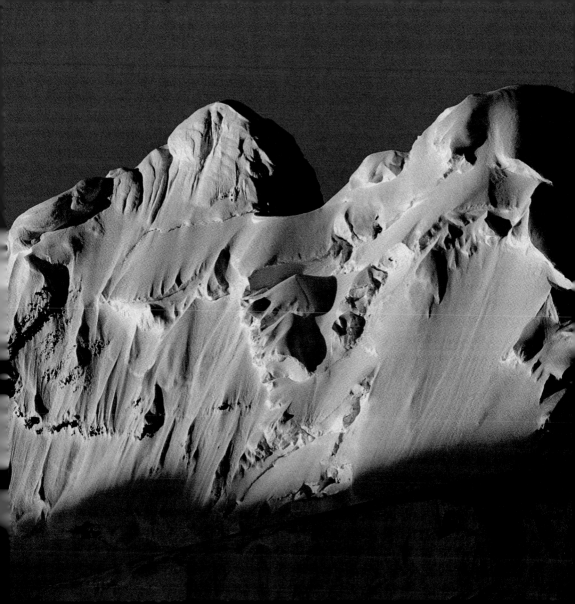

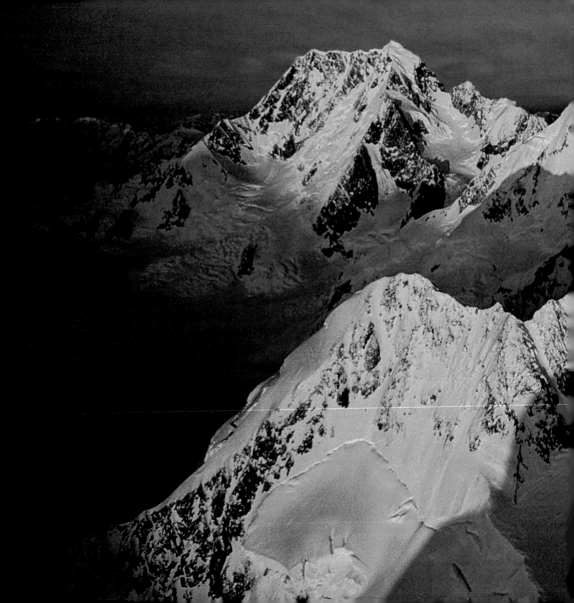

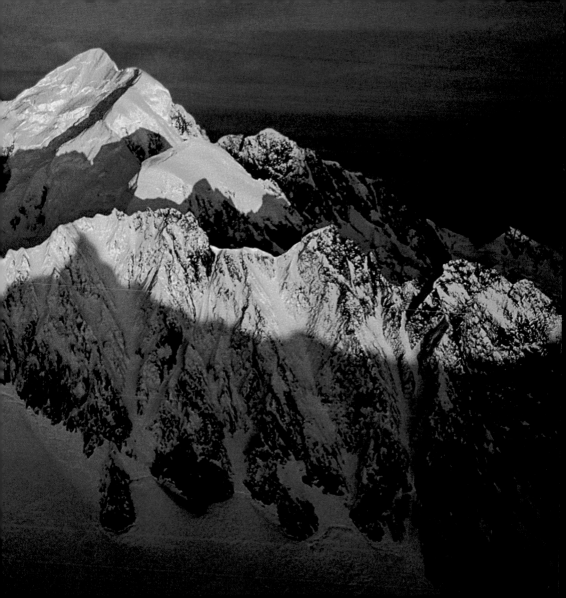

# The BLUE DEPTHS

• Society Islands (French Polynesia) - Bora Bora.

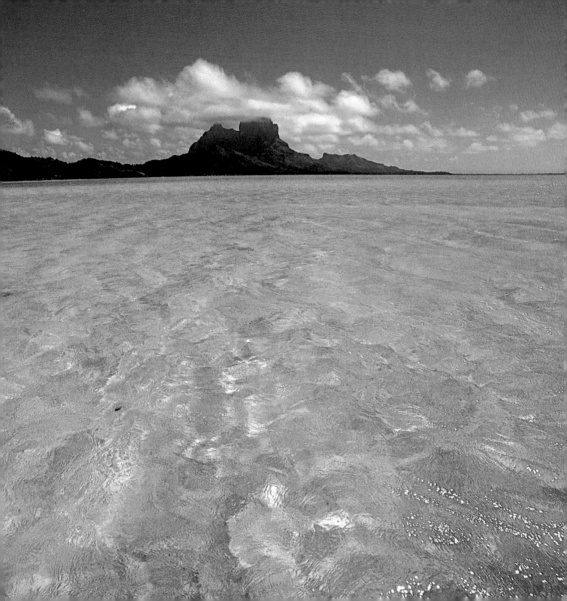

## INTRODUCTION The Blue Depths

SEEN FROM THE SKY, THE THIN SHEET THAT COVERS THE CONTINENTS IS A LUCID VEIL OF PURE SILK TORN HERE AND THERE; THESE RENTS REVEAL A SURFACE THAT IS WHITE, OR YELLOWISH, OR BRIGHT GREEN: DRY LAND. THIS MANTLE HAS MYRIAD NUANCES, ACCORDING TO THE DEPTH, SALINITY AND LATITUDE: GREEN AND LIGHT BLUE OFTEN MERGE WITH LIGHT AND REFLECTIONS, CREATING EXTRAORDINARY PLAYS OF TRANSPARENCY. SEEN FROM THE LAND, THE SEA IS A WAVE THAT CRASHES AGAINST THE CLIFFS, THE WHITE FOAM THAT SLIDES ALONG THE SHORELINE, THE LIGHT OF THE SETTING SUN OR THE MOONLIGHT THAT PAINTS THE SURFACE OF THE SEA AND THEN DIES OUT ON THE SHORE. IT IS A FISHING BOAT UNDER WAY TOWARD THE OPEN SEA, LADEN WITH FISHERMEN AND PRAYERS, A

# INTRODUCTION The Blue Depths

SAILING BOAT ON THE HORIZON FOLLOWED BY SEA-GULLS WHOSE UNFURLED SAIL IS FILLED OUT BY THE WIND, A WAVING PALM TREE IN A DISTANT TROPICAL LOCALE. SEEN FROM THE DEPTHS, THE SEA IS A MYSTERIOUS WORLD FILLED WITH FANTASTIC SIGHTS. THERE ARE NIMBLE PREDATORS WITH THEIR GLASSY LOOK; SINUOUS, MULTICOLORED NUDIBRANCHIAN MOLLUSKS; FISH OF EVERY SHAPE AND COLOR; AND GIGANTIC CREATURES WITH HUGE APPETITES, AS WELL AS CARCASSES OF SHIPWRECKS ENCRUSTED WITH CORAL AND IMPRESSIVE CANYONS AND ABYSSES OUT OF WHICH THERE DART FLUORESCENT ECTOPLASMS, LIKE GHOSTS FROM THE HEREAFTER. FOR MAN, THE SEA MEANS THE SCENT OF BRINE AND THE SALT DEPOSITED ON ONE'S DOOR; IT IS A SHORT-LIVED LOVE STORY, THE LONGING FOR

# The Blue Depths
## Introduction

A LONG WALK ALONG THE BEACH, AN UNFORGETTABLE SONG, HOPE FOR OPPORTUNITIES AND A BETTER FUTURE. THE SEA IS ADVENTURE AND TALES OF HEROISM, IT IS A SAILING VESSEL MOVING OUT INTO THE OPEN WATERS, A SEAGULL FLYING OVER A SHIP THAT HAS BEEN IN THE OPEN OCEAN FOR MONTHS; IT IS THE STRIP OF LAND THAT APPEARS ON THE HORIZON, A HOLD FILLED WITH TREASURES FROM NEW WORLDS, THE BORDERLINE BETWEEN PAST AND FUTURE, BETWEEN A WASTED LIFE AND A LIFE LIVED TO THE FULL.

*97* ● Sardinia (Italy) - Pink Beach, Budelli.

*98-99* ● Micronesia - Foreshore, Lekes Sandspit, Palau.

*100-101* ● Society Islands (French Polynesia) - Aerial view of Bora Bora.

*102-103* ● Society Islands (French Polynesia) - Effects of light in the water at Huahiné.

*104-105* ● Victoria (Australia) - The coast along the Great Ocean Road.

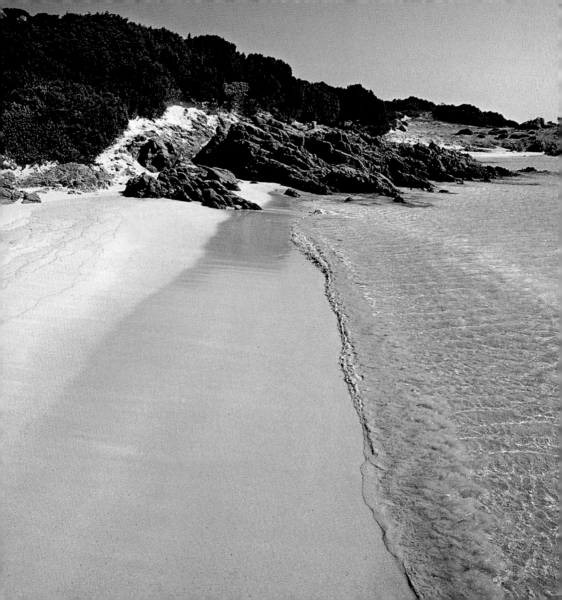

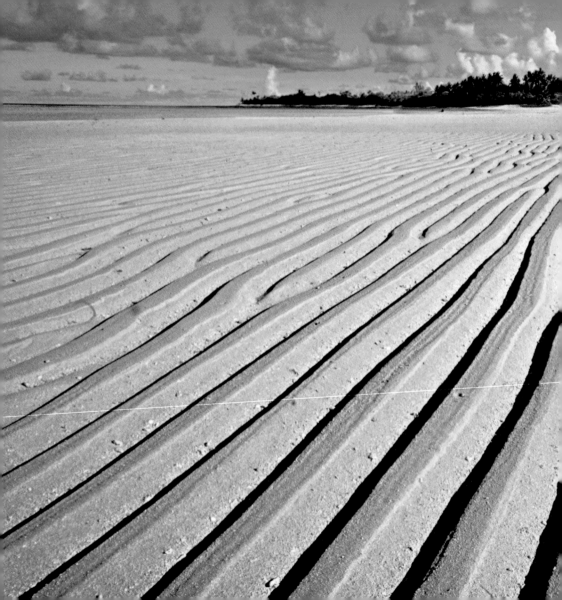

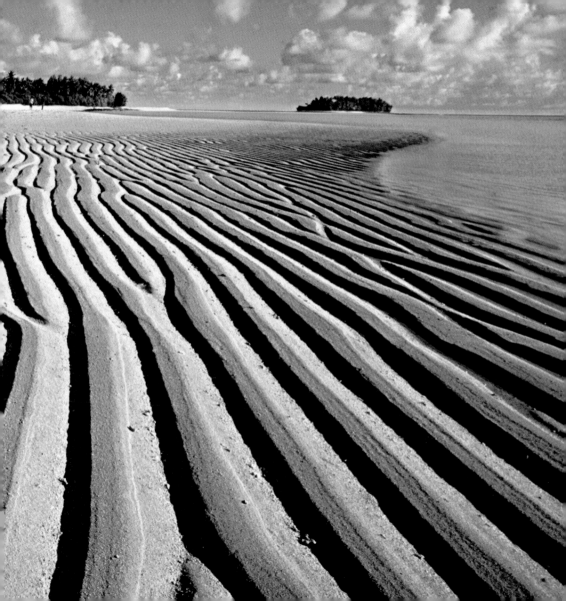

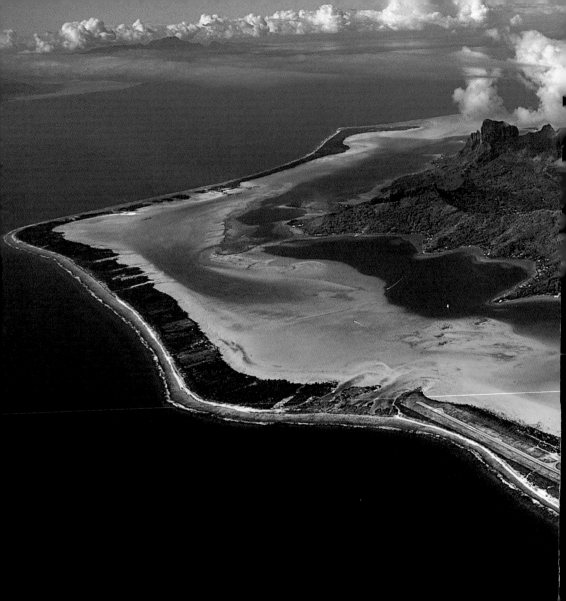

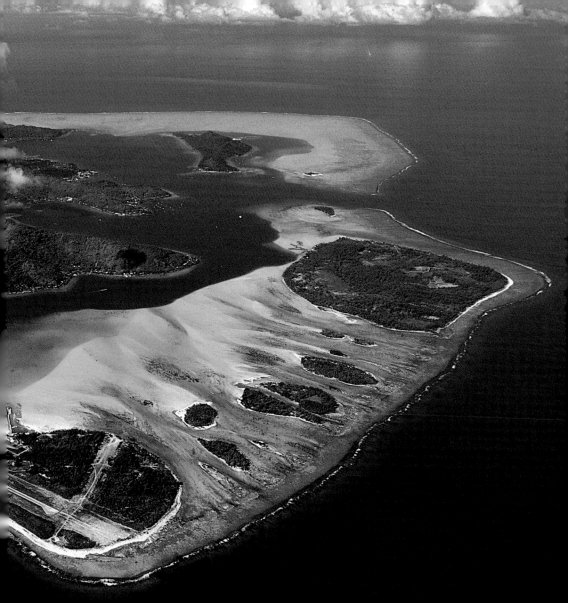

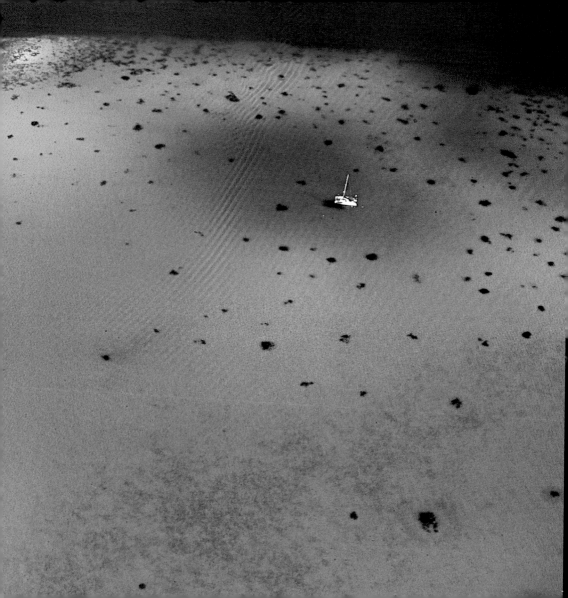

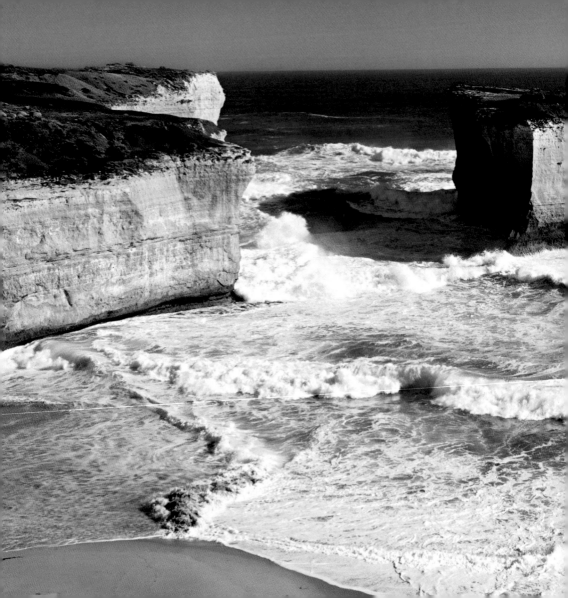

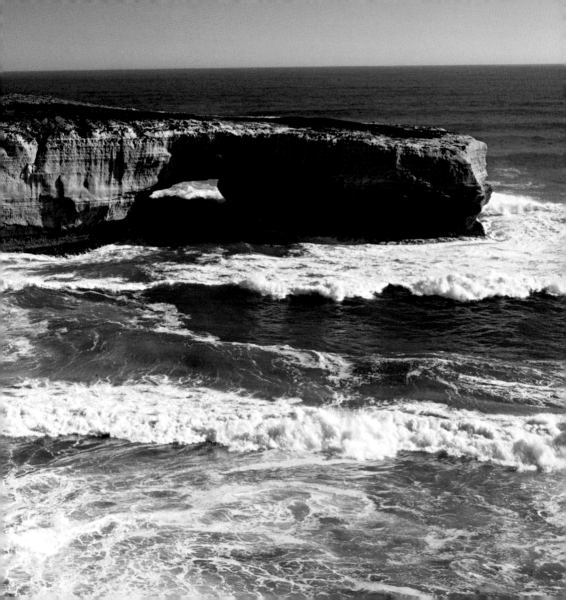

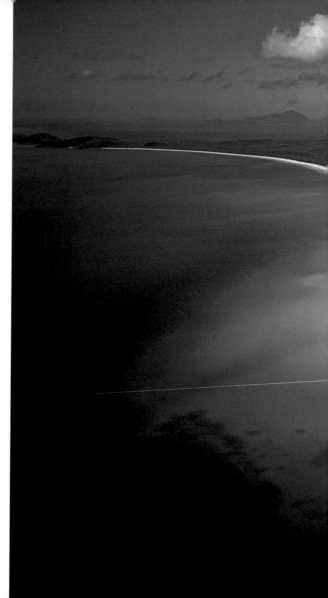

*106-107* ● Queensland (Australia) - Whitsunday Island, Great Barrier Reef Marine Park.

*108-109* ● Seychelles - La Digue.

*110-111* ● Thailand - Rai Lai beach, Krabi.

*112-113* ● Red Sea (Egypt) - Island of Tiran.

*114-115* ● Namibia - Skeleton Coast.

*116-117* ● Sicily (Italy) - Rabbit Beach, Lampedusa.

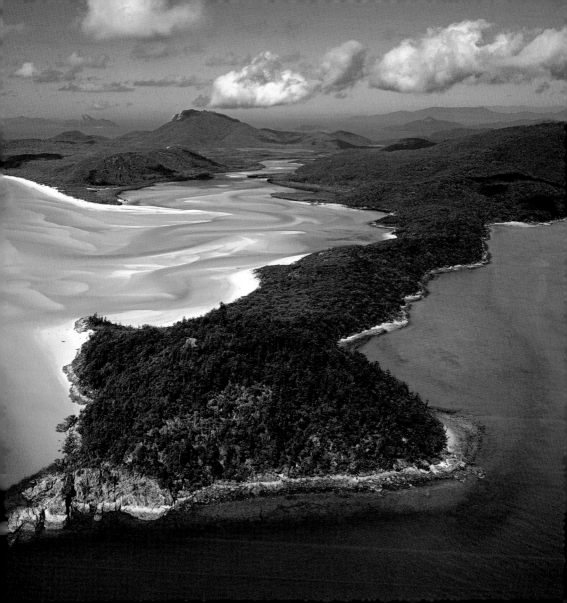

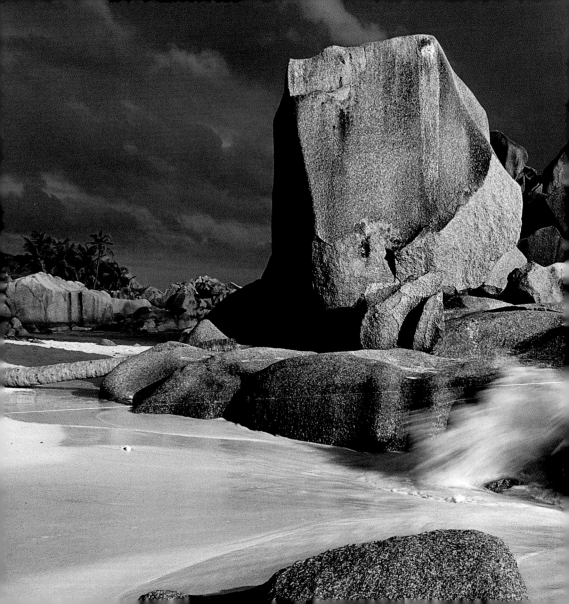

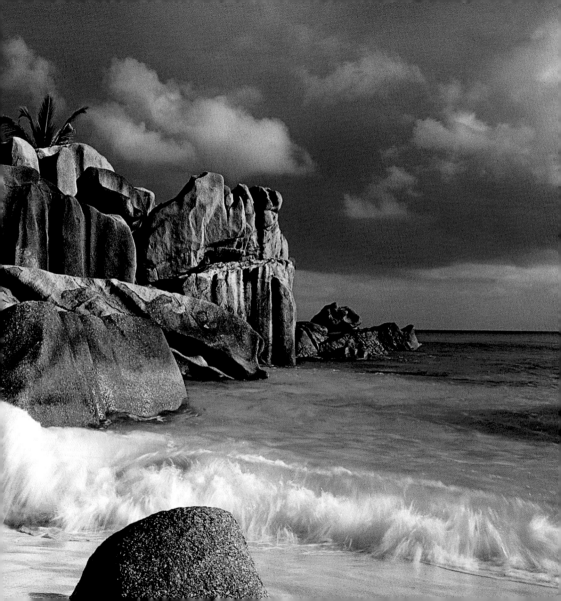

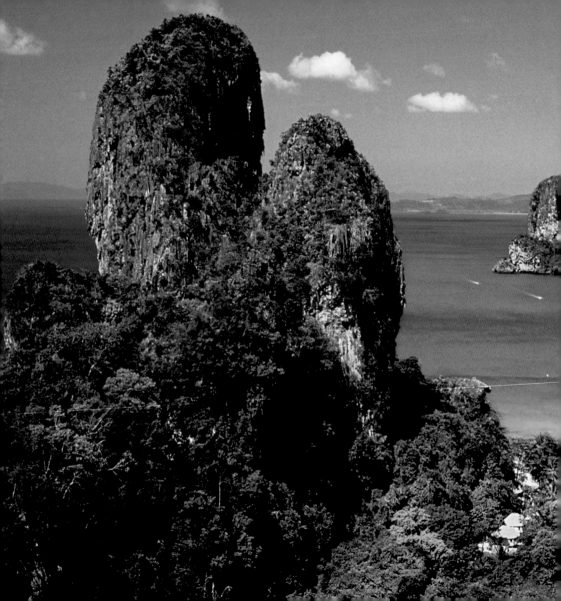

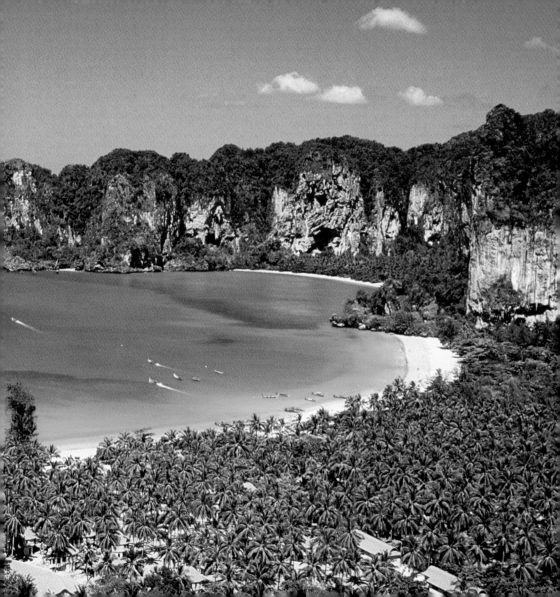

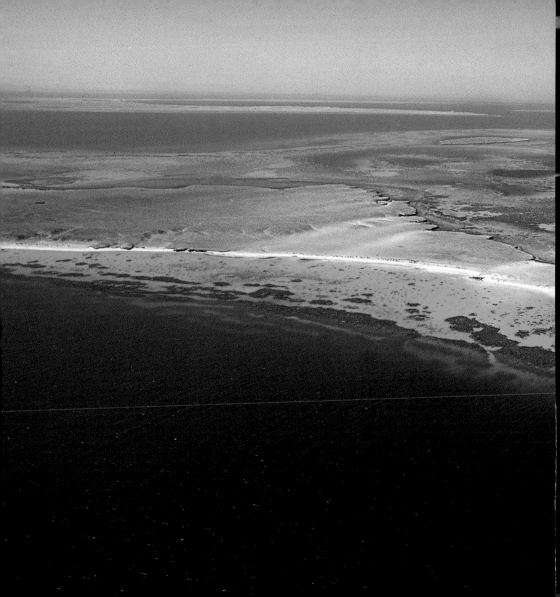

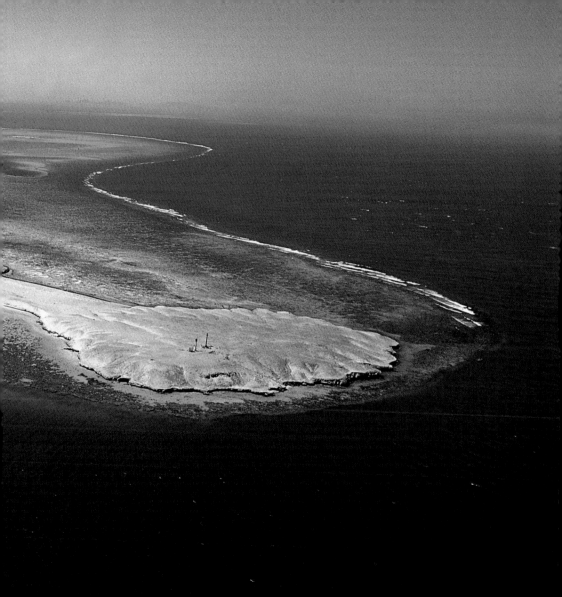

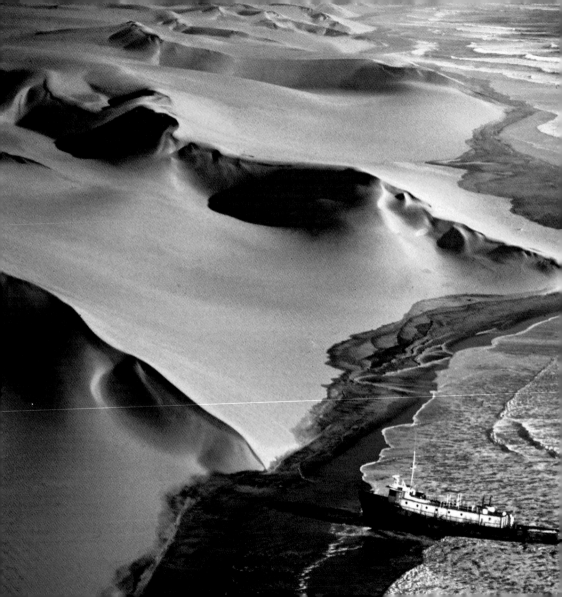

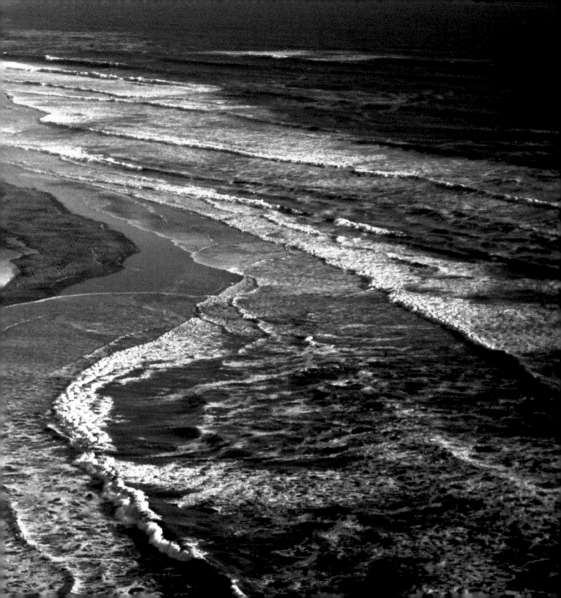

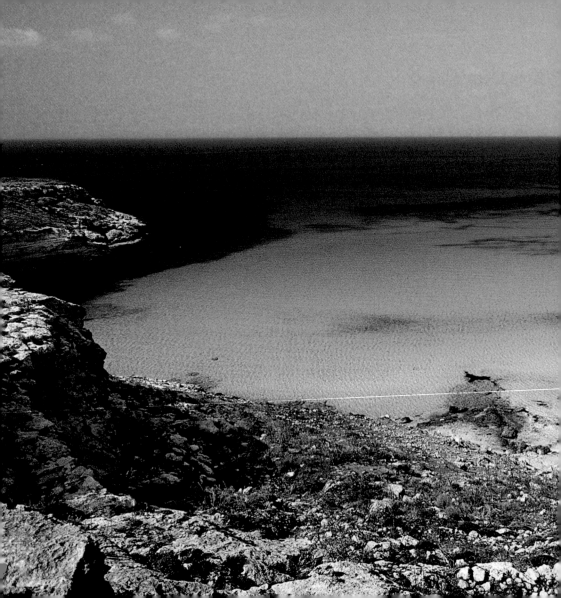

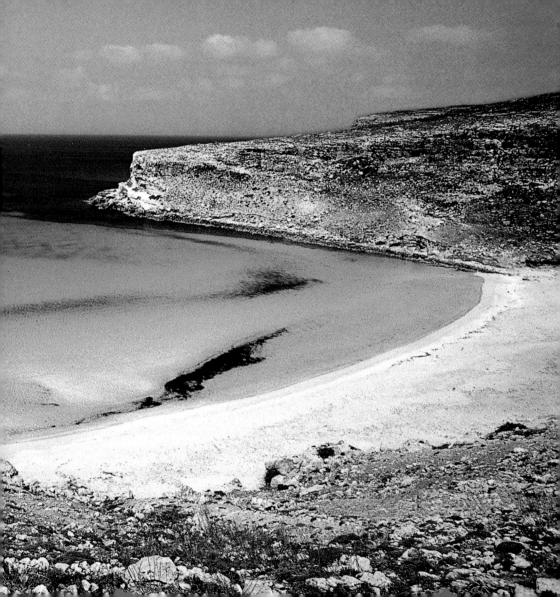

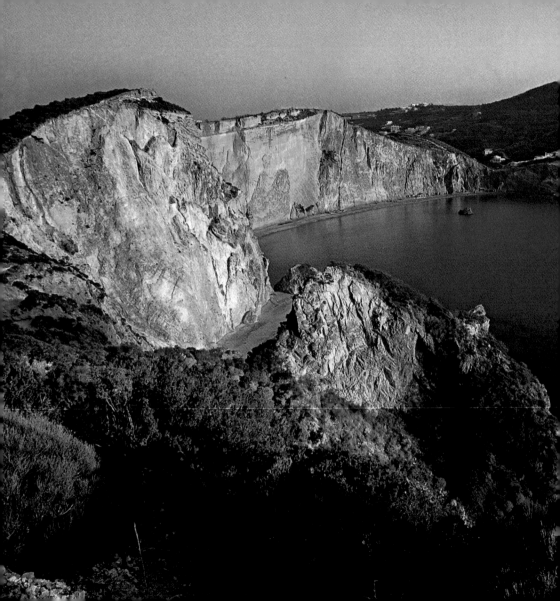

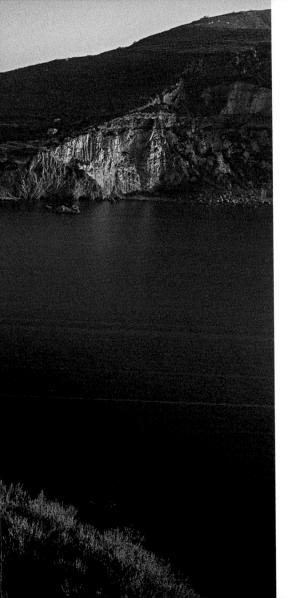

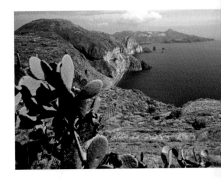

118-119 ● Pontine Islands (Italy) -
Chiaia di Luna, Ponza.

119 ● Lipari Islands (Italy) -
The island of Vulcano.

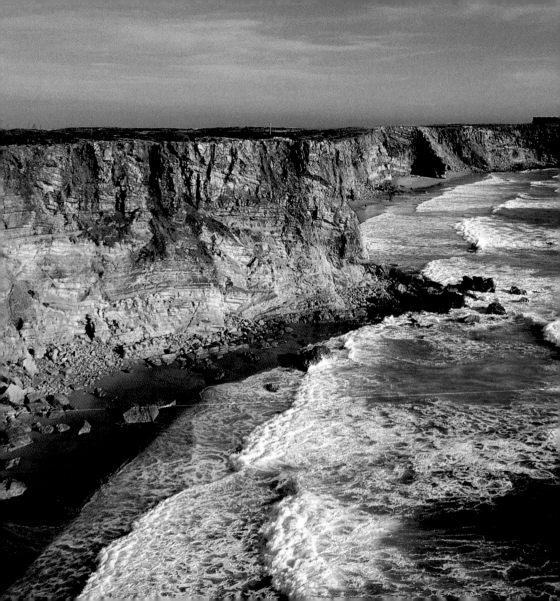

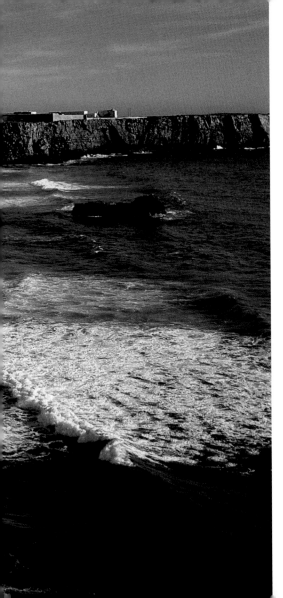

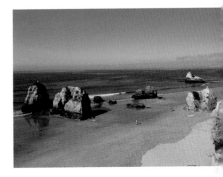

*120-121* ● Algarve (Portugal) - Coastline of Sagres.

*121* ● Algarve (Portugal) - Praia da Rocha.

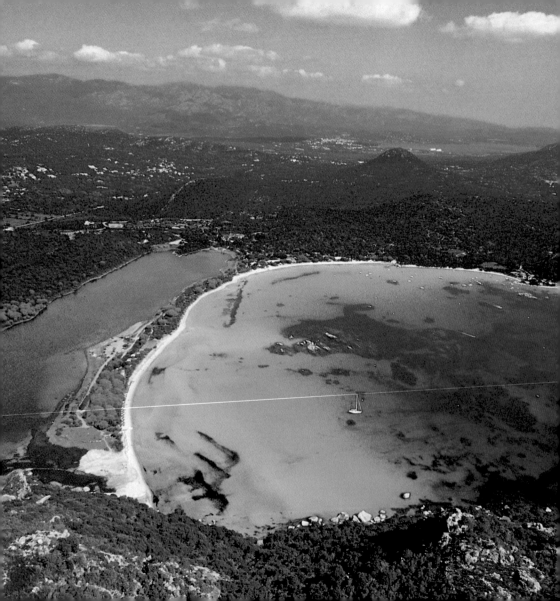

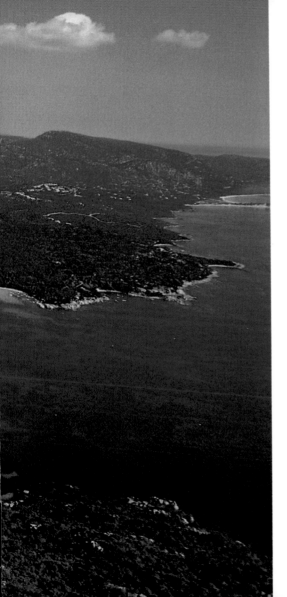

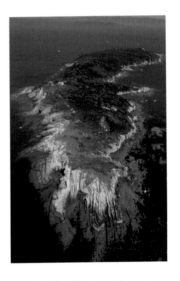

*122-123* ● Corsica (France) -
Southwest coast.

*123* ● Côte d'Azur (France) - Petit
Langoustier, Porquerolles.

*124-125* ● Brittany (France) -
Coastline near Finistère.

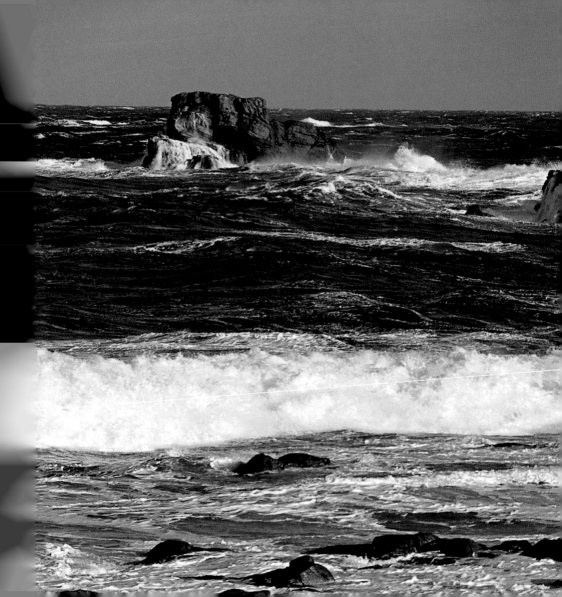

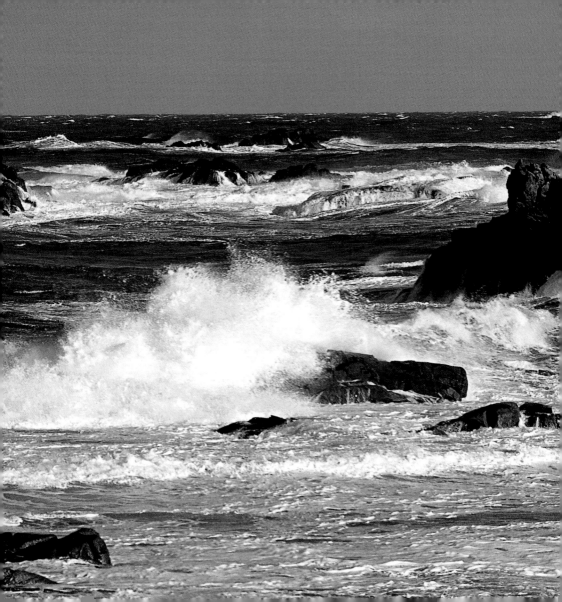

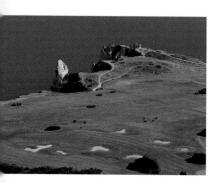

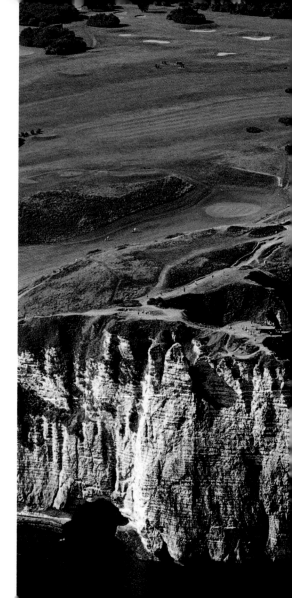

*126* ● Normandy (France) -
Coastline of the Pays de Caux.

*126-127* ● Normandy (France) -
Aval lighthouse, Étretat Bay.

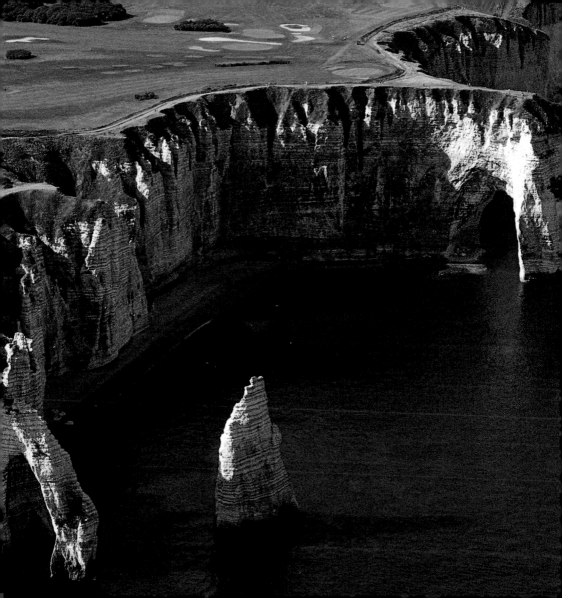

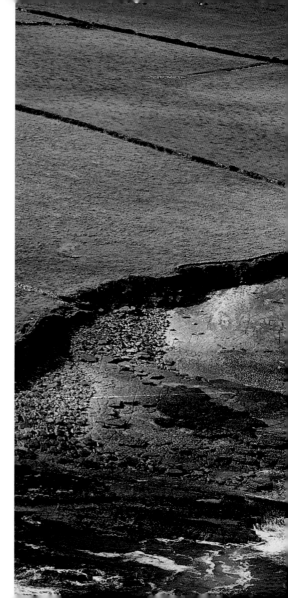

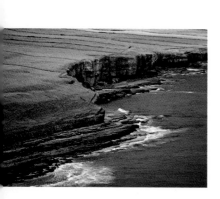

*128 and 128-129* ● County Sligo (Ireland) - Sligo Bay.

*130-131* ● Cuba - Cayo Coco.

*132-133* ● Bahamas - Exuma Cays.

*134-135* ● California (USA) - Big Sur.

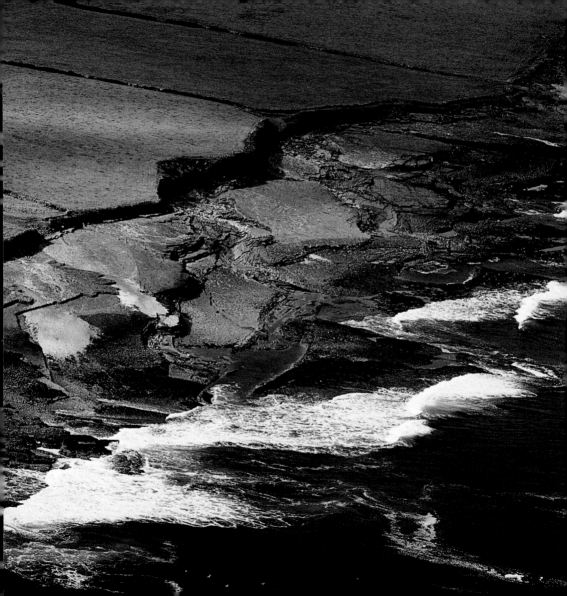

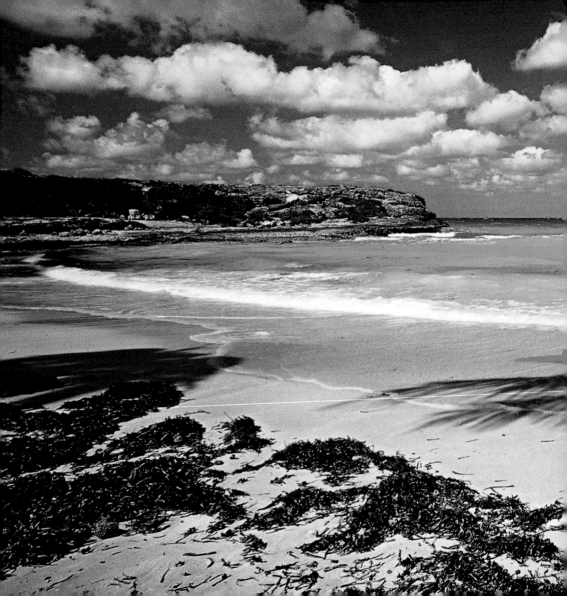

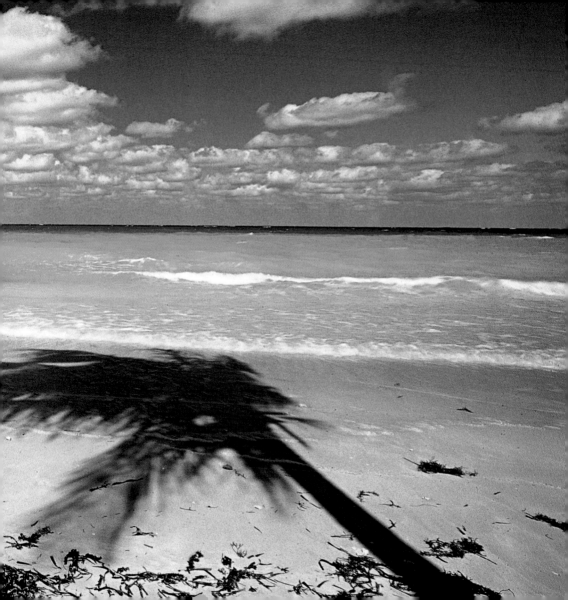

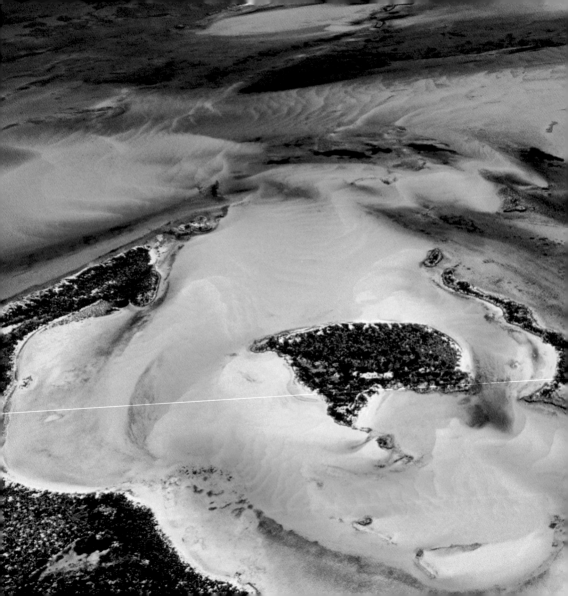

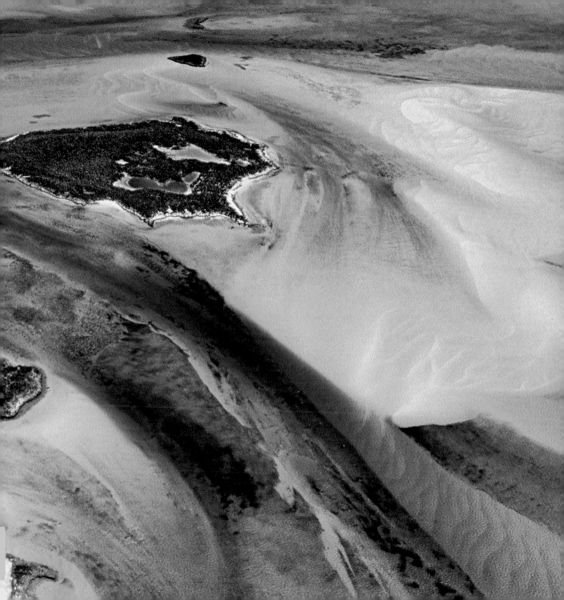

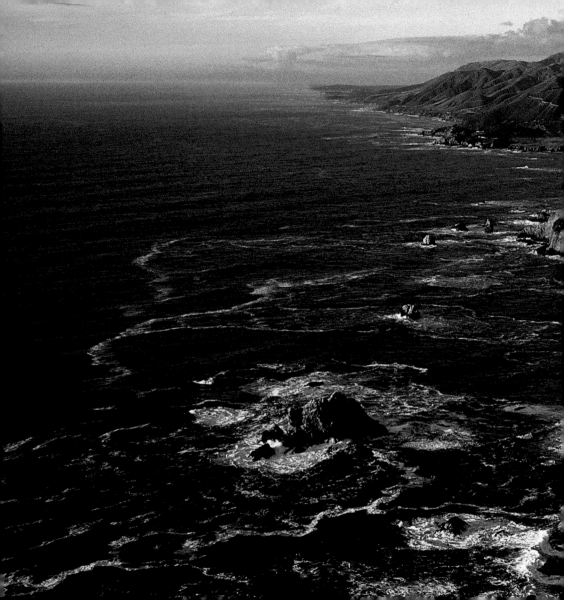

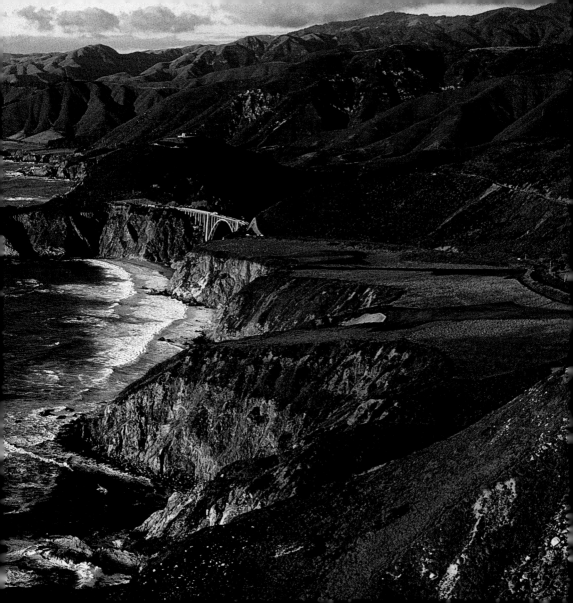

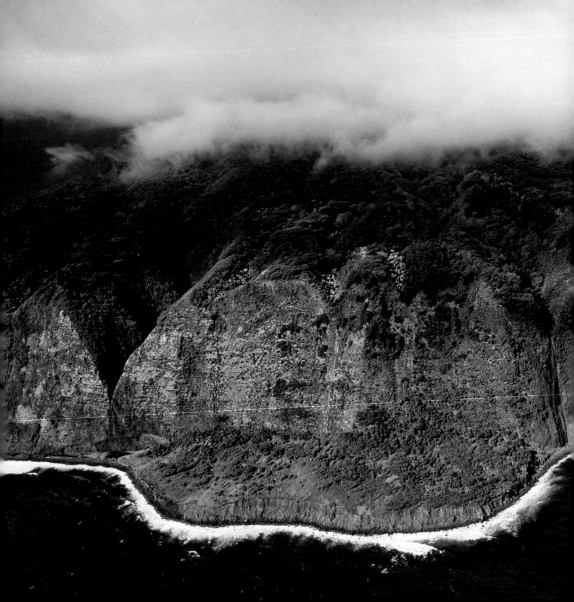

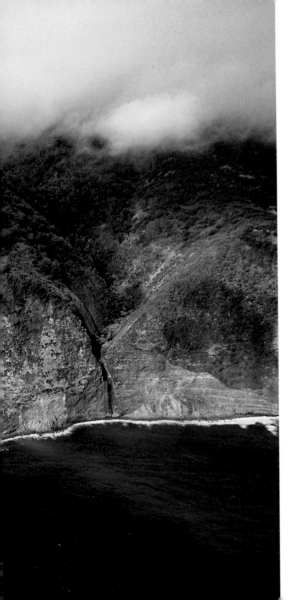

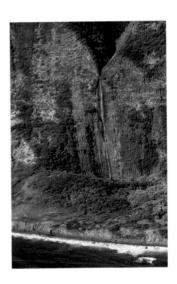

Big Island (Hawaii) -
Waipio Bay.

# SILENT PLANET

• Sinai (Egypt) - Ain Um Ahkmed oasis.

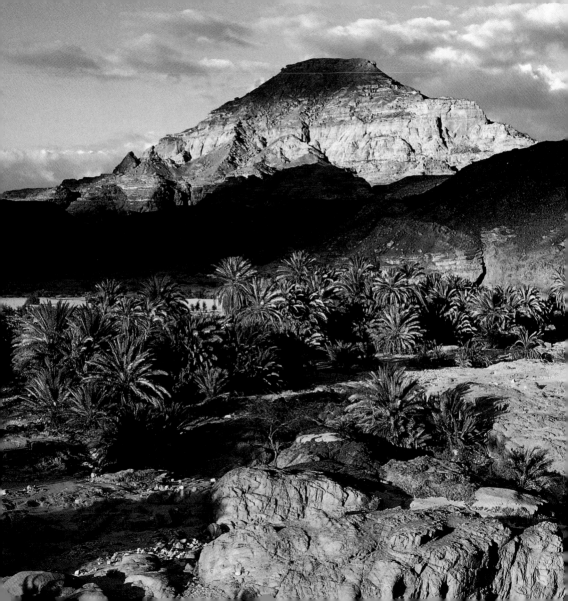

## INTRODUCTION Silent Planet

SAHARA, KALAHARI AND GOBI ARE SYNONYMS FOR LANDS OF NO RETURN, JOURNEYS WITHOUT HOPE, ENDLESS WASTELAND, UNQUENCHABLE THIRST AND DEATH. AND YET, THE ETERNAL EXPANSES OF THE WORLD'S LARGEST DESERTS OFFER A UNIQUE FASCINATION THAT REQUIRES STAMINA AND SENSIBILITY, STRENGTH AND PATIENCE TO BE APPRECIATED. THE MOST BARREN AREAS IN THE WORLD DO NOT FORGIVE THE SUPERFICIAL VISITOR: WE ARE AT THE END OF THE WORLD AND THE LAST SIGN OF WESTERN CIVILIZATION DISAPPEARING BEHIND THE EARTH-COLORED HILLS ARE THE FOUR-WHEEL-DRIVE VEHICLES THAT CAUTIOUSLY VENTURE ALONG PEBBLY TRACKS. THE FEW ROAD SIGNS THAT HAVE SURVIVED THE SANDSTORMS ARE LIKE BOT-

## INTRODUCTION Silent Planet

TLES THROWN INTO THE OCEAN BY A CASTAWAY: MARRAKESH 5,000 KILOMETERS, KUFRA OASES 2,500 KILOMETERS, AIN-BEN-TILI 3,200 KILOMETERS. DESERTS ARE LIKE THE LIGHT THAT FLOODS THEM, CREATING UTTER CONTRASTS: SUFFOCATING HEAT BY DAY AND BITTER COLD AT NIGHT; LONG TREKS INTO WASTELAND AND SUDDEN BURSTS OF LIFE; FIERY REDS, BRIGHT YELLOWS, SKY-BLUES, AS WELL AS THE TYPICAL COLORS OF ASH AND STONE. IN THIS DOMAIN OF BARRENNESS EVERYTHING SEEMS TO BE IN PERPETUAL MOVEMENT: WIND-SWEPT DUNES FOLLOW ONE ANOTHER, FORMING INCREDIBLE PLAYS OF SHADOWS; ROCKS SHAPED BY EROSION ON DISPLAY LIKE BIZARRE SCULPTURES AND ENCHANTED CASTLES; EVIL SPIRITS THAT CREATE AN ENDLESS MIRAGES TO MOCK THIRSTY WAYFARERS; EVEN THE

# Silent Planet

## Introduction

SOUND CREATED BY THE WIND AS IT SHIFTS THE GRAINS OF SAND IN INFINITE MODULATIONS. IN THESE DREAM-LIKE LANDSCAPES, SUBJECT TO CONTINUOUS, UNPREDICTABLE CHANGES, THERE LIVE ELUSIVE, OFTEN MYSTERIOUS CREATURES ABLE TO EXPLOIT SINGLE DROPS OF WATER, LIVING IN A SORT OF SUSPENDED STATE INTERRUPTED BY RARE MOMENTS OF VIGOROUS ACTION. AND THE DESERT PEOPLE ARE EQUALLY MYSTERIOUS, THEIR SKIN AS HARD AS THE LAND ITSELF. REMOTE AND INTANGIBLE, AS ABSOLUTE AS SPACE BUT, LIKE HUMANS, LACKING CER-TAINTY, DESERTS KINDLE OUR IMAGINATION WITH THEIR HARSH AND SPECTACULAR SCENERY. BUT THEY ARE ALSO A WORLD IN WHICH PARADOX BECOMES POETRY.

*143* ● New South Wales (Australia) - 'Wall of China,' Mungo National Park.

*144-145* ● Libya - Variations in the light and shapes of the dunes in the Libyan Desert.

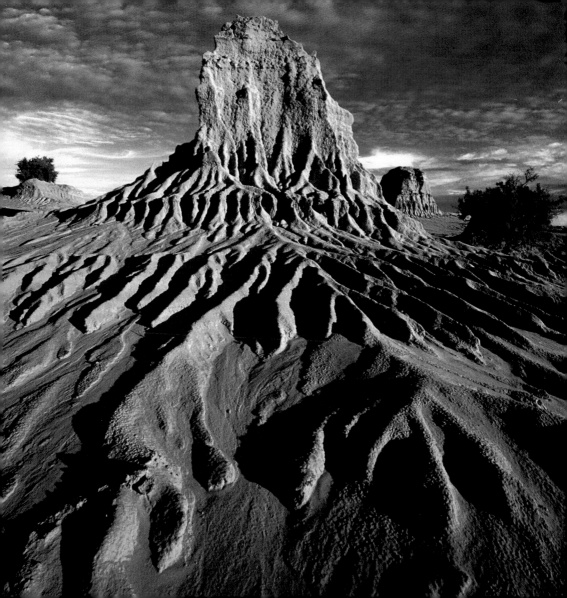

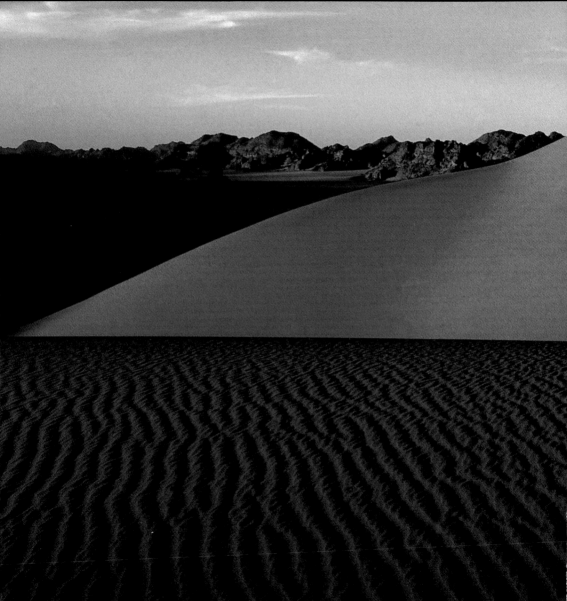

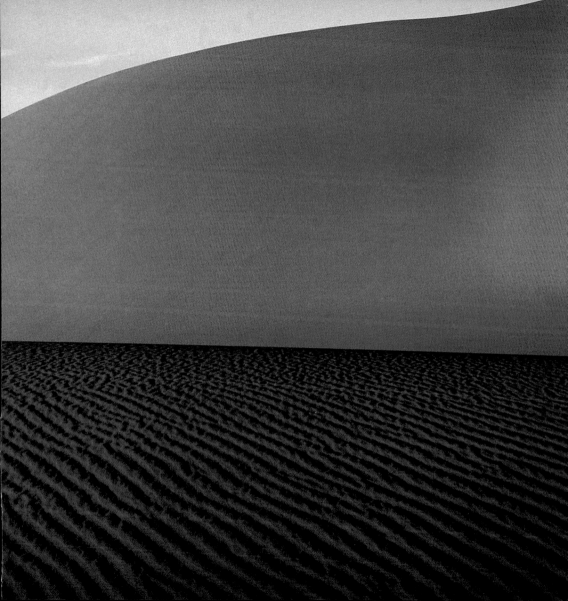

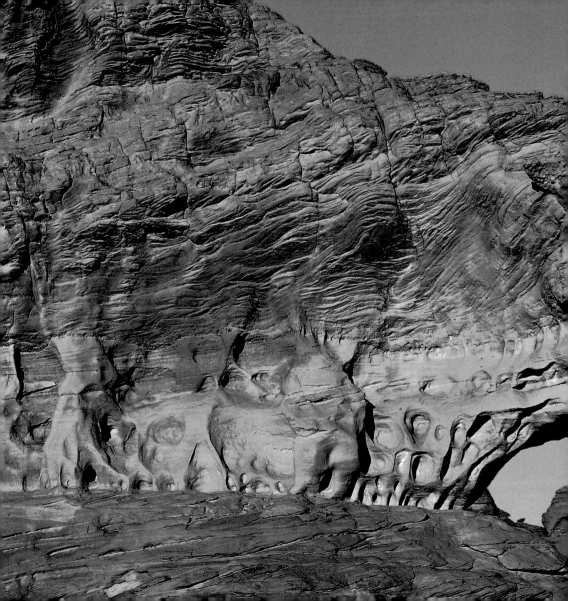

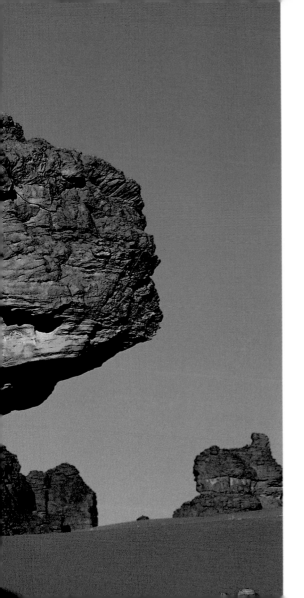

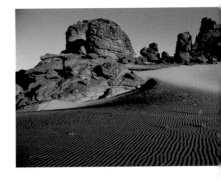

*146-147 and 147* ● Region of
Fezzan (Libya) - Animal-shaped
rocks near Akakus.

*148-149* ● Region of Fezzan
(Libya) - Sebha oasis.

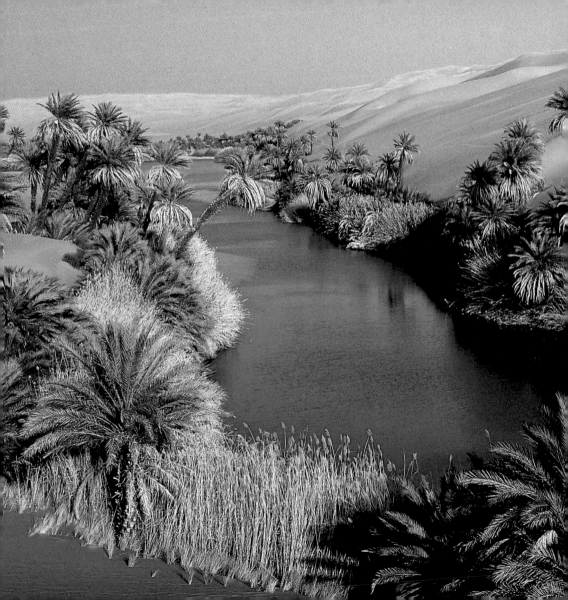

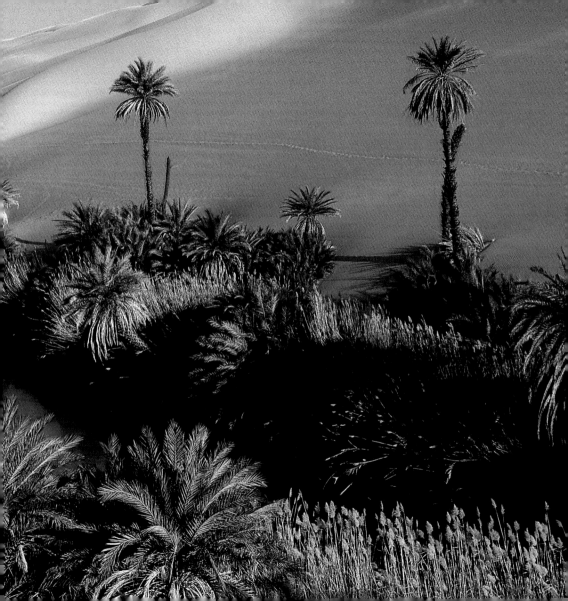

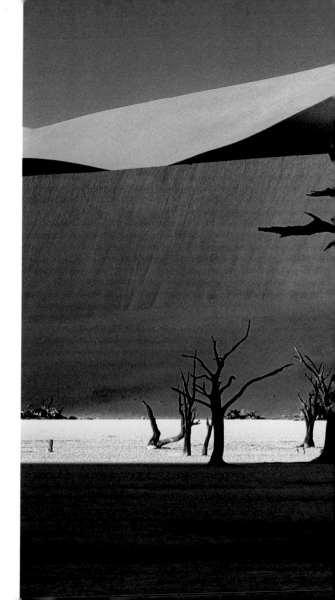

*150-151* ● Namibia - Sussusvlei dunes.

*152-153* ● Namibia - Traces of erosion in the desert to the west of Gamsberg Pass.

*154-155* ● Egypt - Wind-sculpted dunes near Bahariya and Farafra oases.

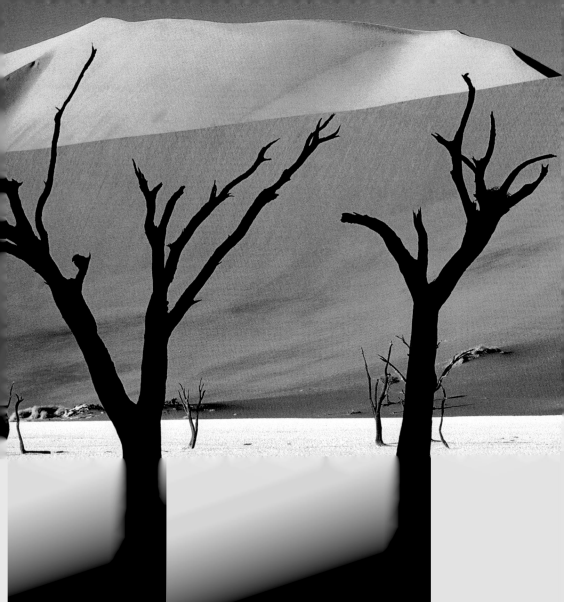

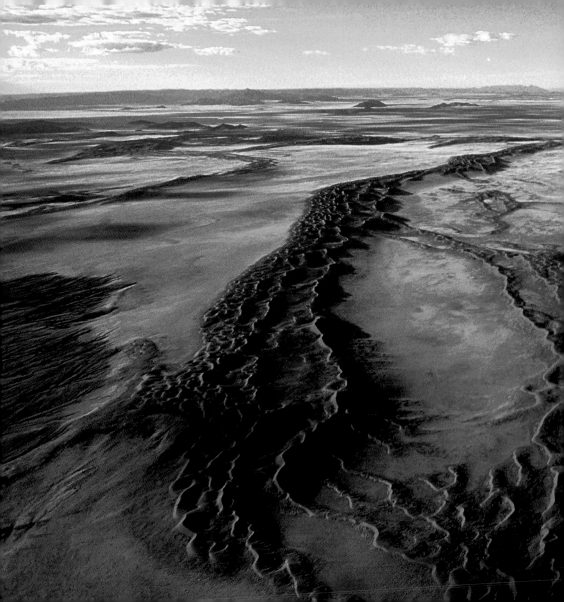

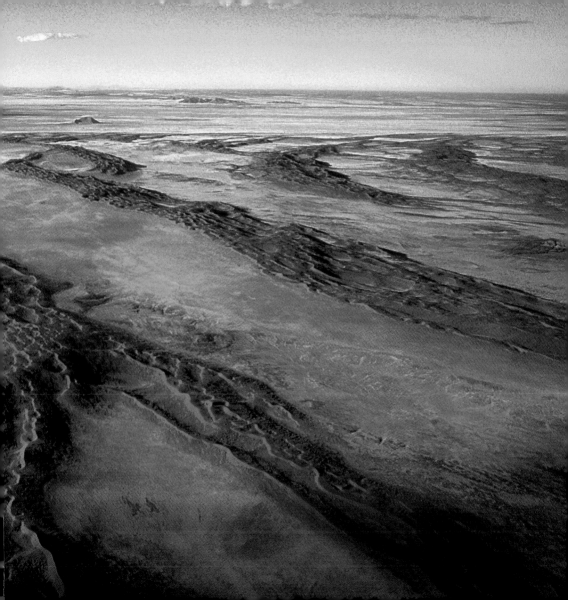

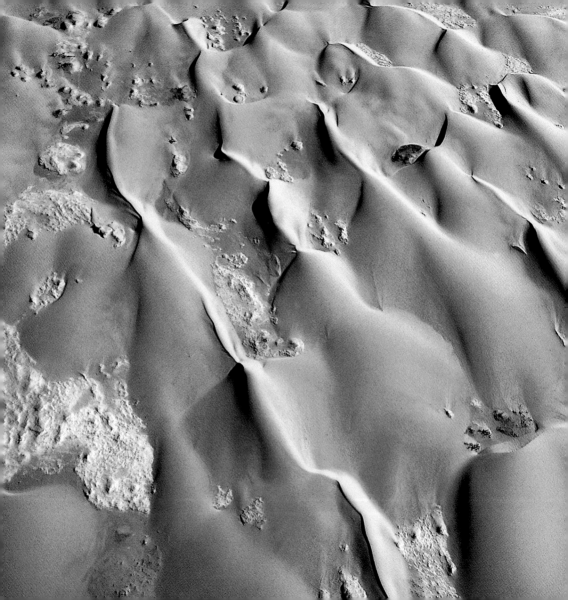

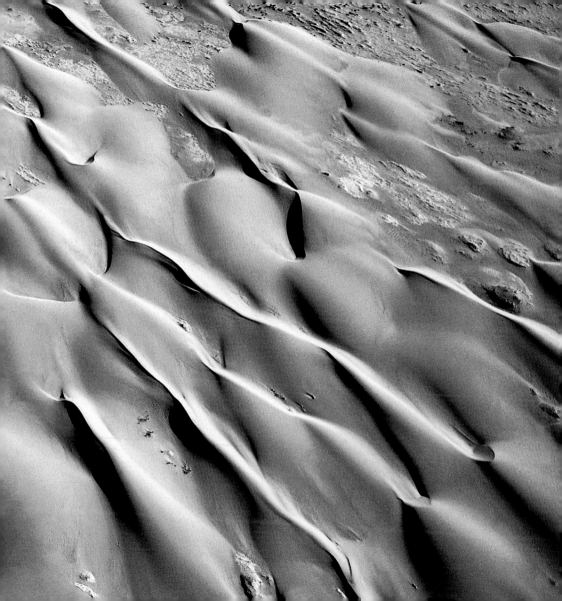

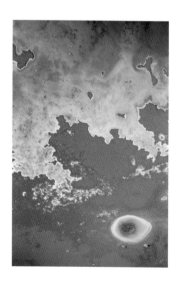

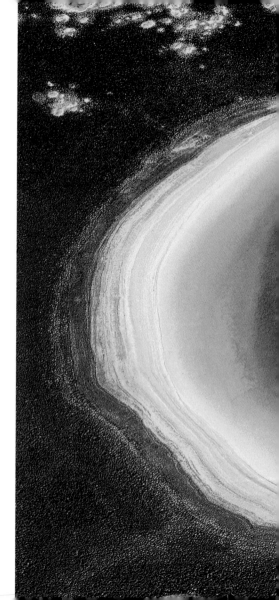

*156 and 156-157* ● Egypt - Salt lakes near Shali, Siwa Oasis.

*158-159* ● Sinai (Egypt) - Jebel Musa.

*160-161* ● Israel - Negev Desert.

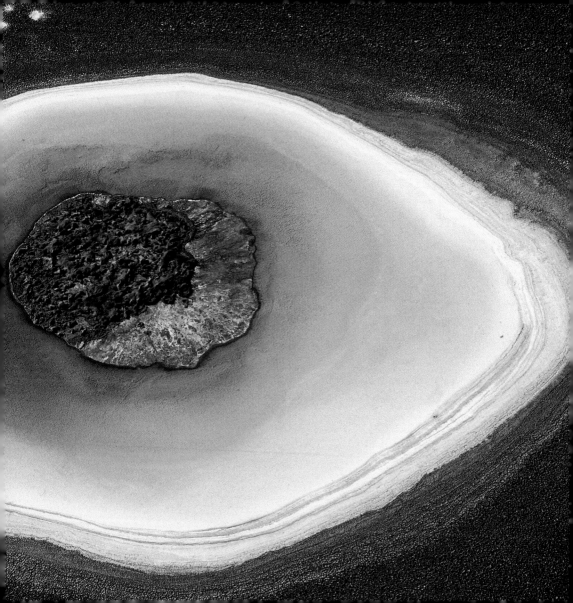

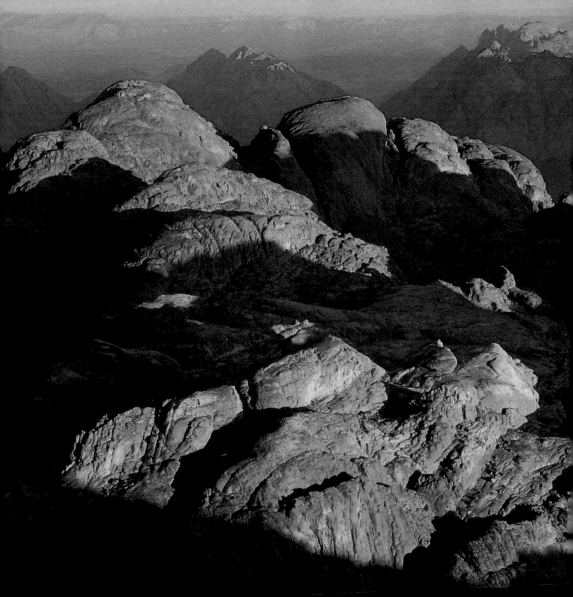

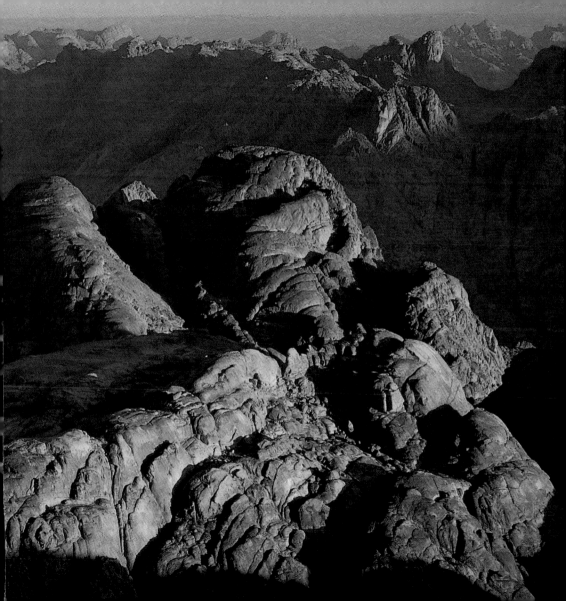

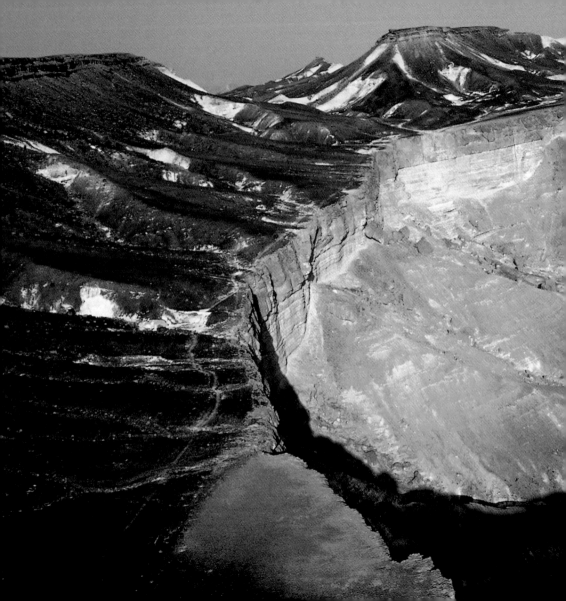

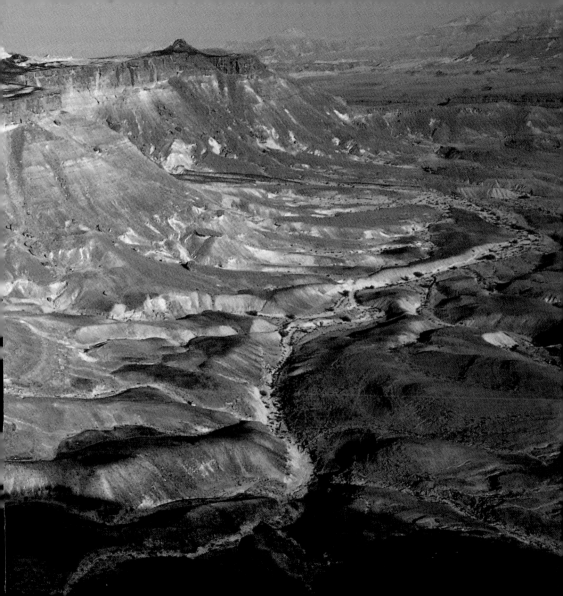

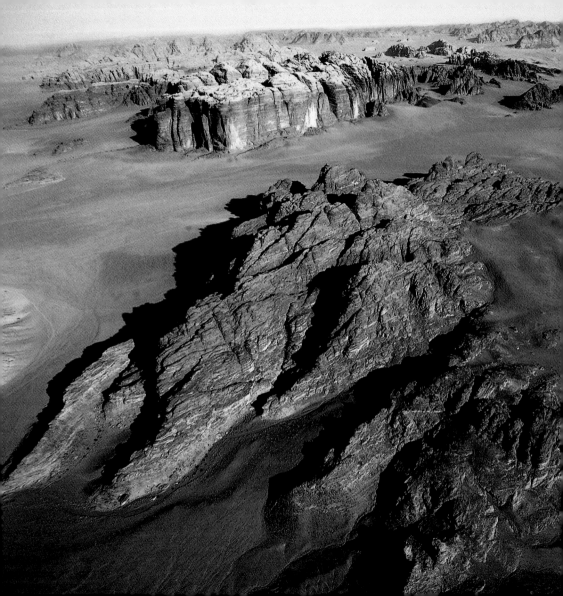

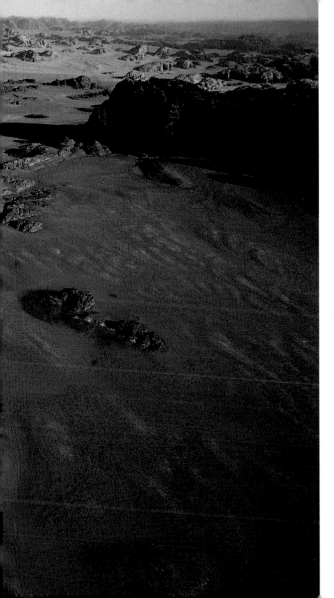

*162-163* ● Jordan - Wadi Rum.

*164-165* ● California (USA) - Death Valley, Zabriskie Point.

*166-167* ● Arizona (USA) - Colorado River Valley.

*168-169* ● Xinjiang Uygur (China) - Erosion-formed valley on the Silk Road.

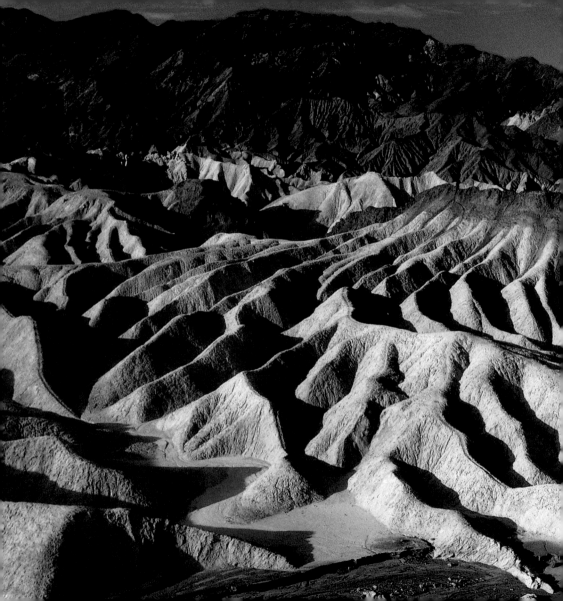

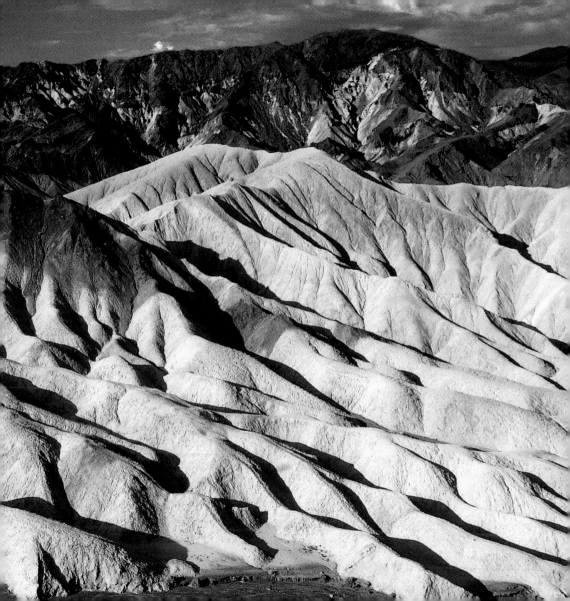

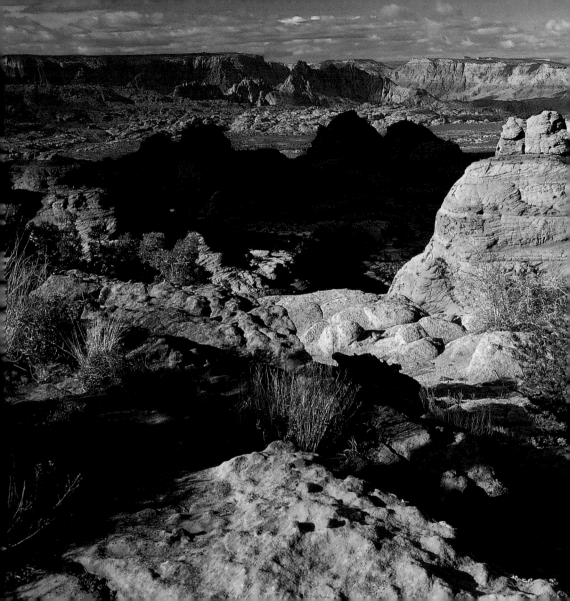

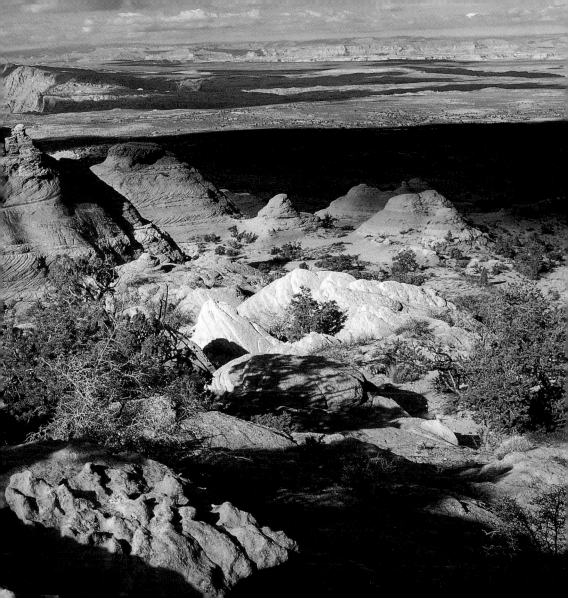

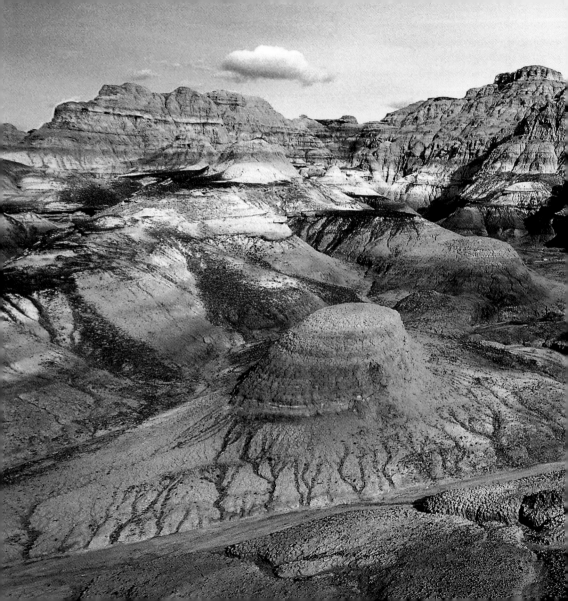

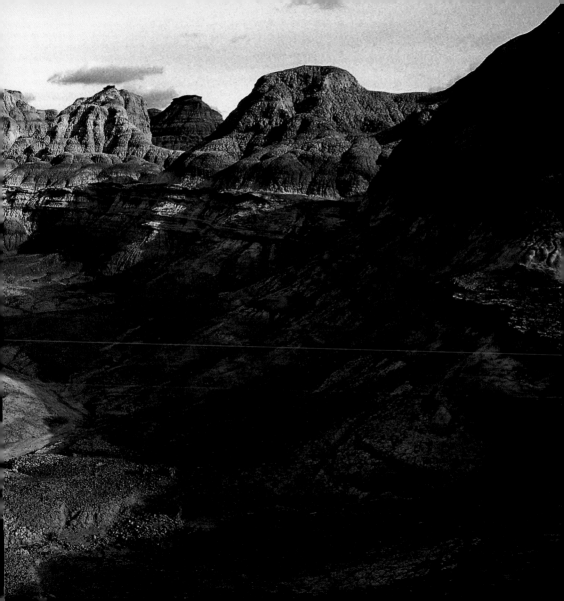

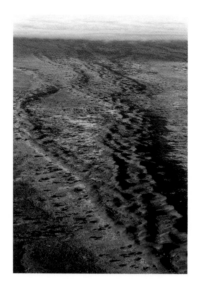

*170* ● South Australia (Australia) - Strzelecki Desert.

*171* ● South Australia (Australia) - Everard Ranges, Great Victoria Desert.

*172-173* ● Western Australia (Australia) - The Pinnacles, Nambung National Park.

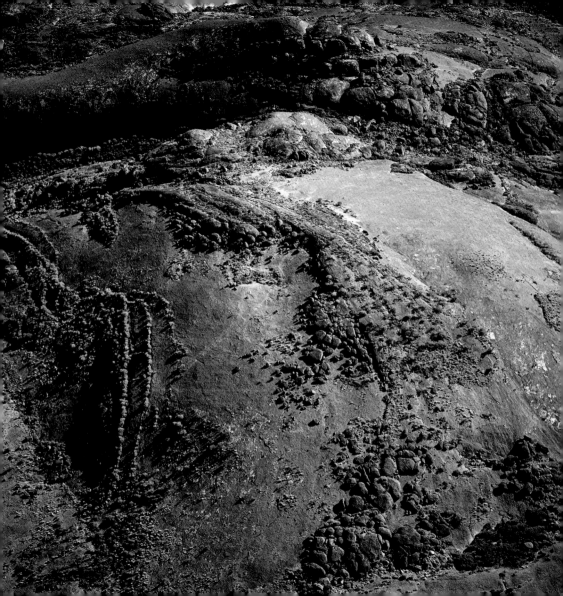

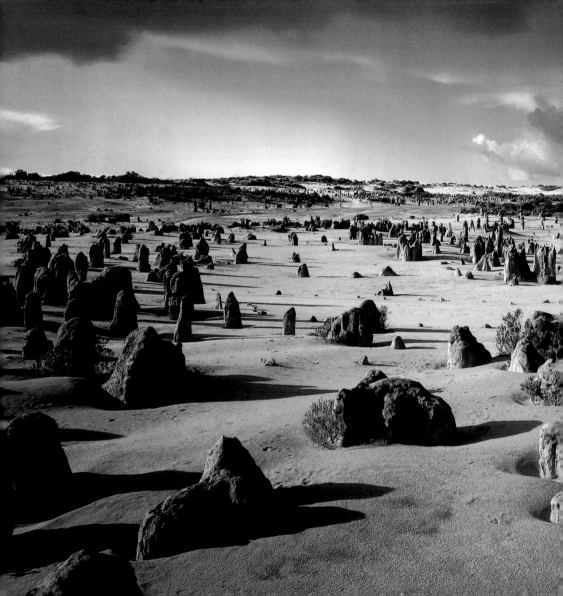

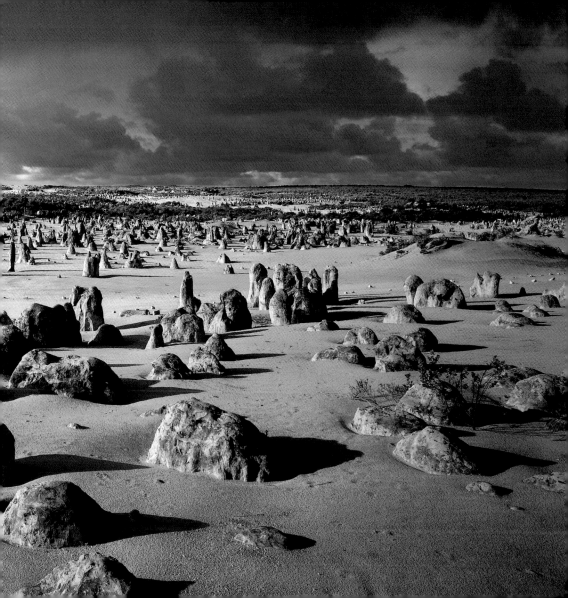

# ROOTS of the WORLD

Nigeria - Jungle in the Niger Delta.

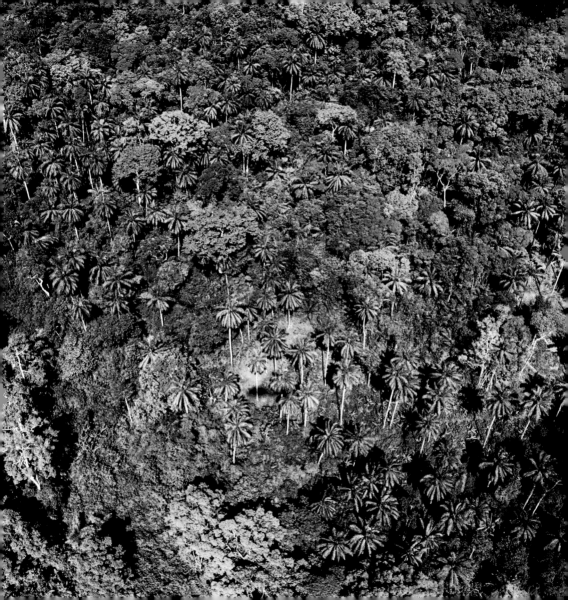

## INTRODUCTION

THE "LUNGS" OF THE EARTH ARE GREEN. A BRILLIANT GREEN LIKE MOUNTAIN WOODS, EMERALD LIKE THE SOUTH AMERICAN PLUVIAL FORESTS, TINGED WITH BLUISH NUANCES LIKE THE CONIFERS IN NORTH EUROPE, BRIGHT LIKE THE SUNNY PATCHES IN THE SOUTH MEDITERRANEAN OR THE DATE PALMS SURROUNDED BY SAND IN NORTH AFRICA. VIEWED FROM THE SKY, FORESTS ARE COLORED CLOUDS, AS THICK AS CARPETS. SEEN FROM GROUND LEVEL, THEY ARE THE LAND OF FANTASY, DREAMS, LIFE ITSELF. IN FACT, FORESTS HAVE ALWAYS BEEN THE SETTING FOR THE MOST FABULOUS FAIRY TALES AND SAGAS; THEY ARE THE HOME, THE WOMB, THE PLACE OFFERING WOOD AND FOOD TO KEEP US WARM AND FEED US, AND SHELTER US FROM RAIN OR HEAT.

## INTRODUCTION Roots of the World

SOMETIMES FORESTS ARE ALSO PLACES OF THE SPIRIT, AS FOR EXAMPLE IN DANTE, WHO VIEWED THE "DARK WOOD" AS THE ABODE OF SIN, TERROR AND EVIL, WHICH ASSAIL HUMANS DURING THEIR JOURNEY TOWARD LIGHT. THIS IS ALSO THE CASE WITH TOLKIEN, WHOSE SWEETEST, MOST INTELLIGENT, STRONGEST AND HEROIC CREA-TURES LIVE IN THE WOODS, WHILE EVIL AND VIOLENCE DWELL IN FLAT STEPPES, ON OMINOUS MOUNTAINTOPS OR IN DARK CAVES. FORESTS LIVE IN SYMBIOSIS WITH WATER. THE BEST EXAMPLES OF THIS ARE TROPICAL FORESTS, WHERE IN CERTAIN SEASONS EVERY CREEK BECOMES A TORRENT AND EVERY TORRENT A FORMIDA-BLE RIVER THAT CARRIES TO THE SEA TONS OF SEDIMENT AND TREE TRUNKS RIPPED AWAY FROM THE BANKS, AND

# Roots of the World

## Introduction

EQUATORIAL JUNGLES, CALLED "CLOUD FORESTS" BECAUSE THEY ARE ALMOST ALWAYS IMMERSED IN THICK RAIN CLOUDS. THE SAME SYMBIOSIS EXISTS BETWEEN WOODS AND THE MYRIAD CREATURES THAT LIVE IN THEM: FLOWERS, BUTTERFLIES, HYMENOPTERA AND COLEOPTERA WITH THEIR DAZZLING COLORS, FISH, REPTILES, AMPHIBIANS, BIRDS, MAMMALS LARGE AND SMALL. A SELF-SUFFICIENT MICROCOSM; A BIOSPHERE IN WHICH THE CHAIN OF LIFE HAS A THOUSAND BEGINNINGS AND A THOUSAND CONCLUSIONS; AN ENVIRONMENT BUFFETED BY LIGHT WHEN IT FILTERS THROUGH THE FOLIAGE IN BROAD SHAFTS, BUT WHICH BECOMES MORE FASCINATING IN DARKNESS AND MYSTERY.

*179* ● Quebec (Canada) - Forest in fall.

*180-181* ● Piedmont (Italy) - Larch woods in Valsesia.

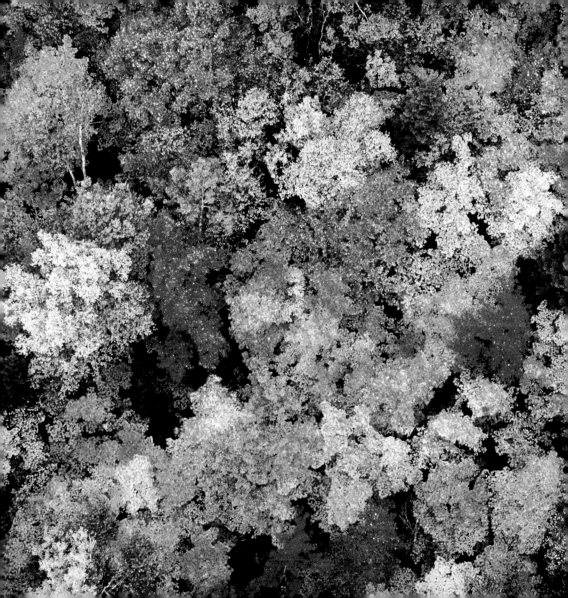

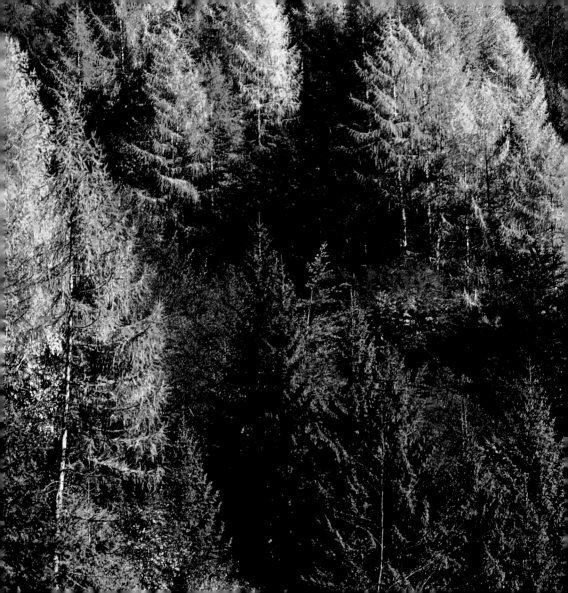

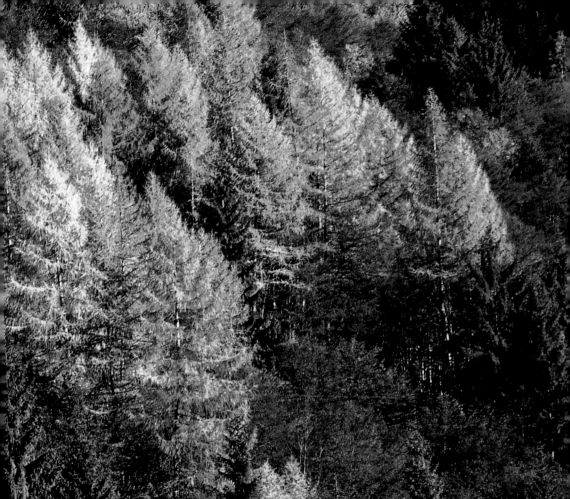

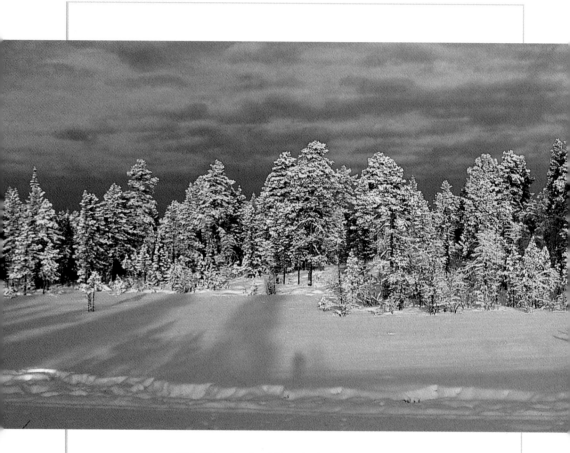

*182-183* ● Lapland (Sweden) - Forest in winter.

*184-185* ● Denmark - Nordskoven Forest.

*186-187* ● Congo - Forest along the Konilou River.

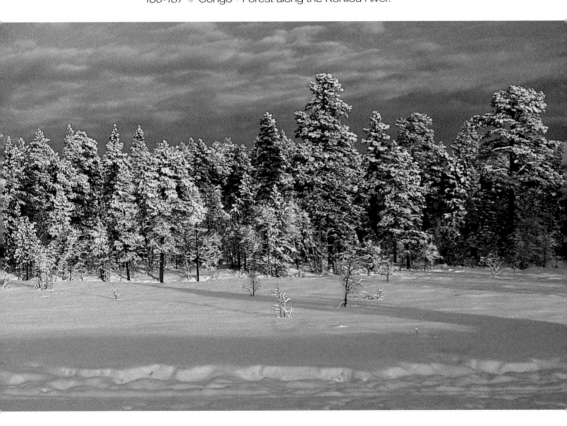

*188-189* ● Congo - Forest of bamboo.

*190-191* ● Congo - 'Gorges de Diosso' at Pointe Noire.

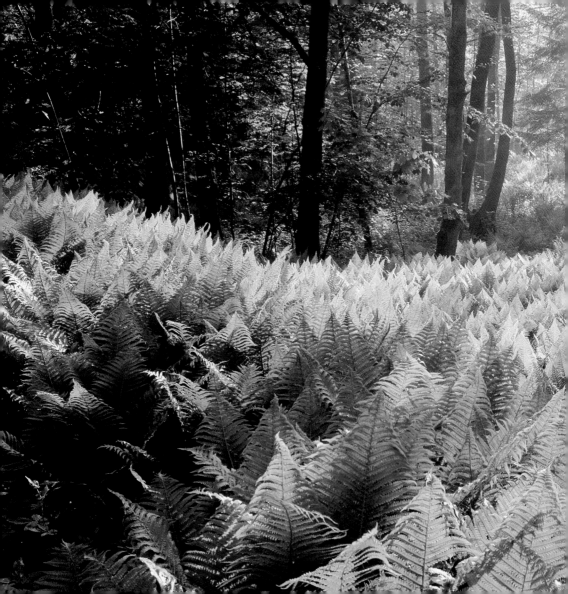

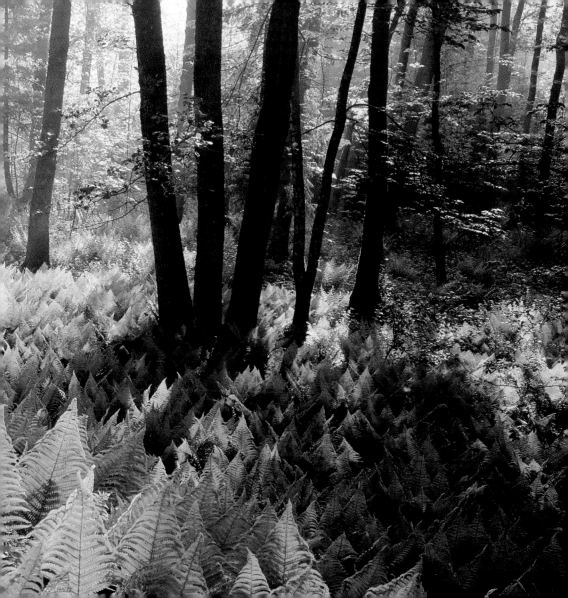

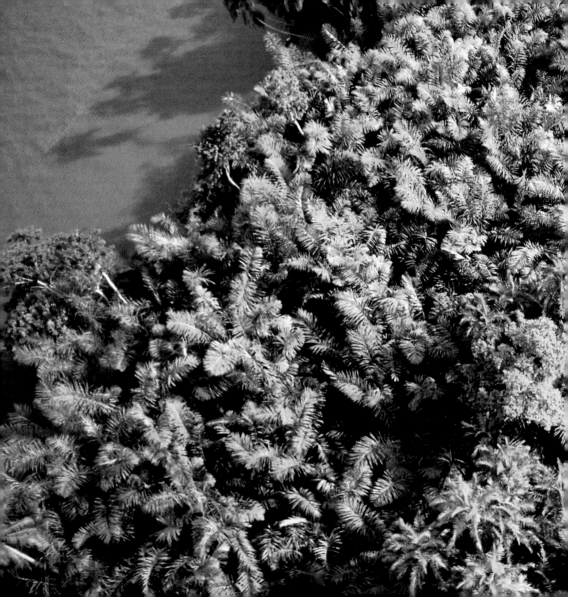

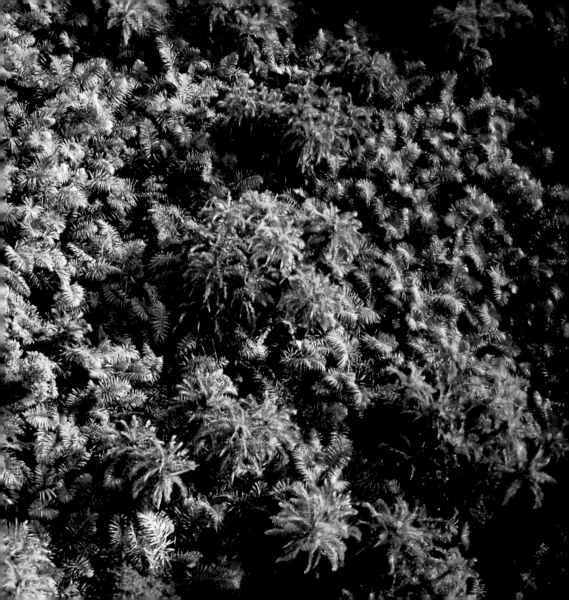

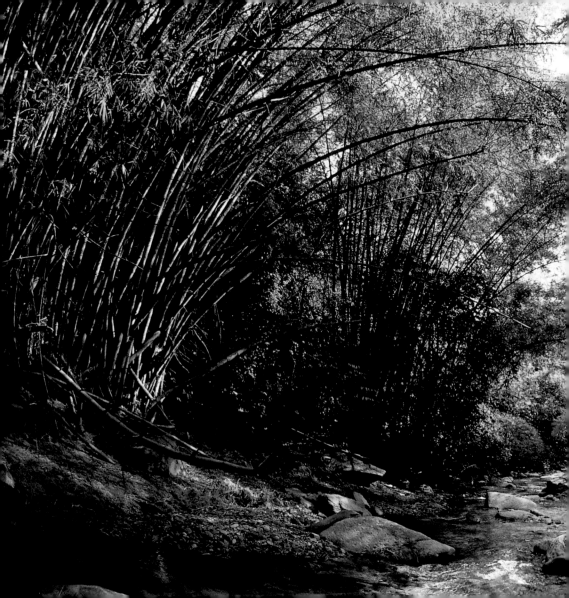

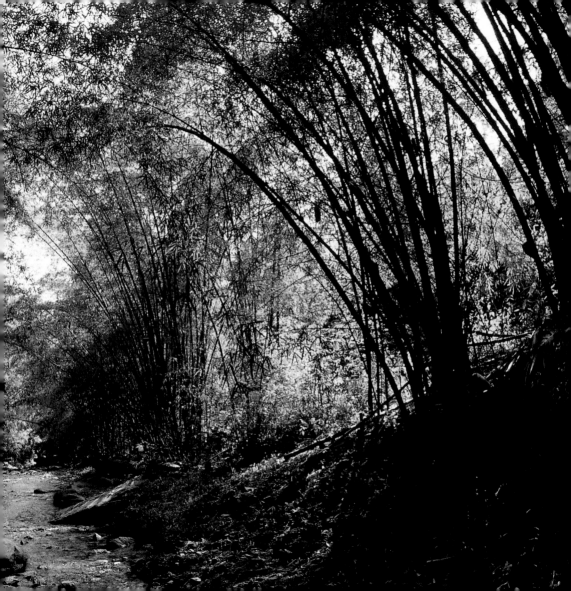

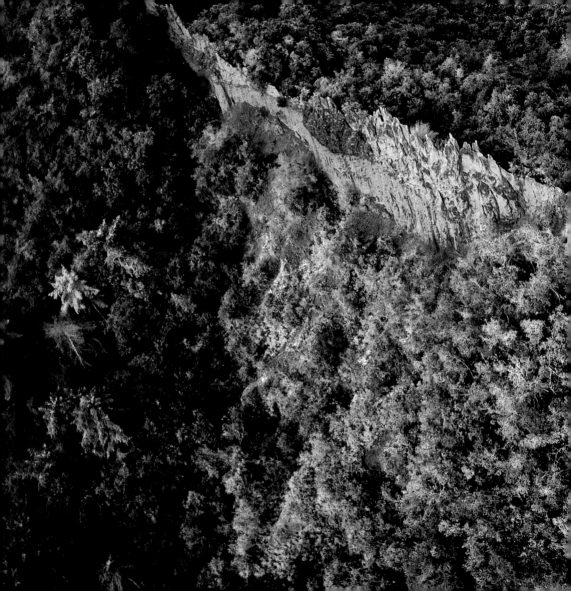

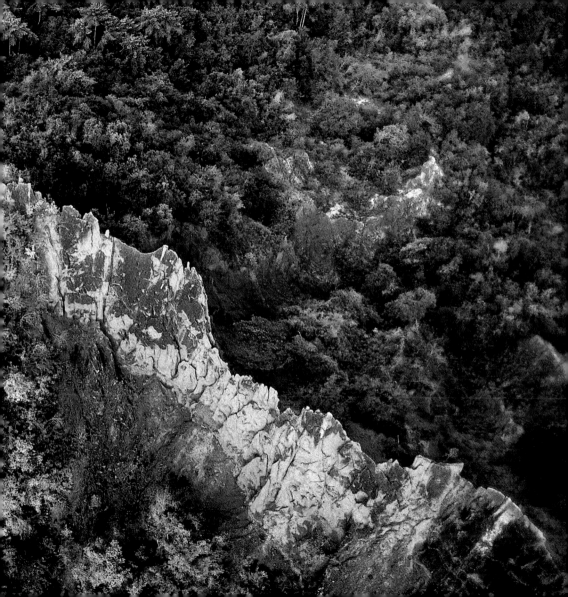

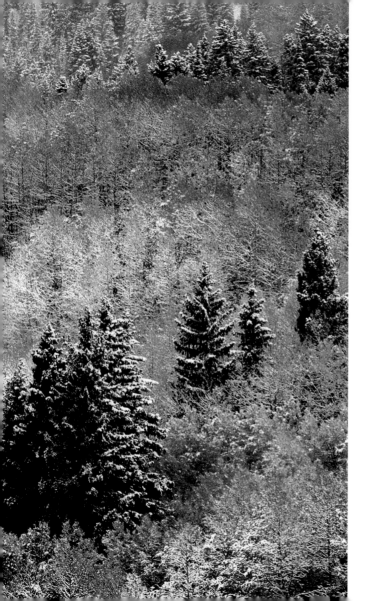

Colorado (USA) - Forest
of poplars and fir
in Aspen.

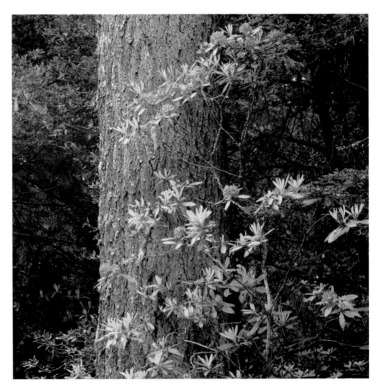

● California (USA) - Redwood National Park.

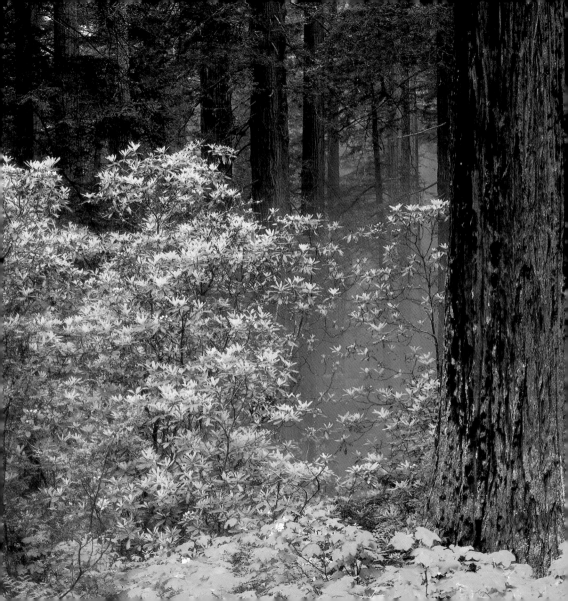

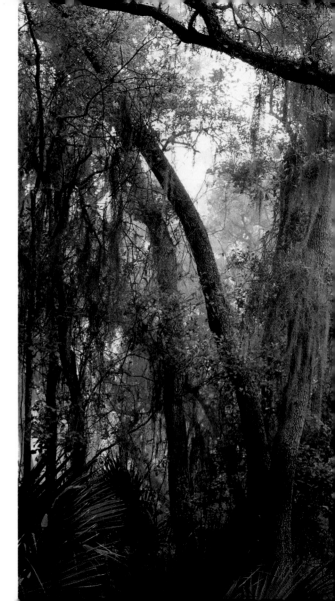

196-197 ● Florida (USA) -
Tropical vegetation in
Lake Woodruff National
Wildlife Refuge.

198-199 ● Costarica -
Monteverde Forest.

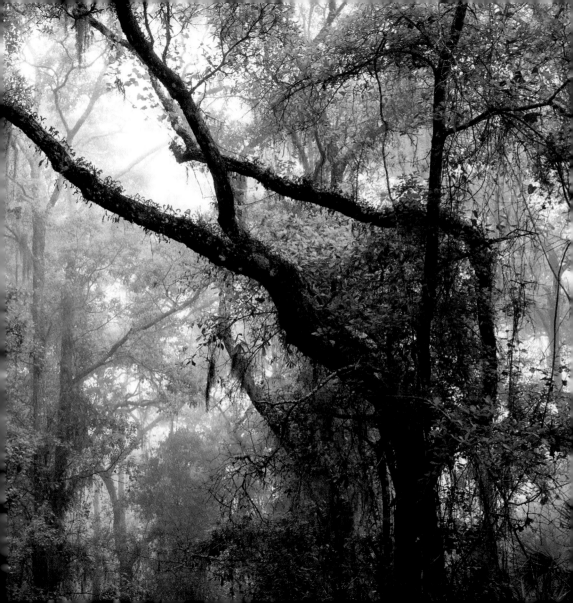

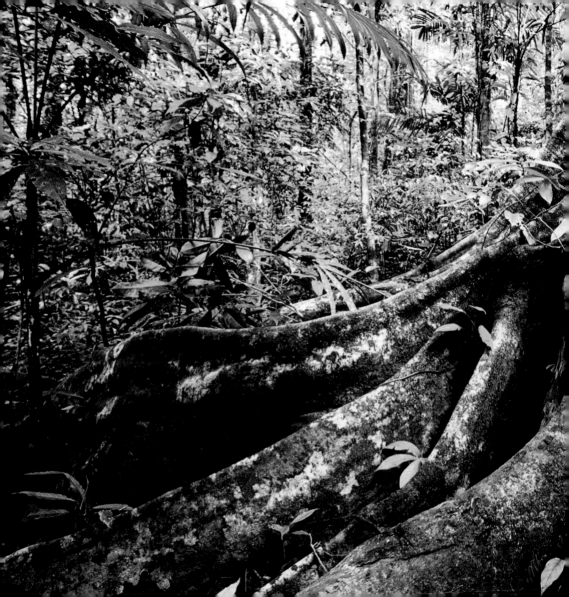

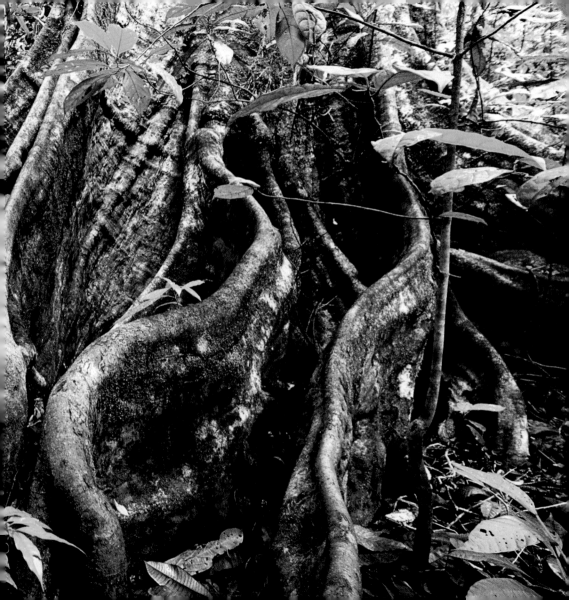

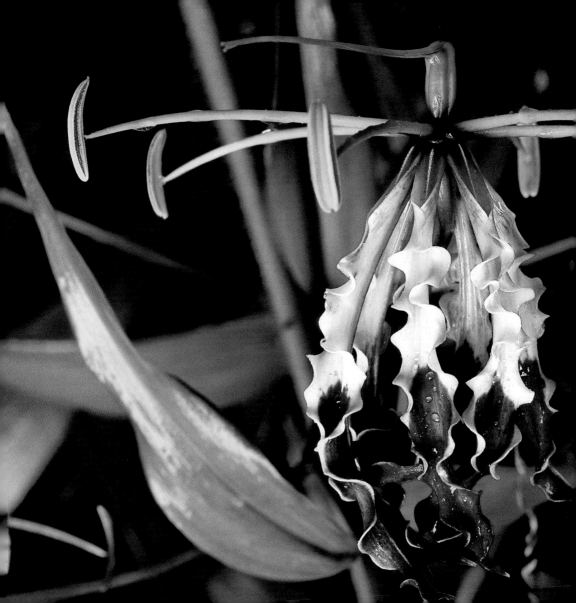

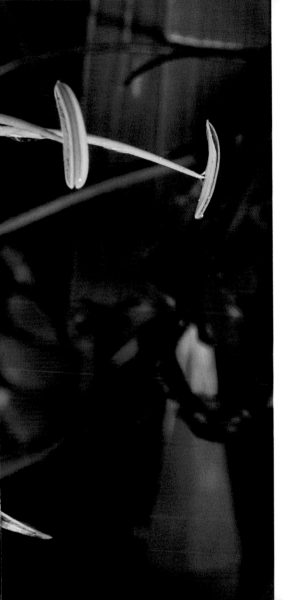

200-201 ● Sri Lanka - The flower of *Gloriosa superba*, Udowattakele Forest Reserve.

201 ● Sumatra (Indonesia) - *Balanophora*, Gunung Leuser National Park.

202-203 ● Borneo (Malaysia) - Sabah Forest.

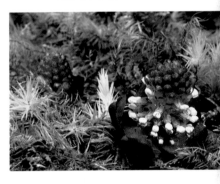

204-205 ● Borneo (Malaysia) - Kinabalu National Park.

206-207 ● Society Islands (French Polynesia) - Huahiné Forest.

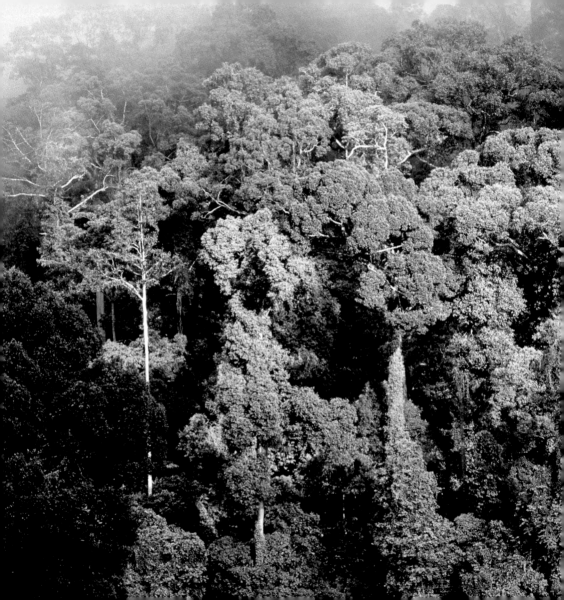

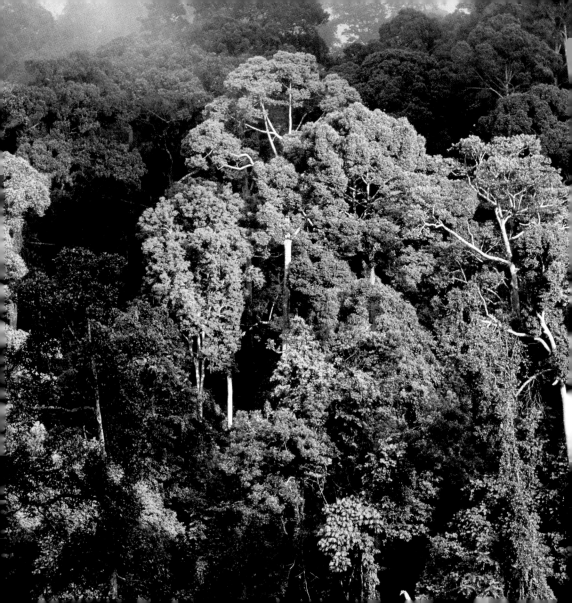

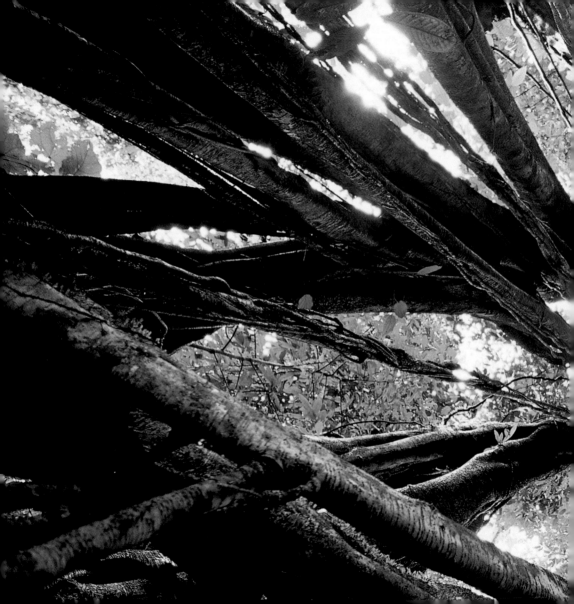

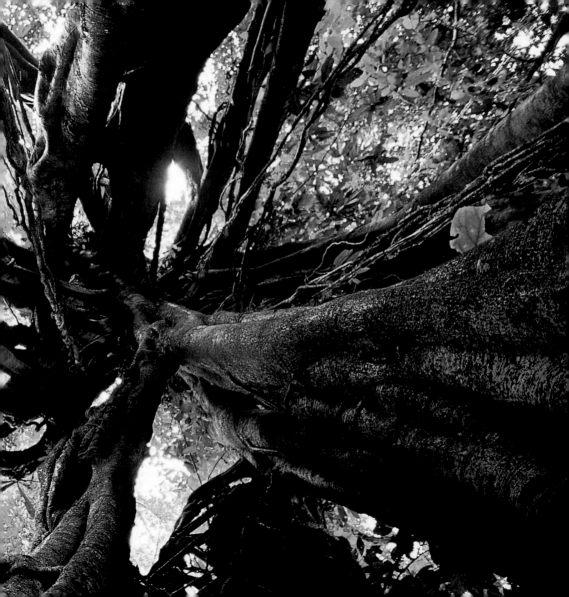

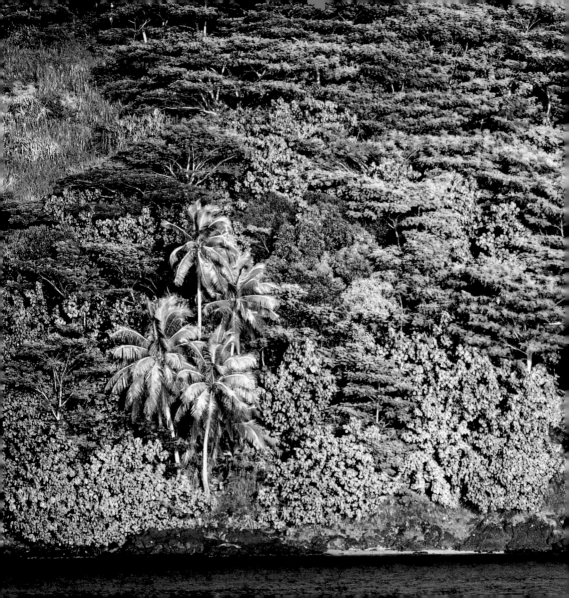

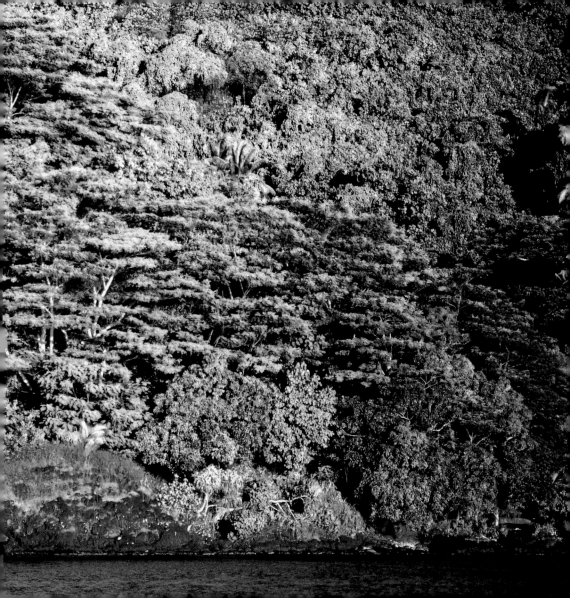

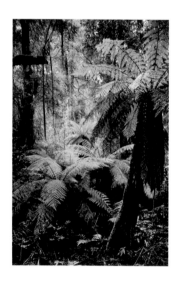

- Victoria (Australia) - East Gippsland
  Errinundra National Park.

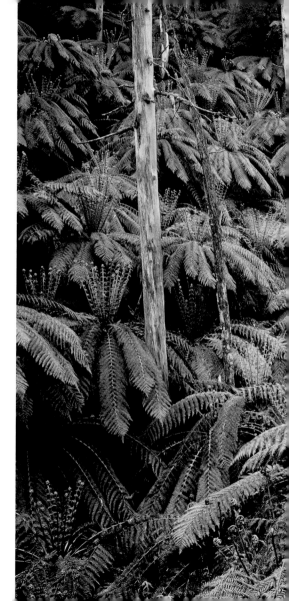

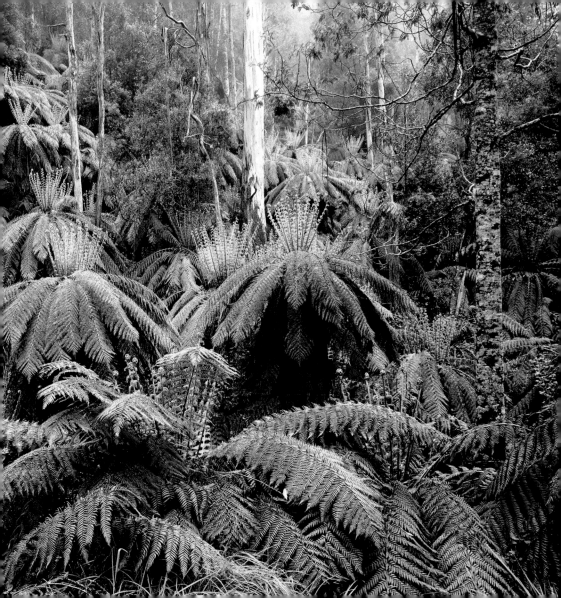

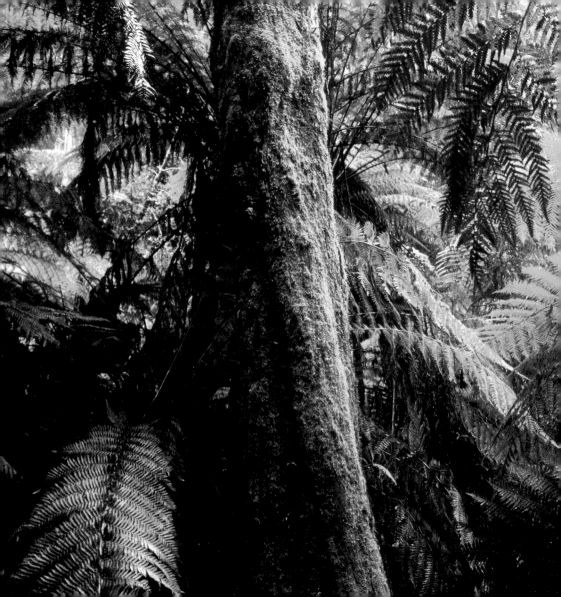

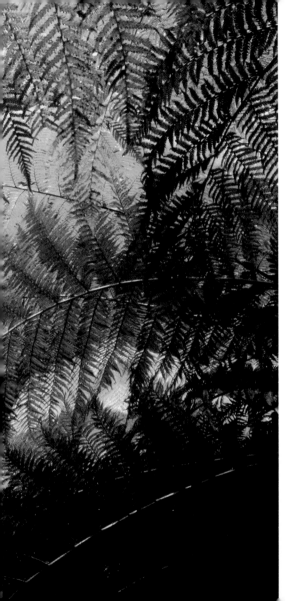

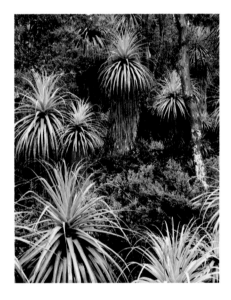

*210-211* ● Tasmania (Australia) -
Pelorus River Scenic Reserve.

*211* ● Tasmania (Australia) - Mount Field
National Park.

# A SENSE of WATER

Canaima (Venezuela) - Angel Falls.

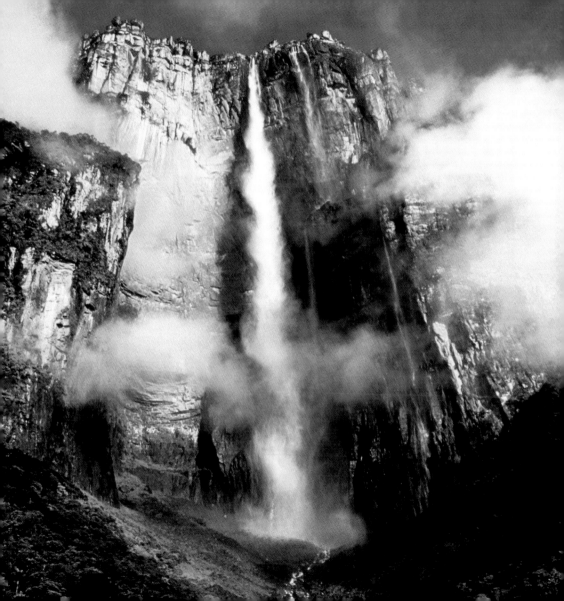

## INTRODUCTION A Sense of Water

IF RIVERS ARE AN ALLEGORY OF LIFE, WATER-FALLS ARE THE MOMENTS IN WHICH LIFE ACCELERATES AND PRECIPITATES, LEAVING US BREATHLESS. STILLNESS AND ROARING, FERTILE STRENGTH AND PURE ENERGY, SLOW TEMPO AND PRESSING RHYTHM .... EVERY WATERWAY EXPRESSES THE CONTRADICTIONS OF EXISTENCE AND IS AT ONCE TENDER AND VIOLENT, PLACID AND ANXIOUS. HOW DIFFERENT THE PARANÁ RIVER IS AS IT TRAVERSES ARGENTINA SO MEEKLY AND THEN BECOMES FEARSOME AS IT PLUNGES OVER THE IGUAZÚ FALLS. HOW DIFFERENT TOO IS THE ST. LAWRENCE RIVER, WITH NIAGARA FALLS AND LAKE ONTARIO TO THE WEST, FLOWING UNHURRIEDLY TO ITS VAST, FRIGID ESTUARY IN THE ATLANTIC OCEAN. A RIVER IS ABUNDANCE

## INTRODUCTION A Sense of Water

AND ARTISTIC BEAUTY. IT IS A PAINTING BY AN 18TH-CEN-
TURY LANDSCAPIST WHO METICULOUSLY DEPICTS THE
WEEPING WILLOWS WHOSE BRANCHES ALMOST TOUCH
THE WATER; CLUSTERS OF LONG, STRINGY GRASS THAT
FLUTTER LIKE A FAIRY'S HAIR IN THE CURRENT; WAVES
THAT SUDDENLY ACCELERATE BECAUSE OF BENDS OR
NARROWS IN THE RIVER AND ARE STREAKED WITH WHITE
FOAM; THE CRYSTAL-CLEAR WATER CARESSING THE
ROCKS .... DOWNSTREAM, WHERE THE WATER FLOWS
MORE SLOWLY, RIVERS BECOME NAÏF PAINTINGS WITH
THE MURKY COLORS OF THE AMAZON RIVER. HERE
THERE ARE NO LONGER THE DARK GREENS OF THE
BANKS, THE LEADEN HUES OF THE DEPTHS, THE FLICK-
ERING REFLECTIONS OF THE MANY RUNNELS CREATED

# INTRODUCTION A Sense of Water

WHEN THE CURRENT BECOMES A BURST OF ELECTRIC ENERGY. THE DOMINATING SHADES ARE NOW BROWN, OCHER AND GRAY, THE LIGHT BECOMES SOFT AND THE AIR IS MORE HUMID. DRIFTS OF FOG SLIDE SLOWLY ALONG THE QUIESCENT WATER, FROM WHICH EMERGE REEDS AND HYDROPHILOUS PLANTS; WE CAN IMAGINE THEIR SUBDUED MUFFLING DROWNED OUT BY THE CRY OF THE BIRDS BICKERING ON EITHER SIDE OF THE RIVER. AT THE ESTUARY THE ABRUPT MIXTURE OF SALT AND FRESH WATER MAKES THE WATER BRACKISH, AND THE SCENT OF ALGAE MINGLES WITH THE STAGNANT RIVER AIR. WATERFALLS ARE THE LYRIC OF A ROMANTIC COM-POSER WHO IMAGINES MAN AWE-INSPIRED BY THE FORCE OF NATURE. FIRST THERE IS A CONTINUOUS AND

# INTRODUCTION A Sense of Water

IMPRESSIVE TREMOR, THEN A SUBDUED RUMBLE COVERED BY THE SOUND OF THE WIND AMONG THE FOLIAGE AND BIRDS SINGING, AND LASTLY A MAJESTIC ROAR AND GUSTS OF WIND. AFTER WHICH THERE IS ONLY THE ENCHANTED HARMONY OF GENERATING POWER IN ITS PUREST FORM, A FABULOUS AND TERRIFYING SPECTACLE OF VAPORIZED DROPS OF WATER THAT CREATE THOUSANDS OF RAINBOWS, SWEET VISIONS THAT CONTRADICT THE HURRICANE-LIKE VIOLENCE OF THE FOAM ON THE ROCKS BELOW. IN THIS RESPECT, WATERFALLS ARE FRAGMENTS OF A LOST PARADISE, PERHAPS OF A LAND OF WHICH WE STILL HAVE ANCESTRAL MEMORIES.

*218-219* ● Friuli Venezia Giulia (Italy) - Fusine River.

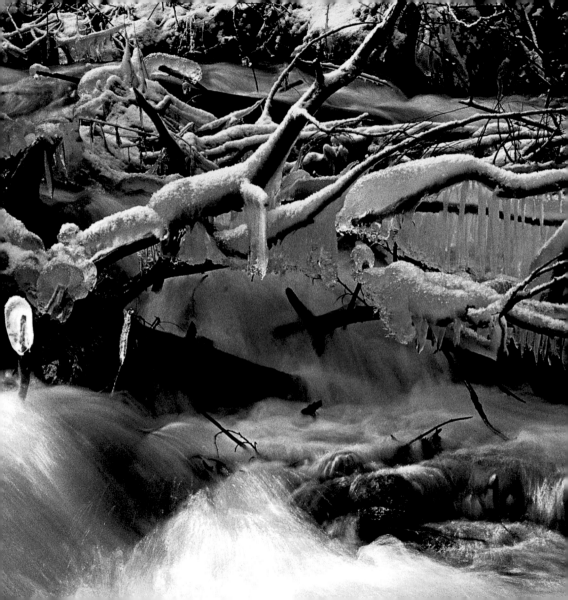

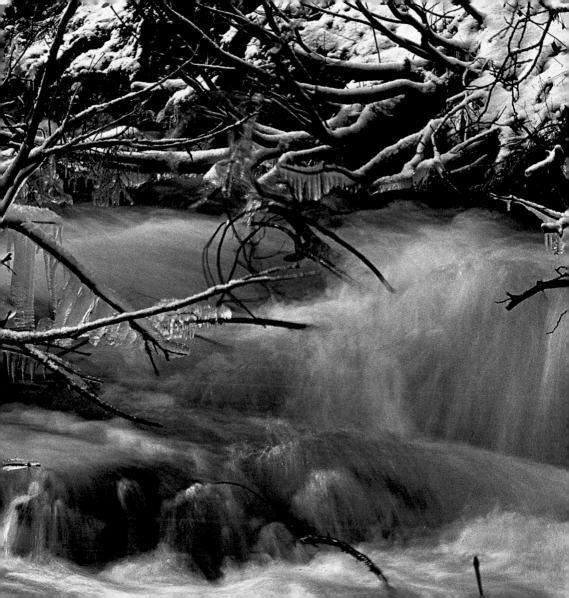

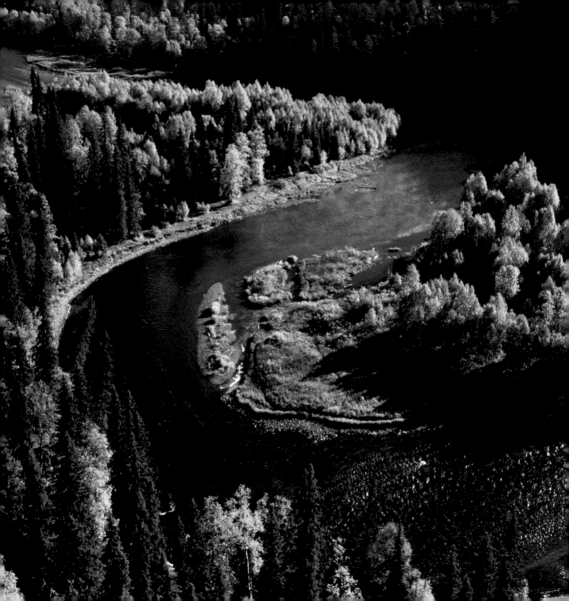

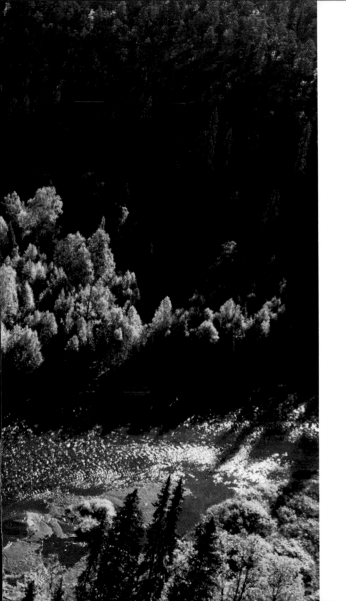

Finland - Oulanka
Joki River, Oulanka
National Park.

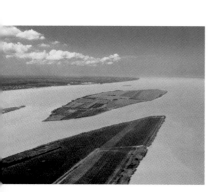

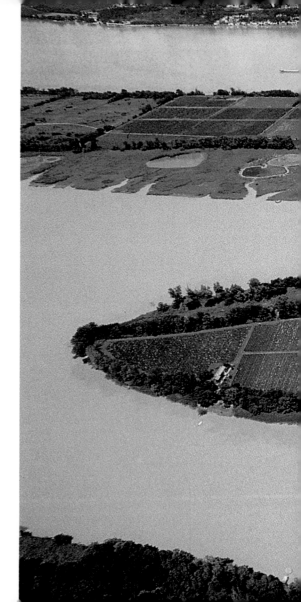

- Gironde (France) -
Gironde estuary.

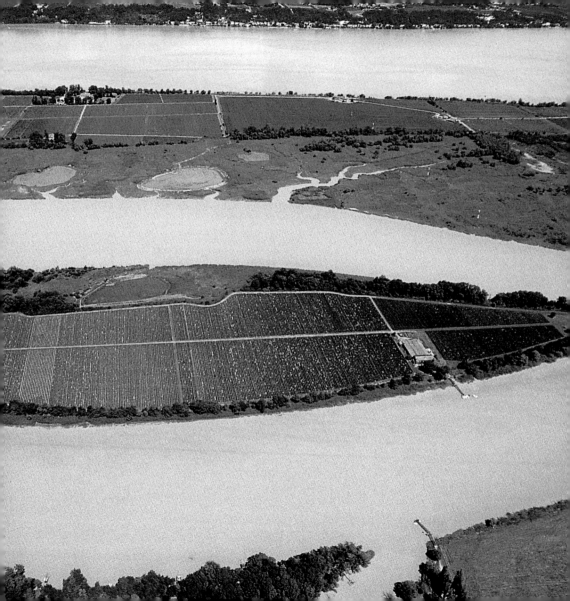

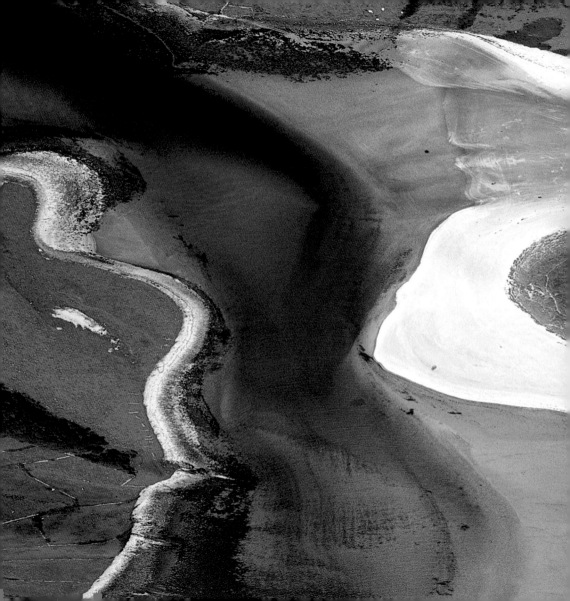

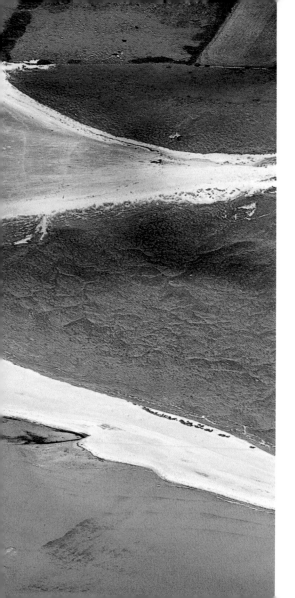

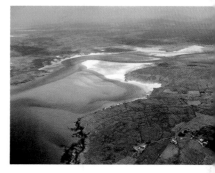

County Donegal (Ireland) -
Mouth of the Gweebarra River.

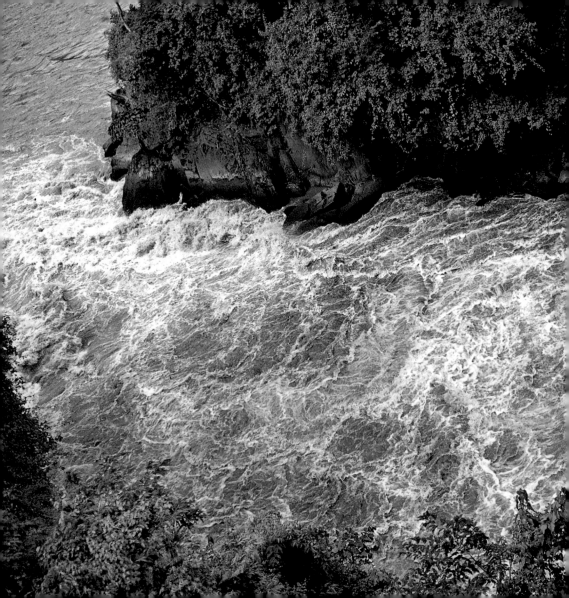

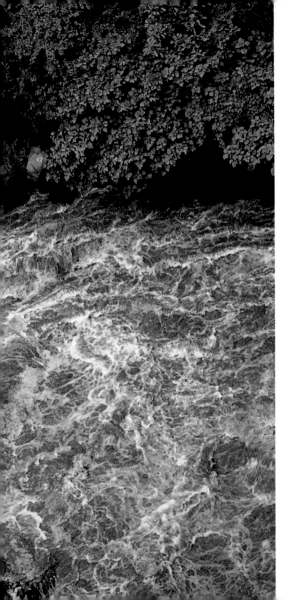

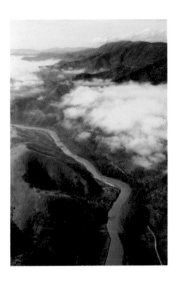

● Rwande - The Kagera.

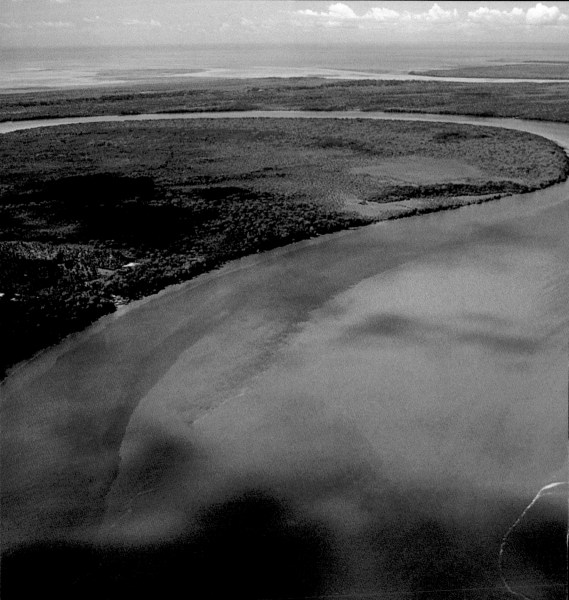

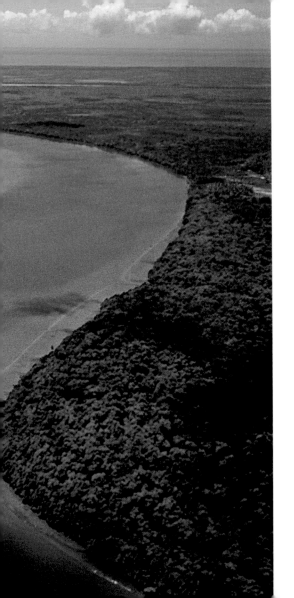

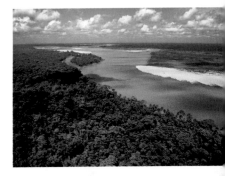

*228-229* ● Tanzania - The Rufiji.

*229* ● Nigeria - The Niger.

*230-231* ● Zimbabwe -
Victoria Falls.

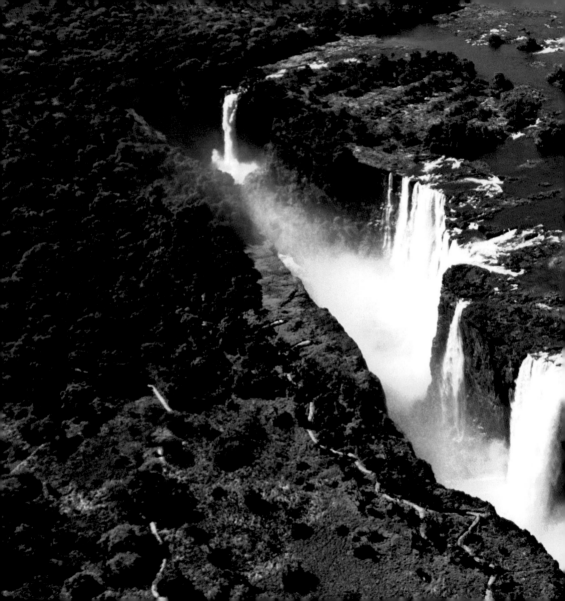

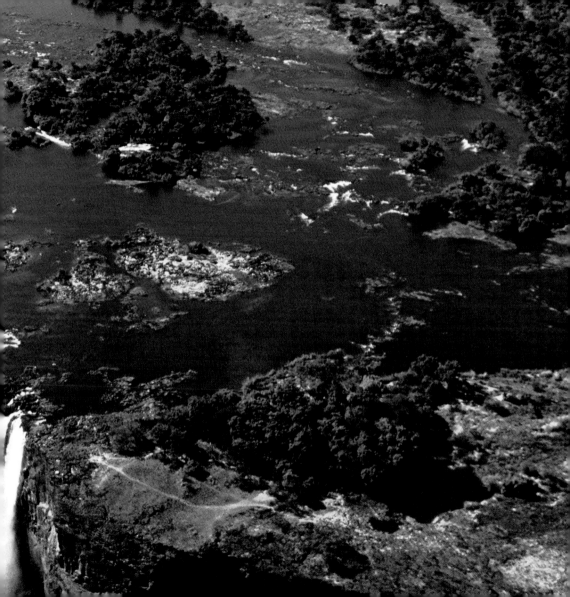

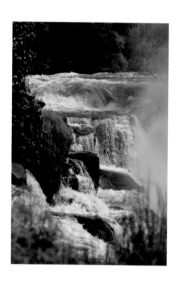

*232 and 232-233* ● Congo -
Loufoulakari Falls.

*234-235* ● Egypt - The Nile.

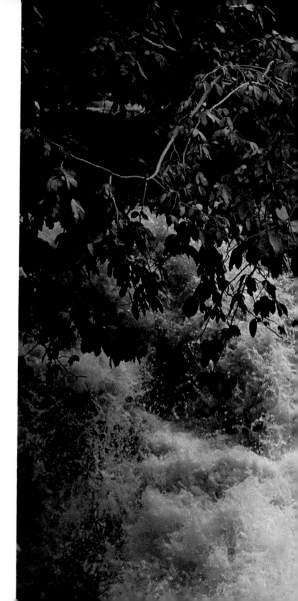

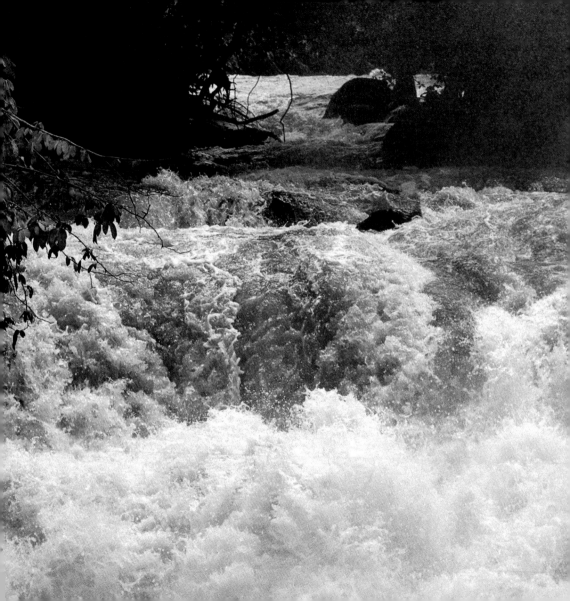

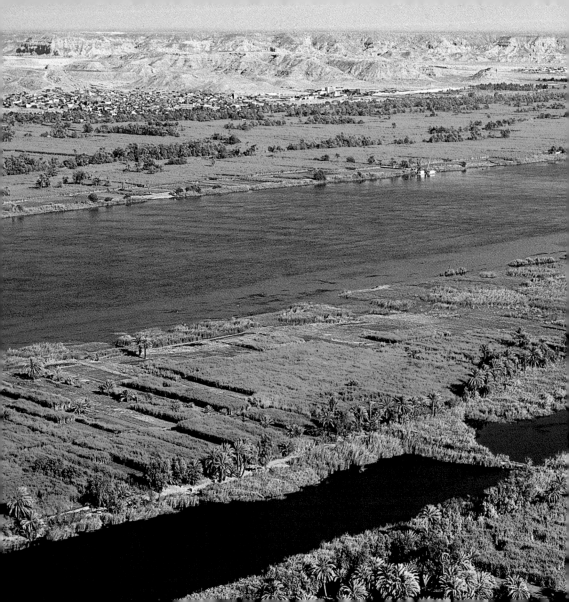

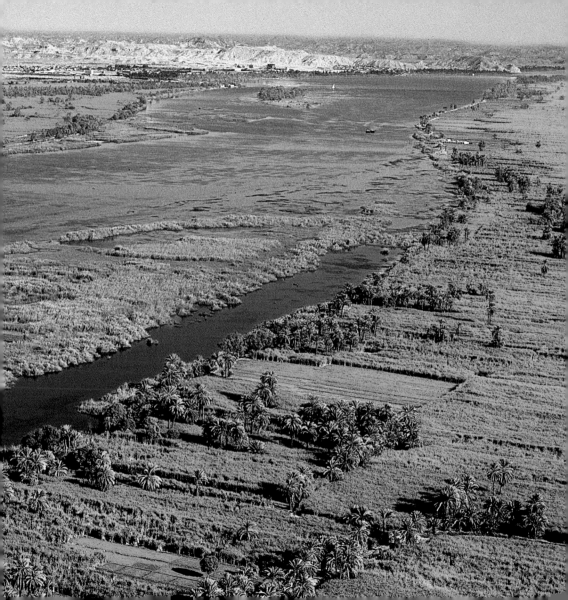

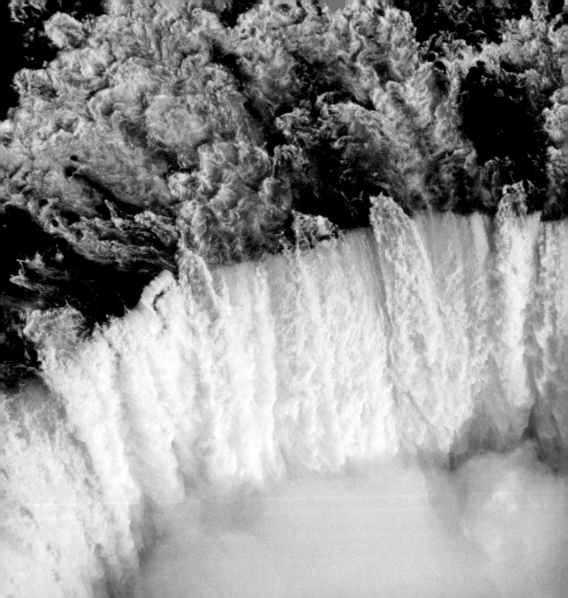

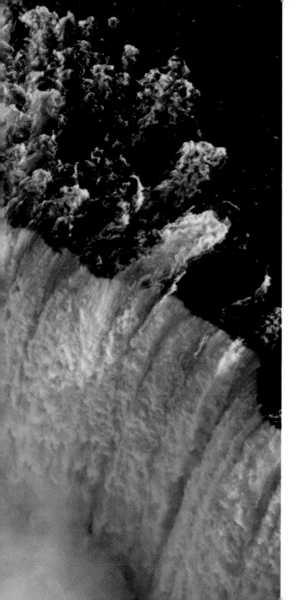

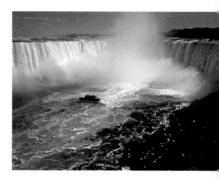

Ontario (Canada) - Niagara
Falls.

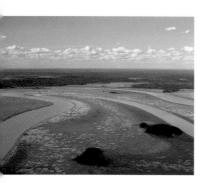

238 • Northwest Territories (Canada) - Peace River Delta.

238-239 • Alberta (Canada) - Slave River.

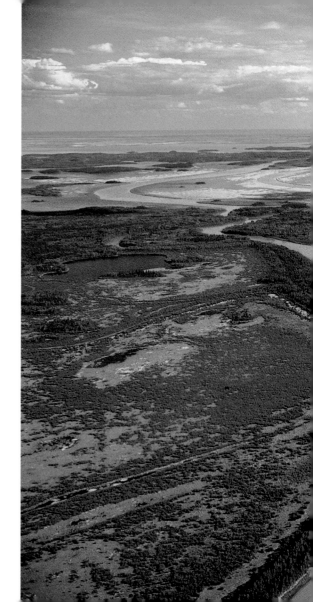

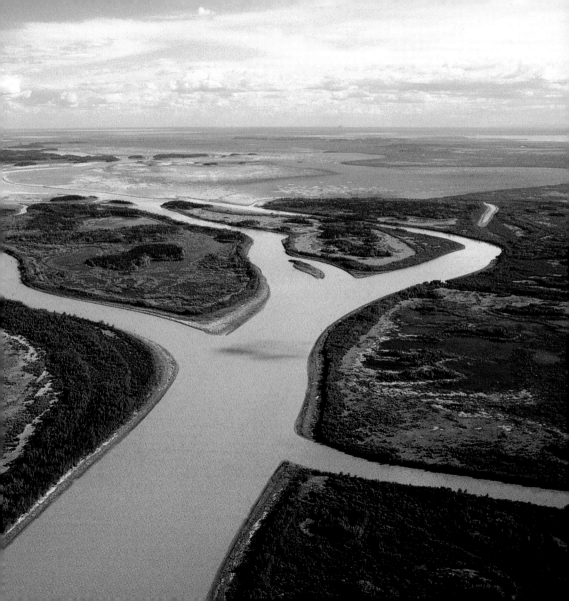

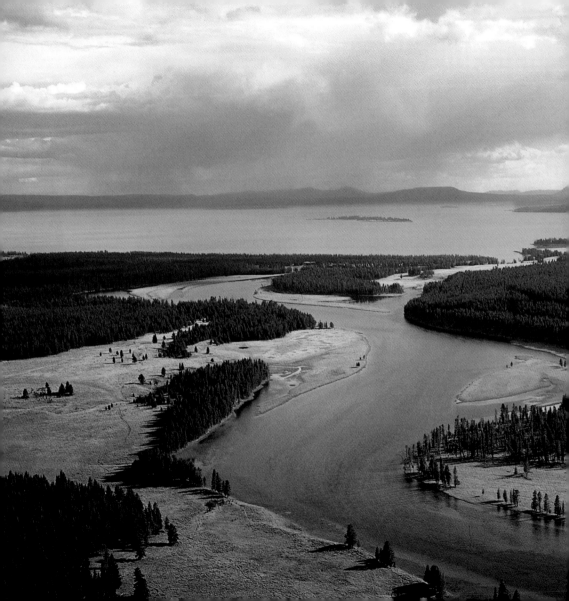

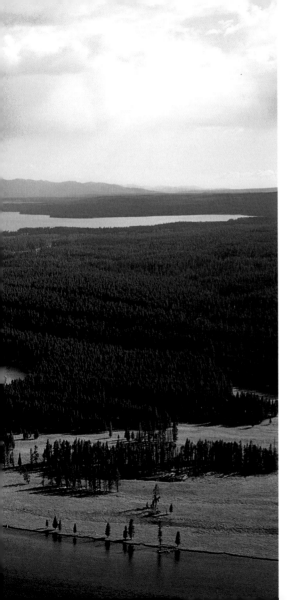

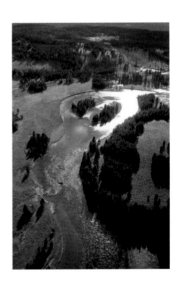

● Wyoming-Montana-Idaho (USA) -
Yellowstone River.

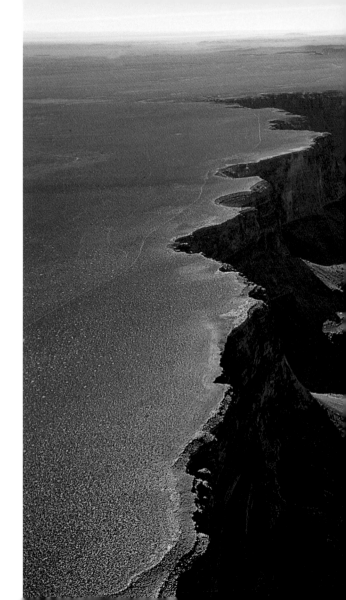

Arizona (USA) - Grand Canyon with the Colorado River, Yavapai Point area.

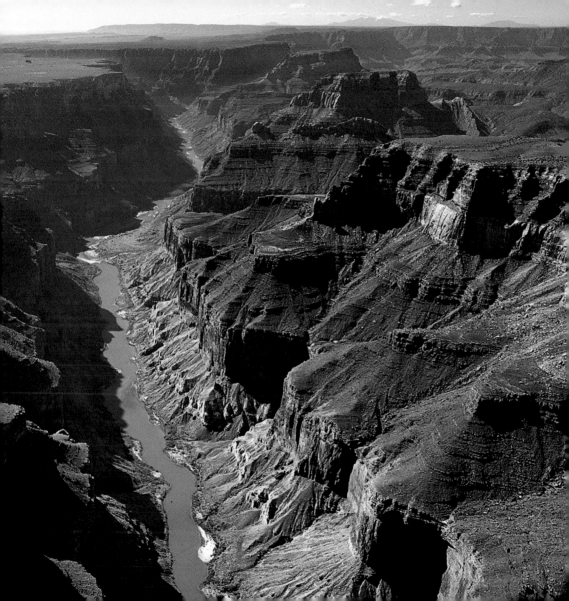

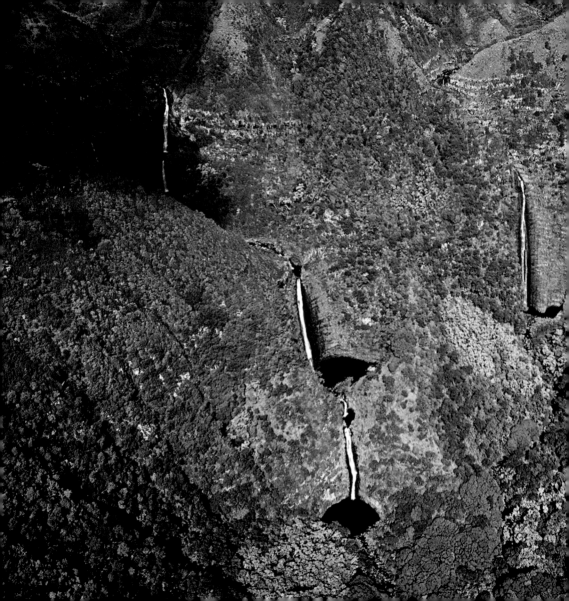

244-245 ● Molokai (Hawaii, USA) - Waterfall in Kalaupapa National Historical Park.

245 ● Kauai (Hawaii) - Waterfalls on the sides of the Waialeale volcano.

246-247 ● Brazil - Rio Negro and Arcipelago Anavilhanas.

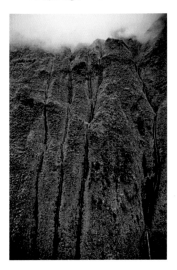

248-249 ● Paranà, (Brazil) - Iguazú Falls.

250-251 ● Venezuela - Sand banks on the Orinoco.

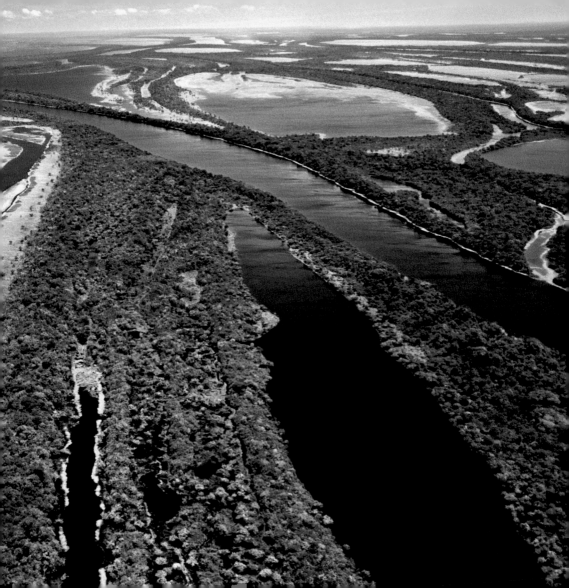

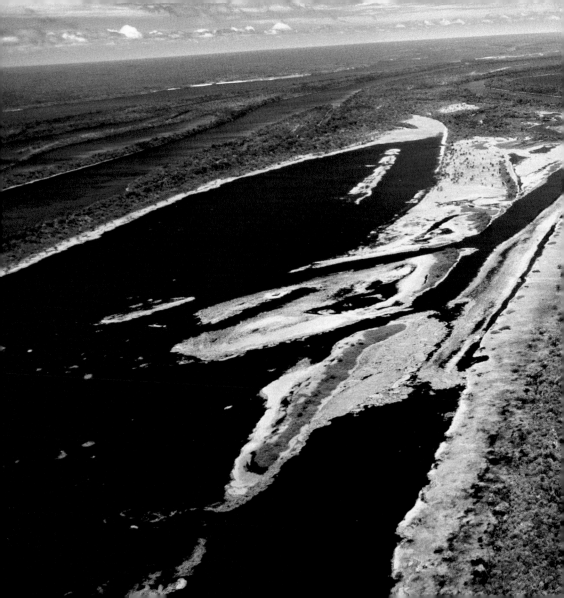

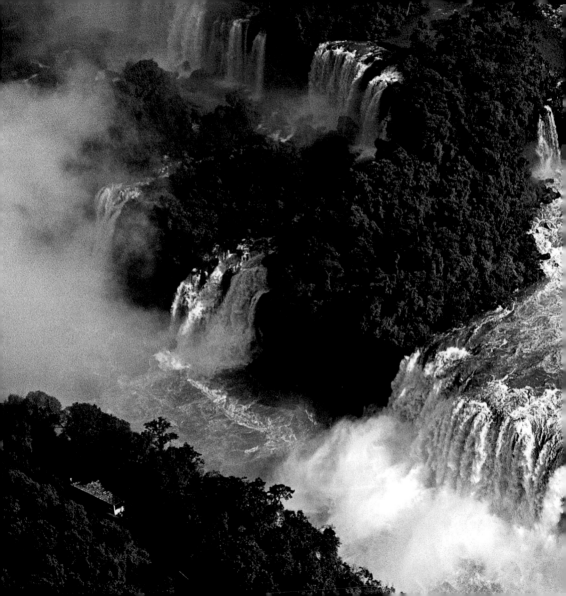

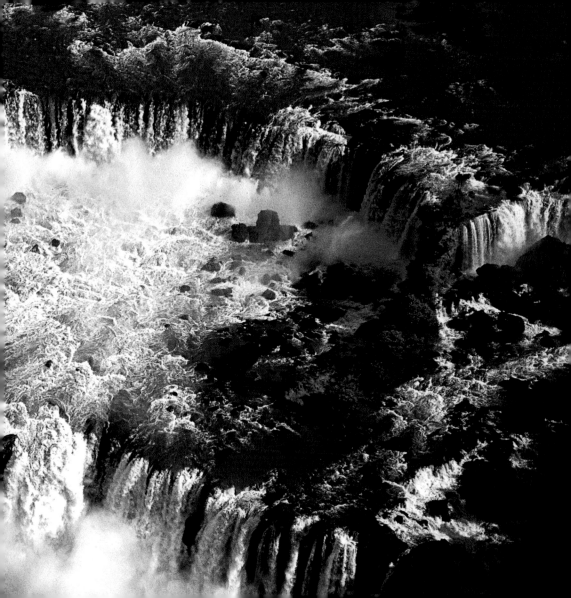

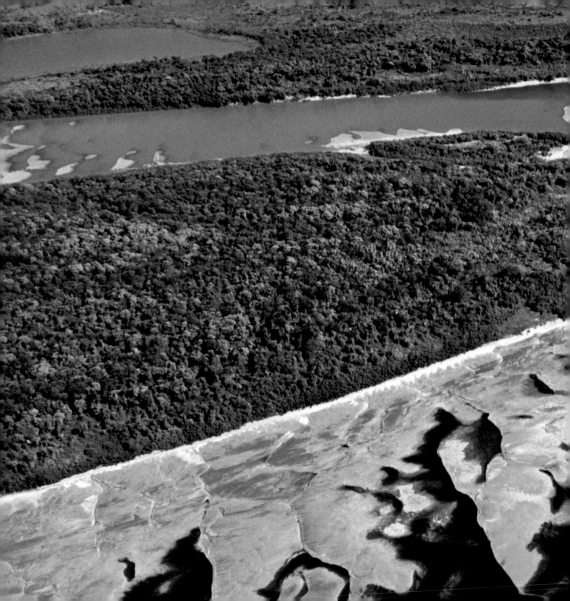

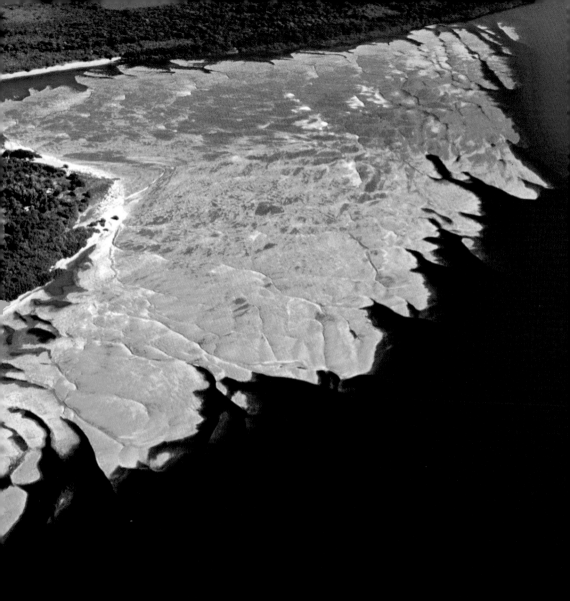

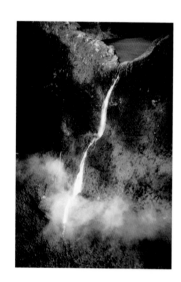

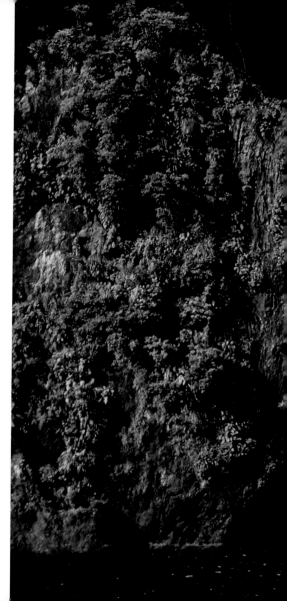

*252* ● South Island (New Zealand) -
Sutherlands Falls.

*252-253* ● South Island (New Zealand) -
Bowen Falls.

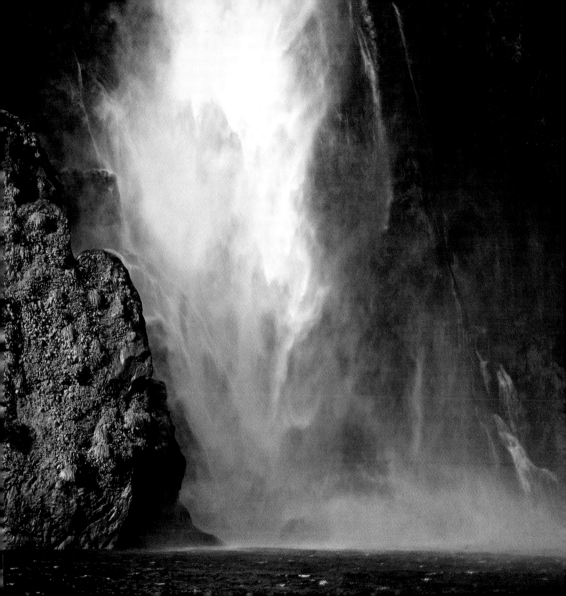

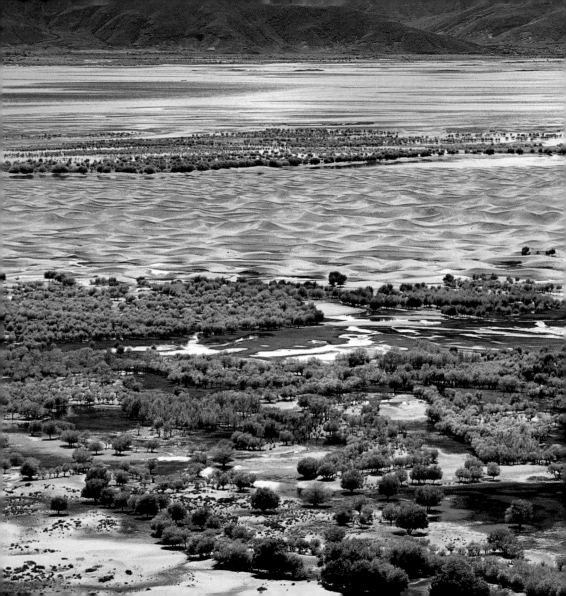

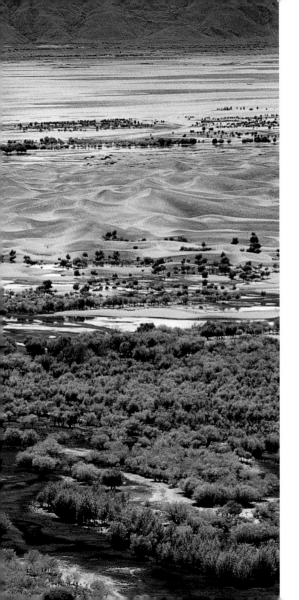

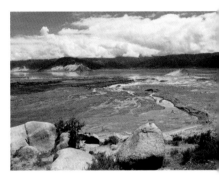

*254-255 and 255* ● Tibet (China) -
The Brahmaputra Valley.

*256-257* ● Tibet (China) -
The wide bed of the
Brahmaputra.

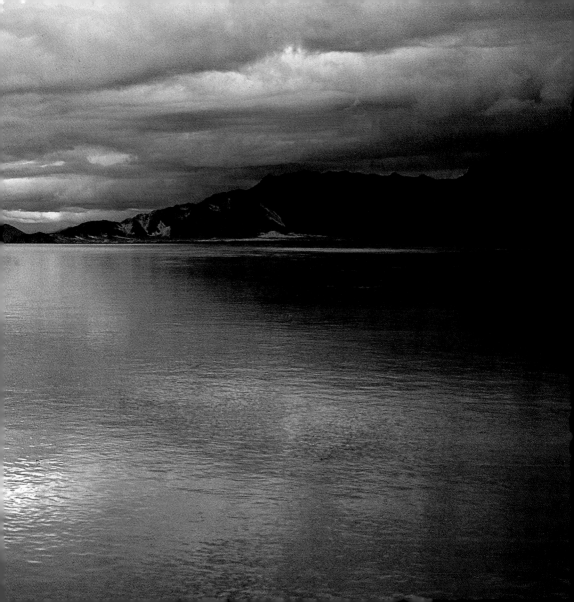

# The MIRRORS of the SKY

- Arizona (USA) - Lake Powell.

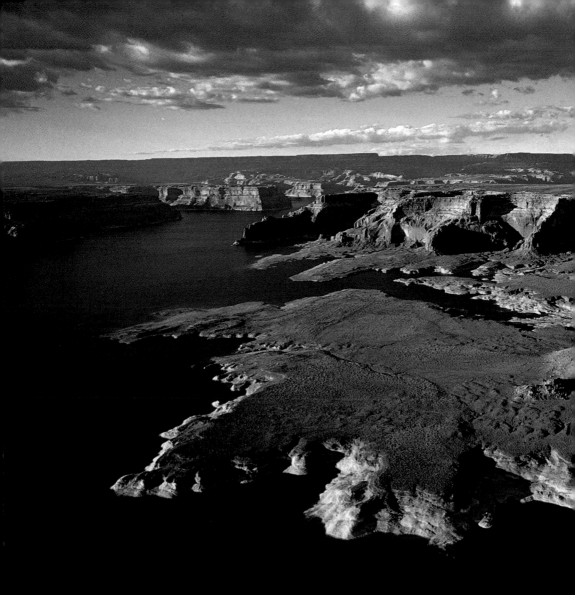

# The Mirrors of the Sky
## Introduction

BEEN SET ALONG ITS BANKS. MANY LESSER LAKES ARE KNOWN ONLY TO SHEPHERDS AND HIKERS. OTHERS SEEM TO HAVE BEEN CREATED BY THE DREAM OF A LOVING GOD, WITH THEIR TURQUOISE HUES, GOLDEN REFLECTIONS, THICK VEGETATION, MOUNTAINS MIRRORED IN THE WATER, AND EVERYTHING ELSE THAT MAKES FOR A PICTURE POSTCARD. YET OTHERS CONCEAL ARCHEOLOGICAL TREASURES OR HAVE TRIGGERED TENDER OR VIOLENT LEGENDS. IN ANY CASE, MOST LAKES ARE THE HOME OF ECOLOGICAL WONDERS THAT ALSO HOST ARTISTIC OR ARCHITECTURAL GEMS. THEY ARE BODIES OF WATER THAT FOR MILLENNIA HAVE REFLECTED THE SKY ABOVE AND THE EVENTS OF HUMAN HISTORY BELOW.

- Yukon Territory (Canada) - Kluane Lake.

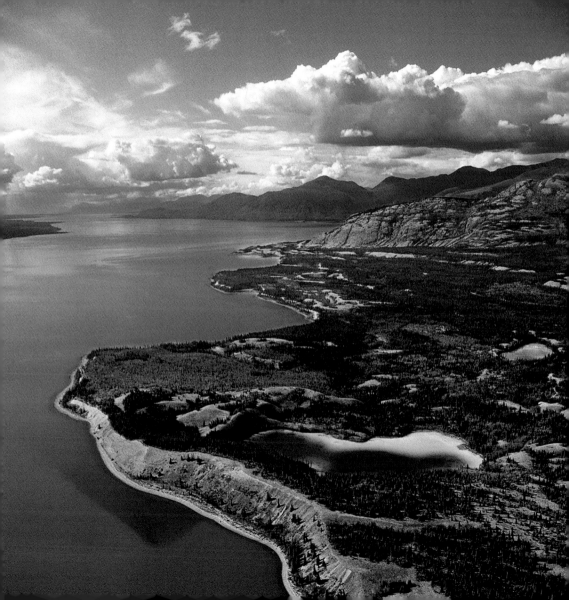

*264-265* ● Alberta (Canada) - Wedge Pond and Mount Kidd.

*266-267* ● Maine (USA) - Moosehead Lake.

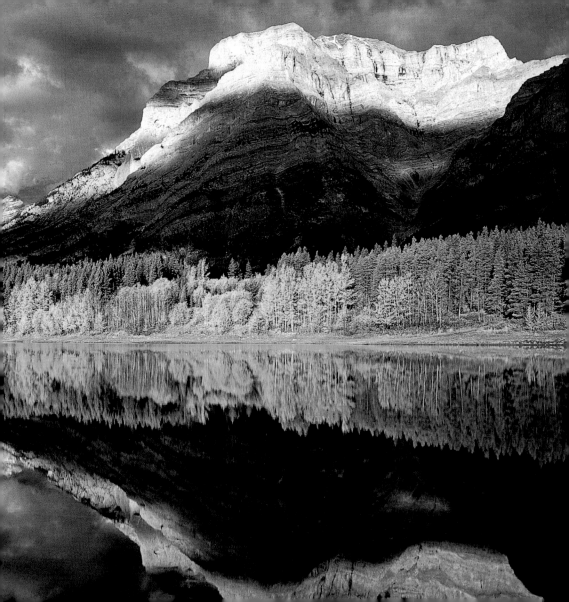

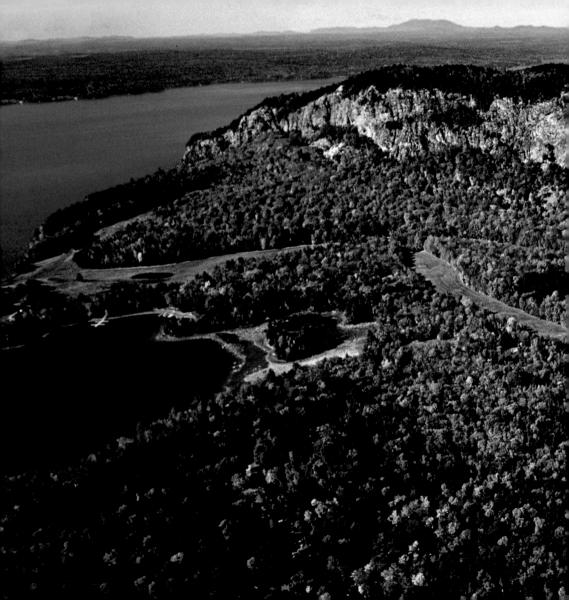

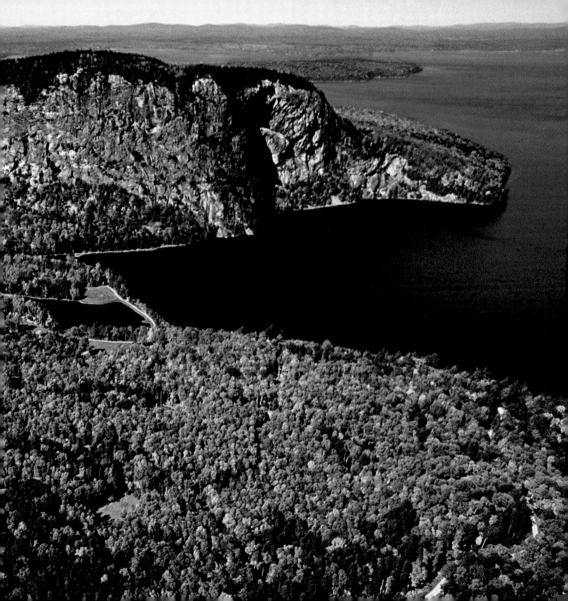

*268* ● Alberta (Canada) - Moraine Lake, Banff National Park.

*269* ● British Columbia (Canada) - O'Hara Lake, Yoho National Park.

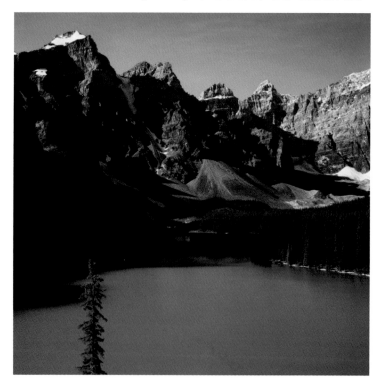

*270-271* ● Arizona (USA) - Lake Powell.

*272-273* ● Chile - Lake Pehoe, Torres del Paine National Park.

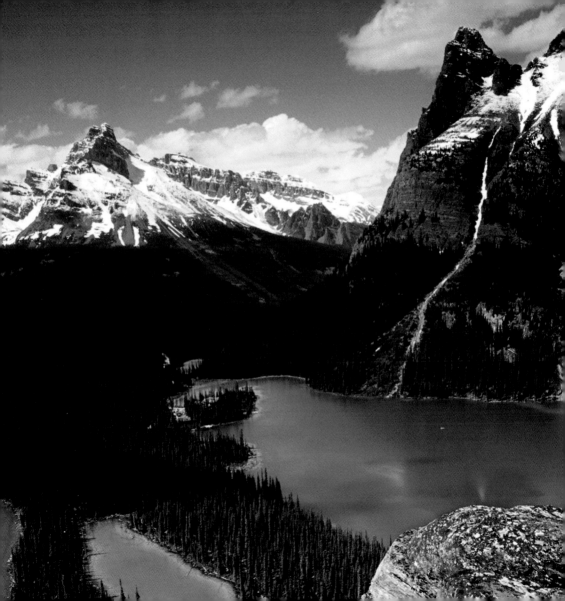

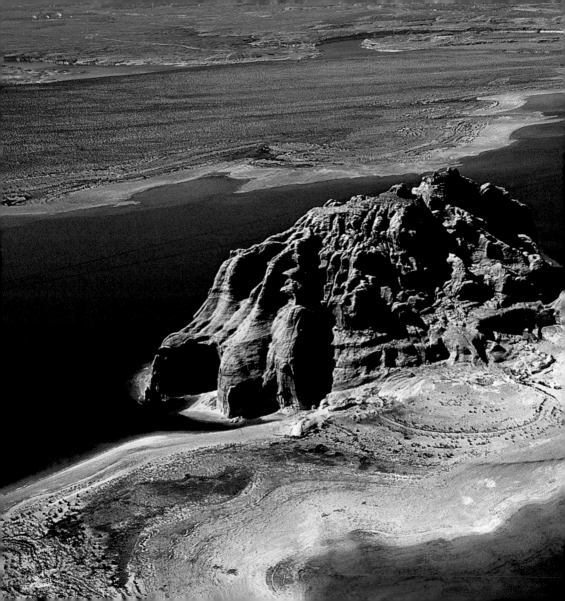

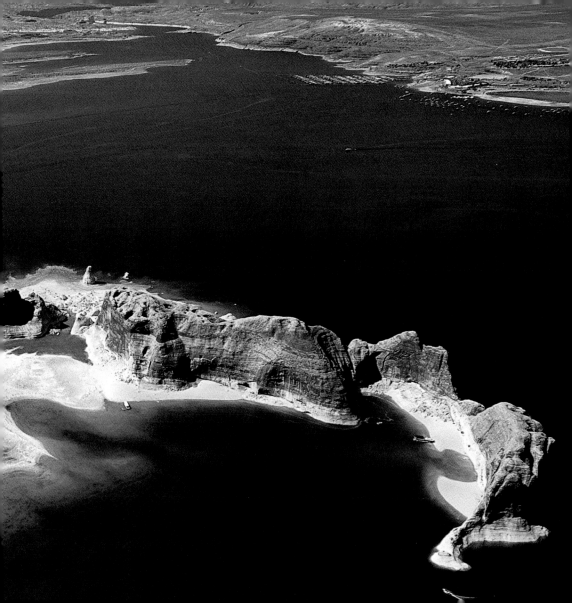

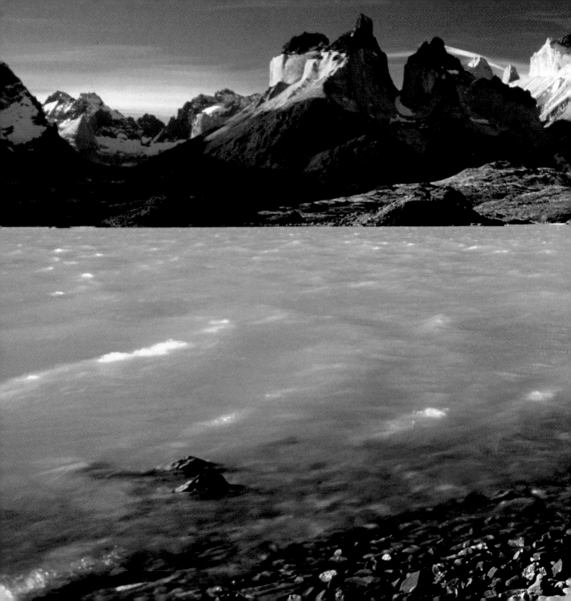

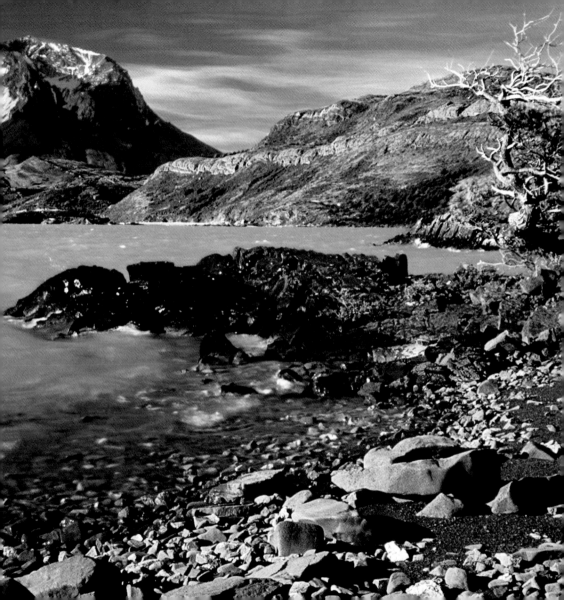

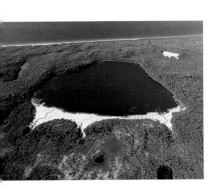

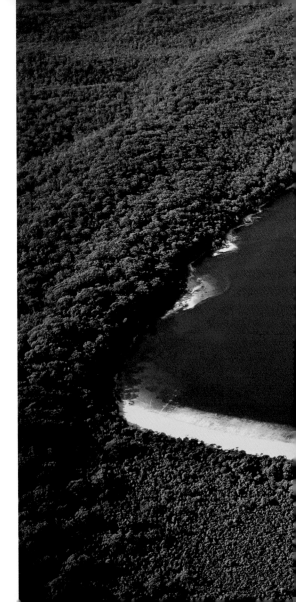

274 ● Queensland (Australia) -
Lake Boomanjin, Fraser Island.

274-275 ● Queensland (Australia)
- Lake McKenzie, Fraser Island.

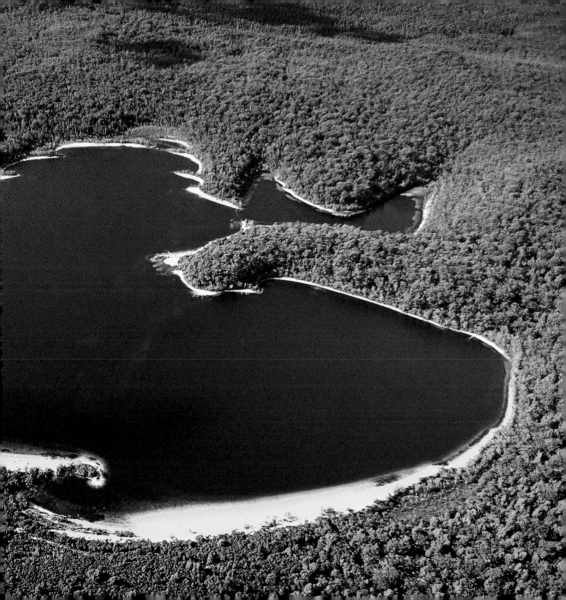

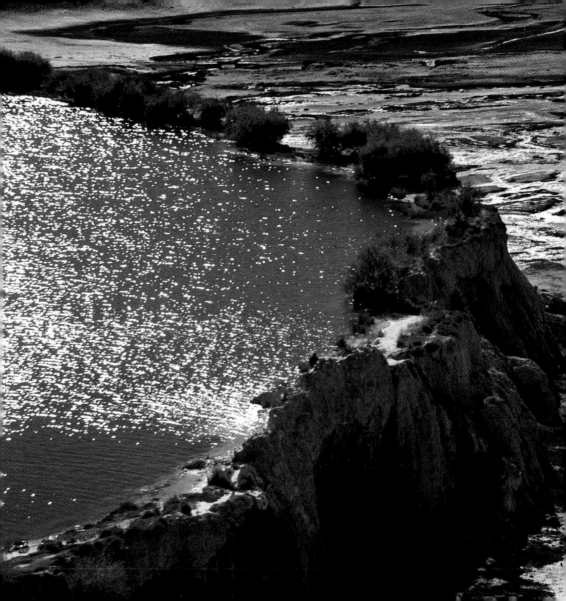

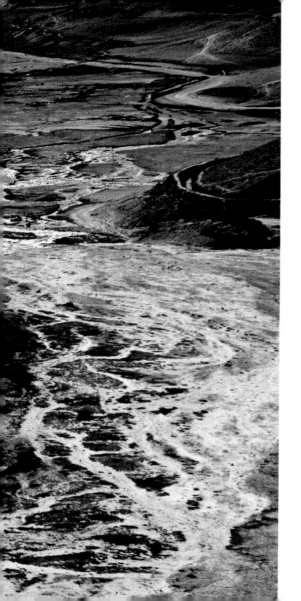

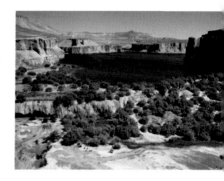

*276-277 and 277* ● Afghanistan -
Lake Band i Amir.

*278-279* ● Tibet (China) -
Lake Yamdruk.

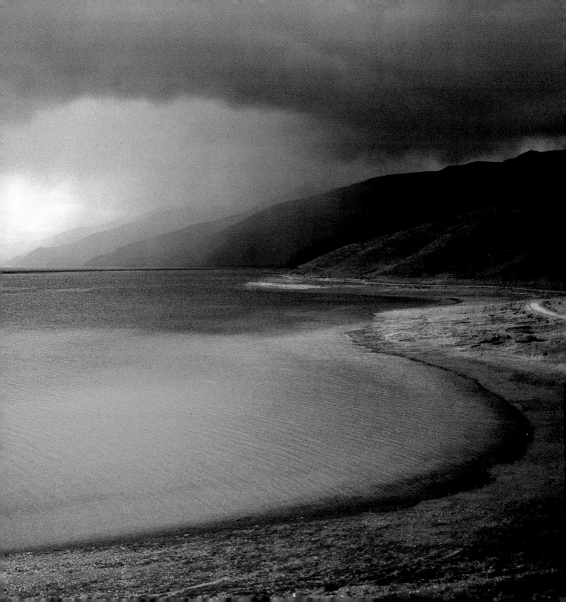

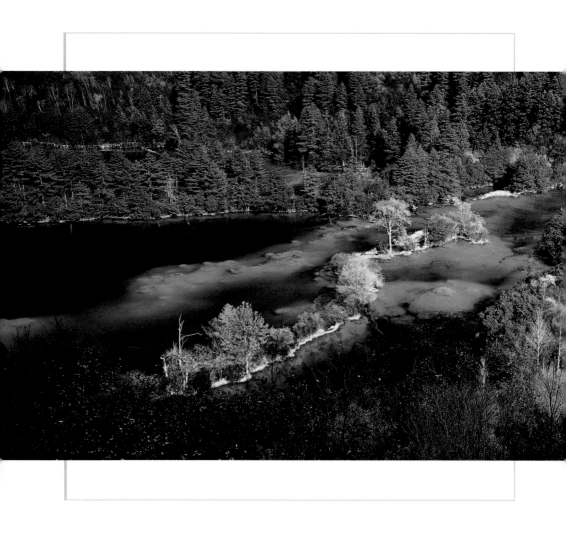

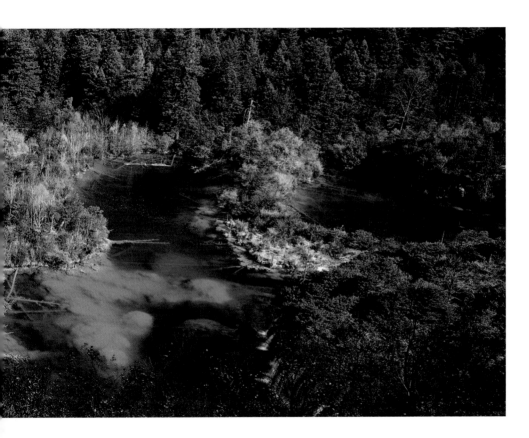

Sichuan (China) - Lake Shuzheng.

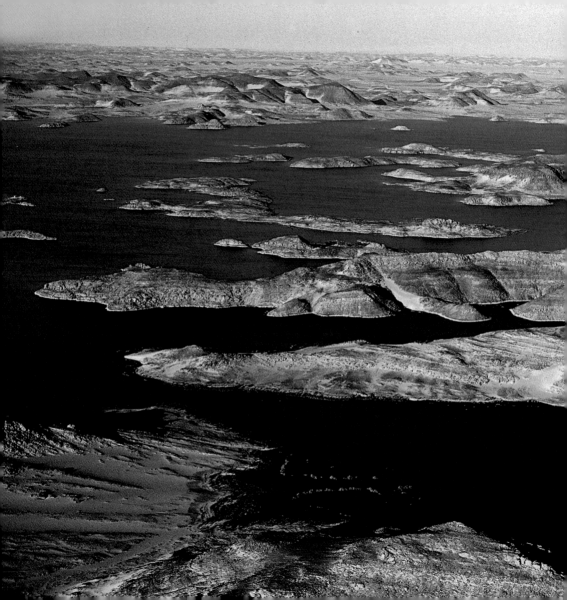

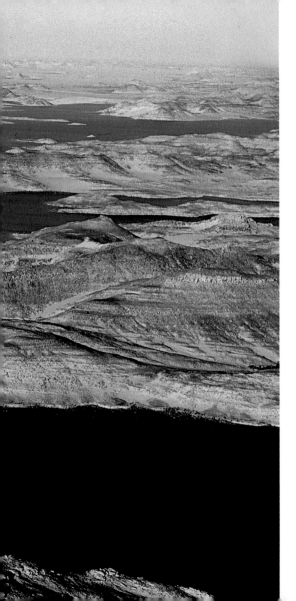

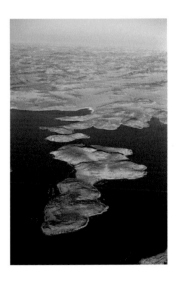

*282-283 and 283* ● Nubia (Egypt) -
Lake Nasser.

*284-285* ● Egypt - Jebel Bayda and
Lake Siwa.

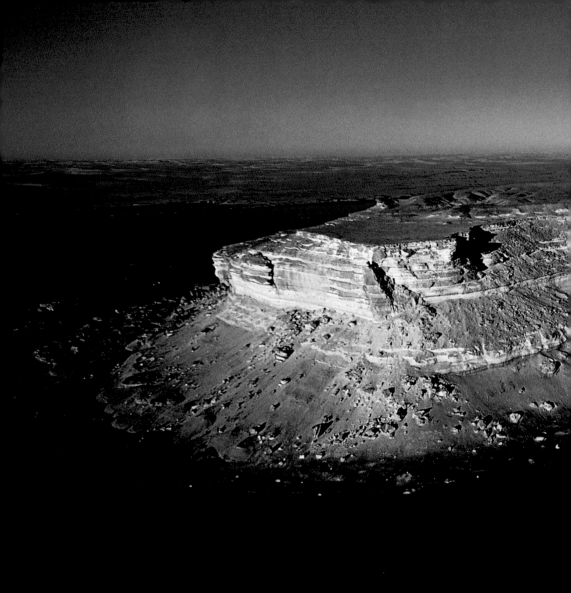

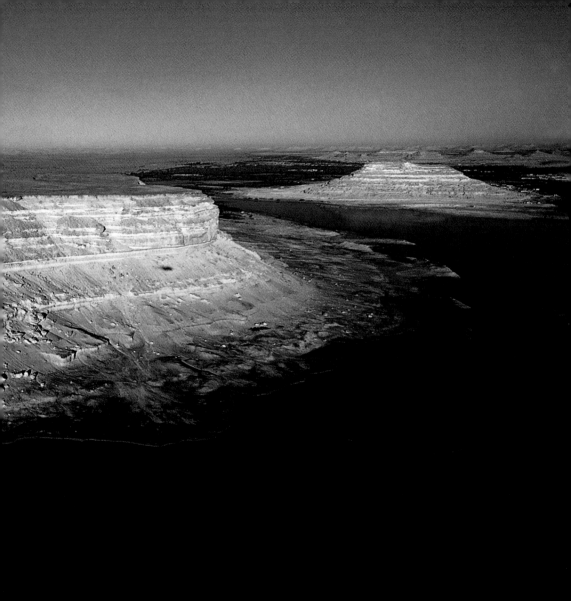

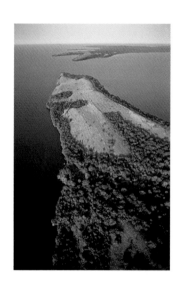

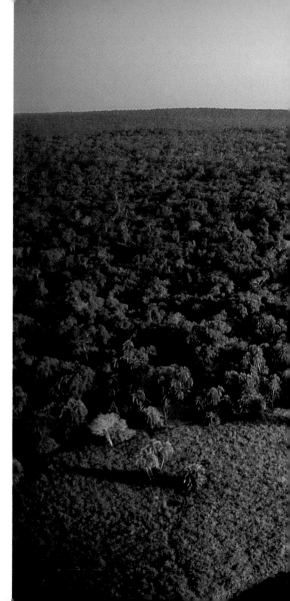

*286 and 286-287* ● Tanzania - Lake Victoria.

*288-289* ● Tanzania - Lake in Serengeti National Park.

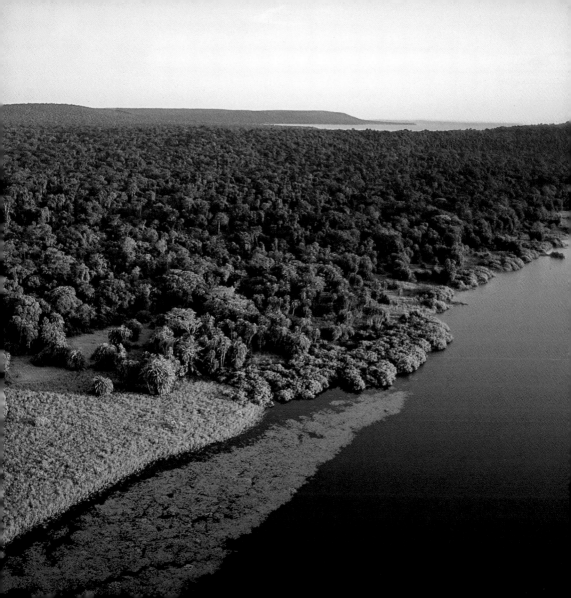

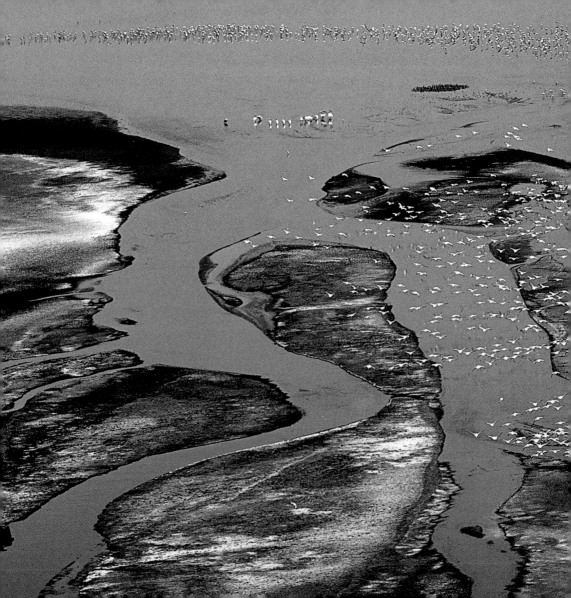

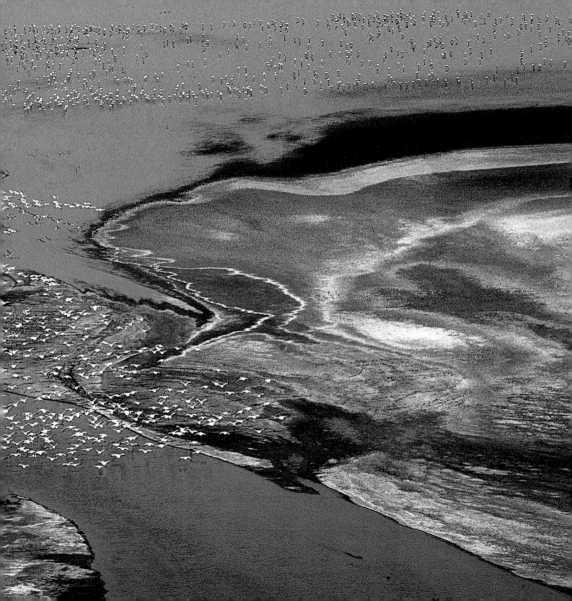

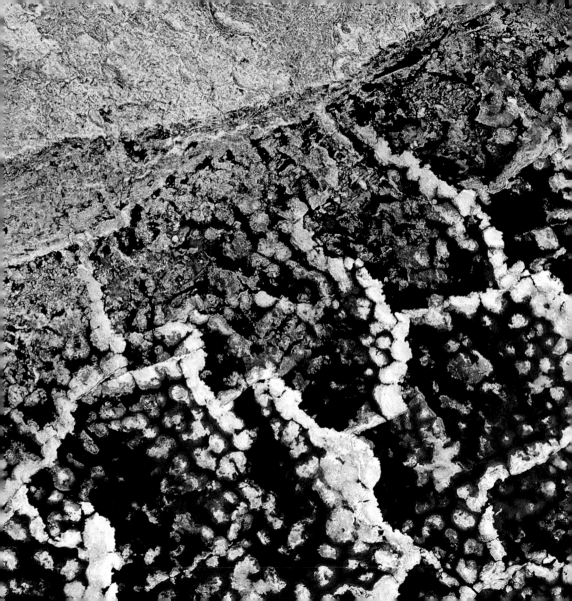

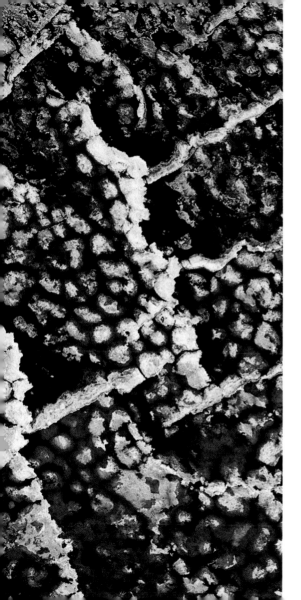

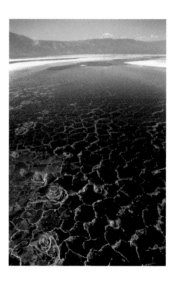

Tanzania - Patterns formed by salt crystals on the banks of Lake Natron.

*292 and 292-293* ● Friuli Venezia Giulia (Italy) - Fusine Lakes Natural Park.

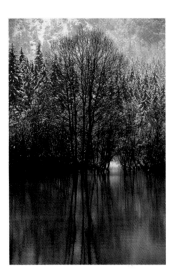

*294-295* ● England (United Kingdom) - The lakes of Tarn Hows, Lake District, Cumbria.

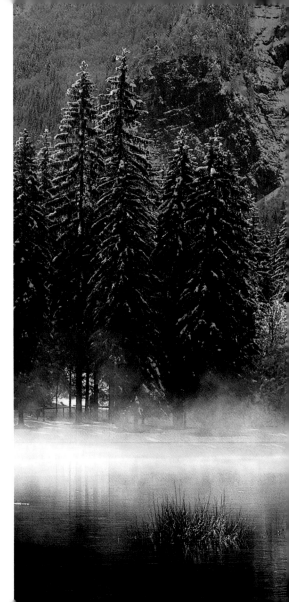

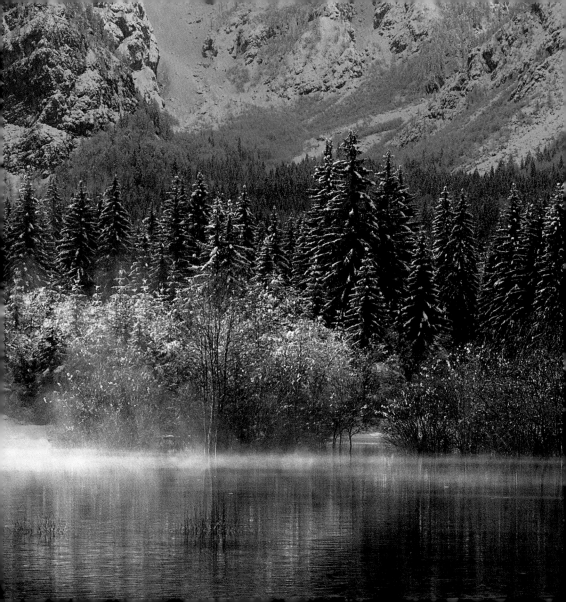

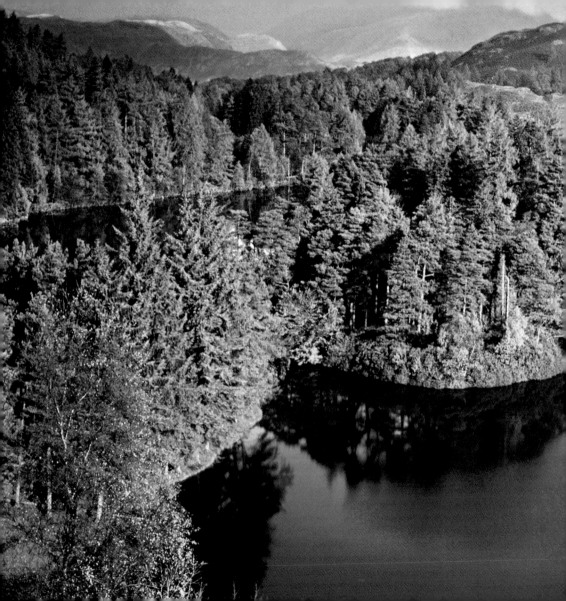

# The GODS of FIRE

Sicily (Italy) - Eruption of Etna.

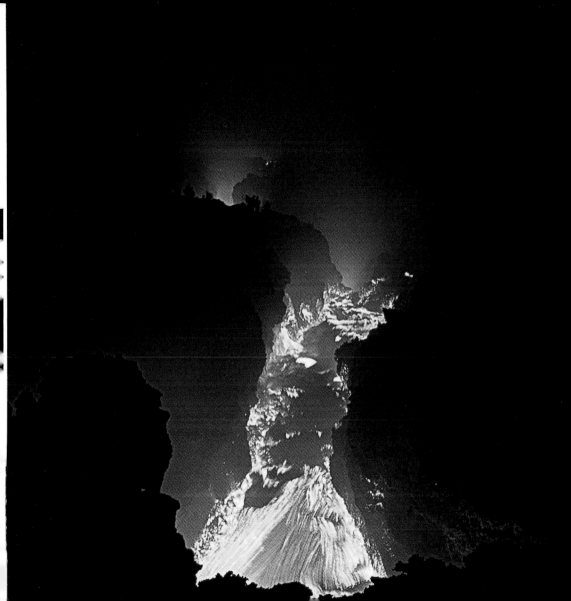

# The Gods of Fire

## Introduction

ARE THE ABODE OF ONI, A SNEERING RED MONSTER WHO THRASHES ABOUT AND HURLS STONES DURING ERUPTIONS. IN THE HAWAIIAN ISLANDS THE CULT OF PELÉ, THE POLYNE-SIAN GODDESS OF FIRE, IS STILL QUITE POPULAR. AFTER A VI-OLENT ARGUMENT WITH HER SISTER, PELÉ WAS OBLIGED TO SWIM TO THE SOUTH, AND EVERY TIME SHE EMERGED FROM THE WATER AN ISLAND WAS BORN, THUS CREATING THE HAWAIAN ARCHIPELAGO. PELÉ'S PRESENT HOME IS THE HALEMAUMAU CRATER ON THE KILAUEA VOLCANO. WHEN PELÉ GETS ANGRY, SHE STAMPS HER FOOT ON THE GROUND, CAUSING THE CRUST TO BREAK AND LAVA TO SPEW OUT, A "CAPRICIOUS" SPECTACLE THAT HAS AFFORDED SOME OF THE MOST BEAUTIFUL PICTURES EVER TAKEN OF A VOLCANO.

*301* ● Hawaii (USA) - Mouth of Kilauea, Hawaii Volcanoes National Park.

*302-303* ● Washington (USA) - Mount St. Helens.

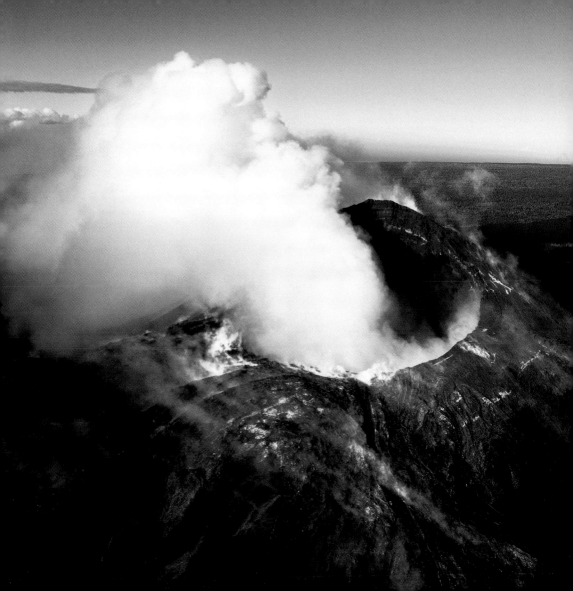

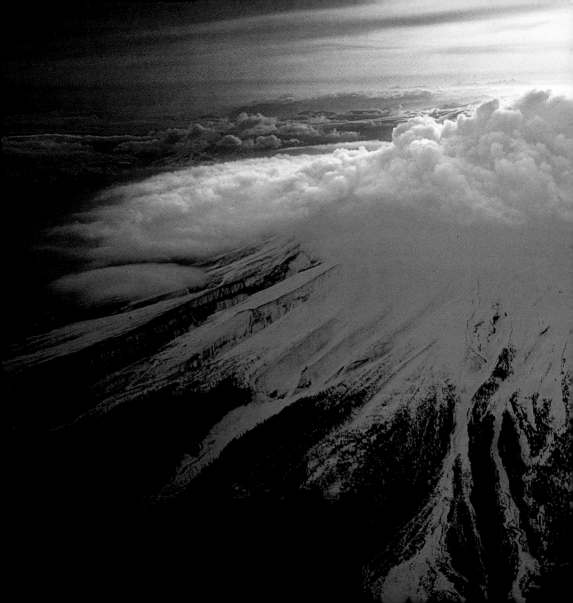

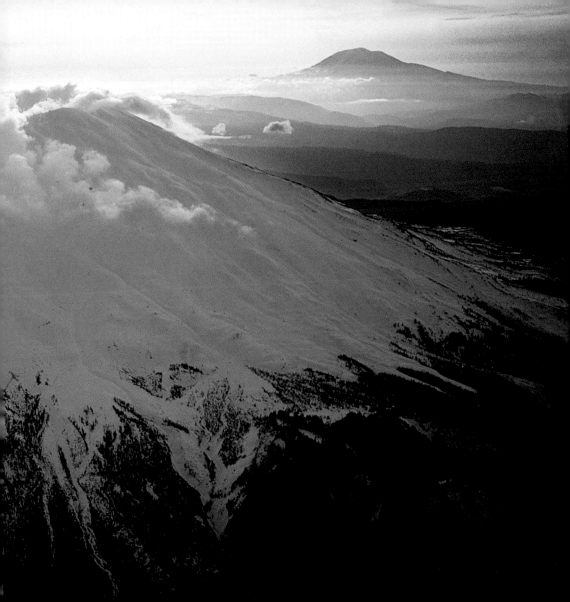

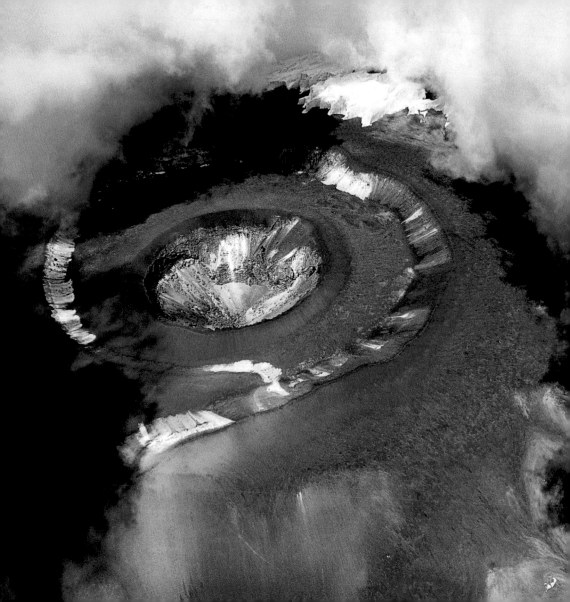

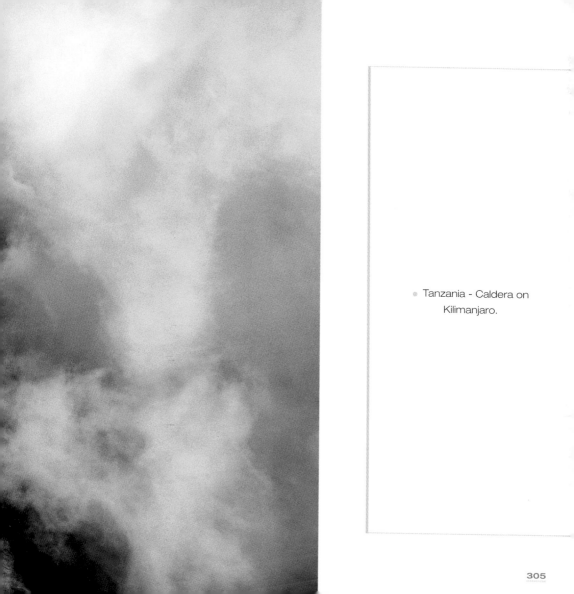

Tanzania - Caldera on Kilimanjaro.

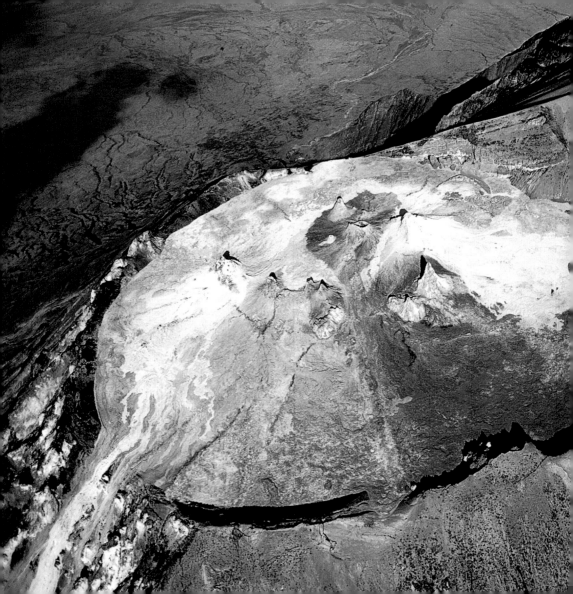

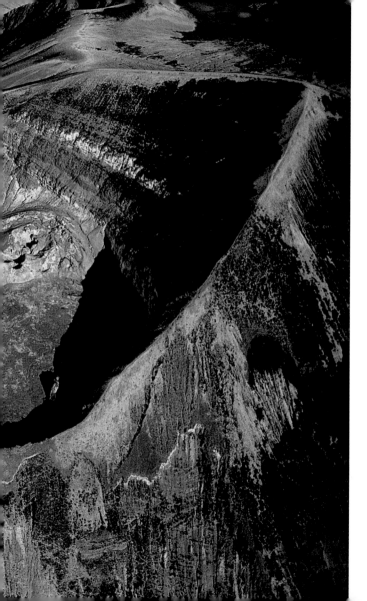

Tanzania - Crater of Oldonyo Lengai.

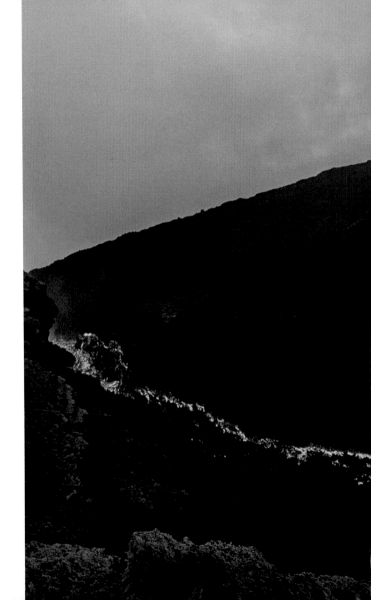

*308-309* • Sicily (Italy) - Lava flow on Etna.

*310-311* • Hawaii (USA) - Lava flow on Kilauea, Hawaii Volcanoes National Park.

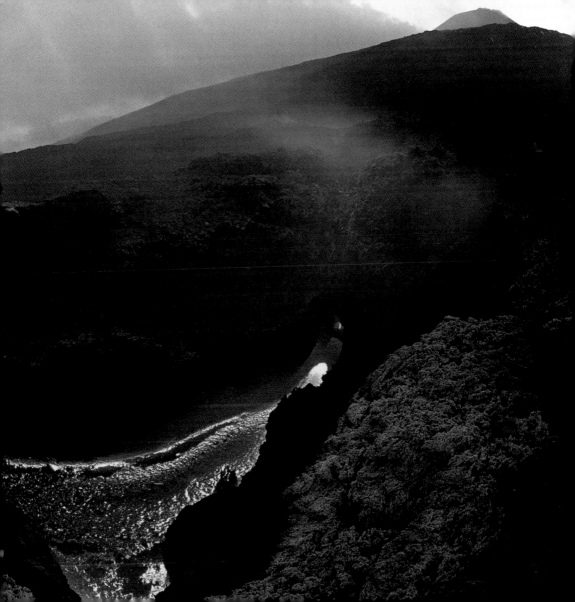

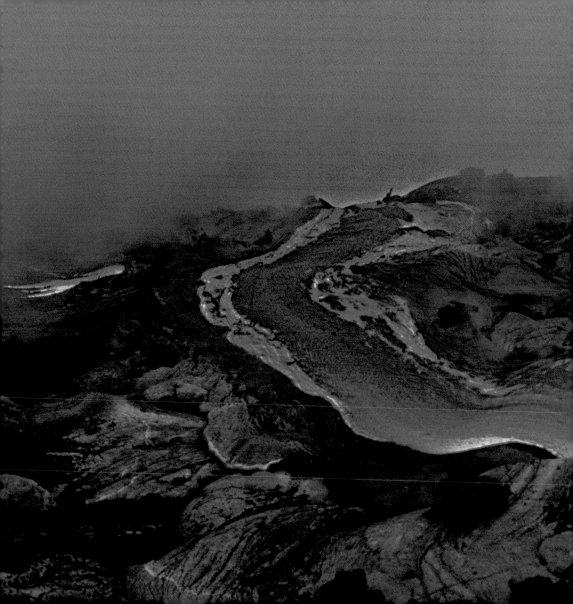

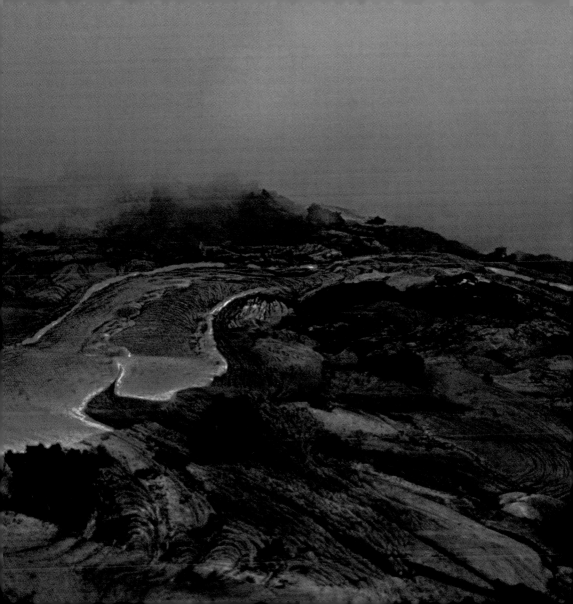

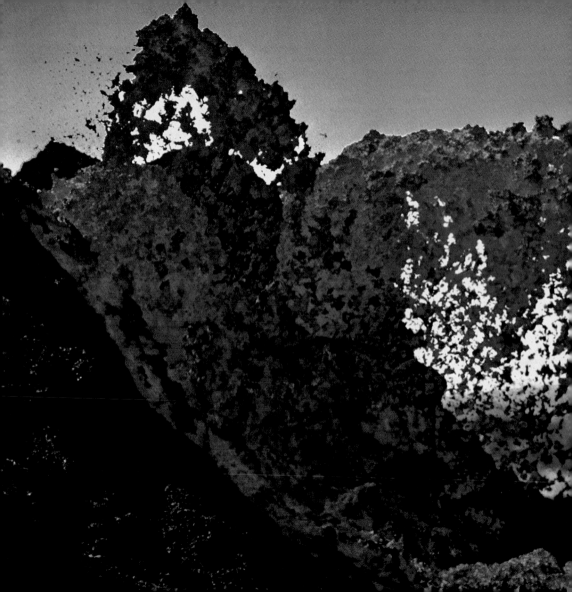

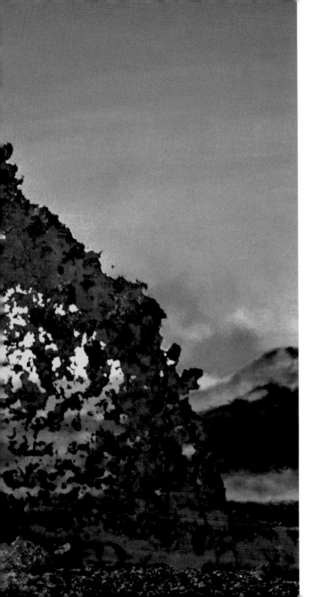

" EARTH AND FIRE. POWER AND VIOLENCE. IMMENSE FORCES UNLEASHED BY IMPERCEPTIBLE MOVEMENTS BENEATH THE EARTH'S CRUST SEND MAGMA TOWARDS THE SURFACE. THE ERUPTION IS ONLY THE LAST ACT IN PHYSICAL ACTIVITY THAT HAS LASTED FOR MILLENNIA, AND WHICH REGARDS THE NATURE OF THE PLANET ITSELF. "

Hawaii (USA) - Lava spout on Kilauea, Hawaii Volcanoes National Park.

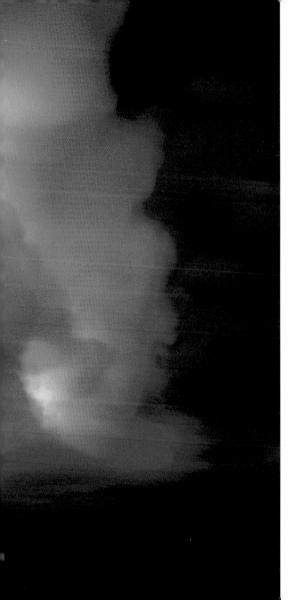

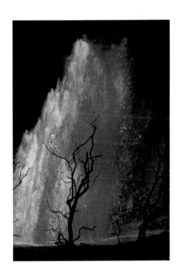

*314-315* ● Hawaii (USA) - Lava flow from Kilauea crater, Hawaii Volcanoes National Park.

*315* ● Hawaii (USA) - Lava spout on Mauna Ulu, Hawaii Volcanoes National Park.

# The ICE KINGDOM

Australian Antarctic Territory - Iceberg.

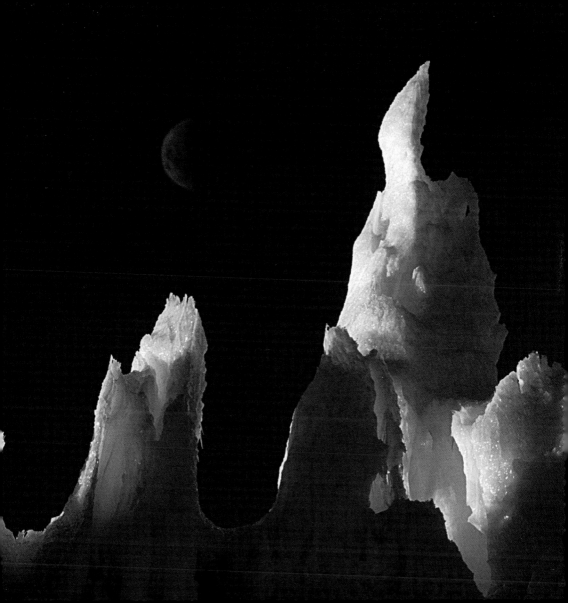

## INTRODUCTION The Ice Kingdom

AMONG THE CRYSTAL TOWERS AND ALONG THE WIND-SWEPT PASSAGES IN THE WORLD OF GLACIERS, THE RULES OF LIFE LOSE THEIR MEANING: THERE REMAIN THE DIMENSIONS OF THE REAL AND IMAGINARY, WHICH MINGLE SOMEWHERE BETWEEN THE TRUE AND FALSE, WAKEFULNESS AND DREAM. TWO DIMENSIONS THAT ATTEST TO THE VAST WHITE EXPANSE THAT IS BLINDING ON SUNNY DAYS, MILKY ON CLOUDY DAYS, AND MURKY AND UNDECIPHERABLE UNDER THE MANTLE OF THICK, ICY FOG. THE THIRD DIMENSION IS A GIFT THAT CANNOT BE PERCEIVED AT THIS LATITUDE: HERE, WHERE THERE IS NO VEGETATION AND THE SOLID ICE IS ALWAYS COVERED WITH SNOW, THE BLINDNESS CAUSED BY THE LACK OF REFERENCE POINTS ANNULS

## INTRODUCTION The Ice Kingdom

ONE'S PERCEPTION OF DEPTH, TRIGGERING A SORT OF VERTIGO. THE THIRD DIMENSION IS ALSO MUDDLED BY MIRAGES, WHICH OBLITERATE DISTANCES, MAKING THE SIGHT OF VERY DISTANT OBJECTS SUCH AS AN ISLAND, MOUNTAIN CHAIN, SHIP, THE SEA OR A VILLAGE SEEM CLOSE AT HAND.

THE DIMENSION OF TIME FADES AWAY IN POLAR SUM-MERS AND WINTERS, WHEN EVEN AT MIDNIGHT THE SUN DOES NOT DESCEND BELOW THE HORIZON AND DAYS SEEM TO BE SUSPENDED IN PERPETUAL LIGHT.

THE FIFTH DIMENSION IS THAT OF DREAMS, SO TO SPEAK, WHICH CONTINUOUSLY PRODUCE THE MOST MAGICAL VISIONS THAT THE POLAR REGIONS HAVE IN STORE FOR AMAZED OBSERVERS: SOLAR HALOES,

# The Ice Kingdom
## Introduction

MOCK SUNS AND MOCK MOONS, THAT IS, THE MAGICAL APPEARANCE OF TWO, THREE AND SOMETIMES FOUR SUNS AND MOONS AT THE SAME TIME, THE TRICK OF A DIVINITY THAT SEEMS TO ENJOY POKING FUN AT HUMANS. THEN THERE ARE THE AURORAS, THE SOUTHERN AND NORTHERN LIGHTS, WHICH APPEAR SYMMETRICALLY IN THE SOUTHERN AND NORTHERN HEMISPHERE, CONSISTING OF A PALE "DRAPE" OF FLOWING LINES DELICATELY COLORED GREEN, RED AND PINK. THOSE FORTUNATE ENOUGH TO SEE THESE MAGIC DISPLAYS OF LIGHT MAY BE LED TO BELIEVE THAT THESE DRAPERIES TOUCH THE HORIZON AND COME FROM A DISTANT WORLD.

*321* • Weddell Sea (Antarctica) - Midnight sun.

*322-323* • Argentina - Perito Moreno Glacier.

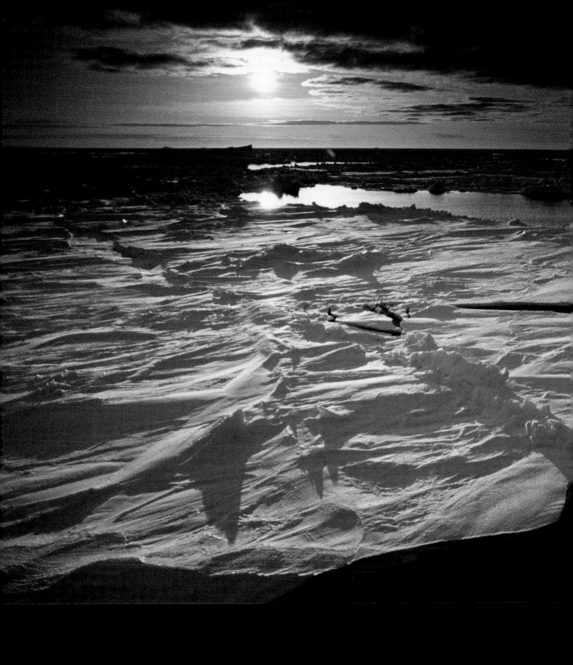

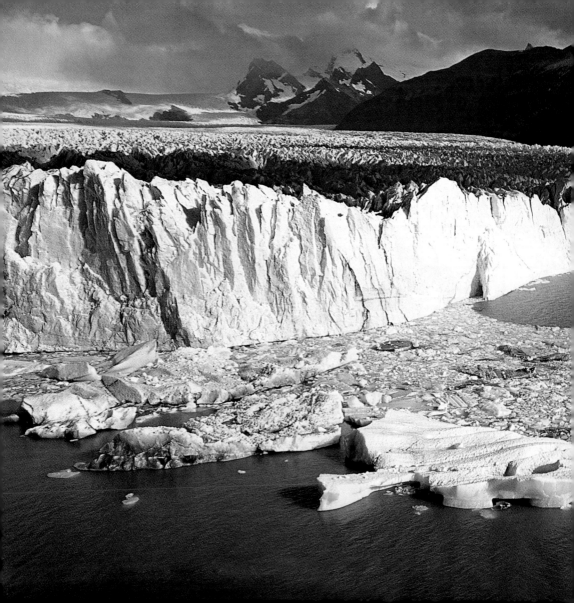

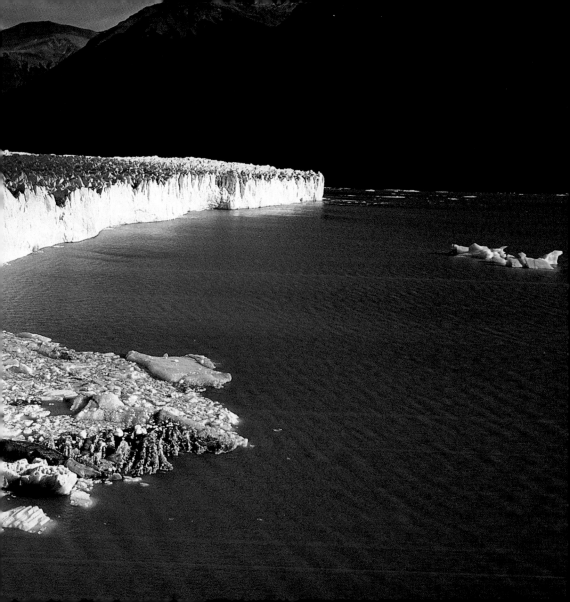

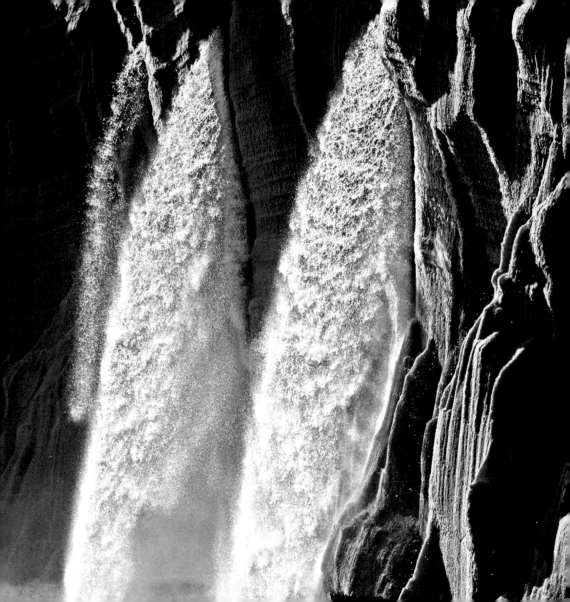

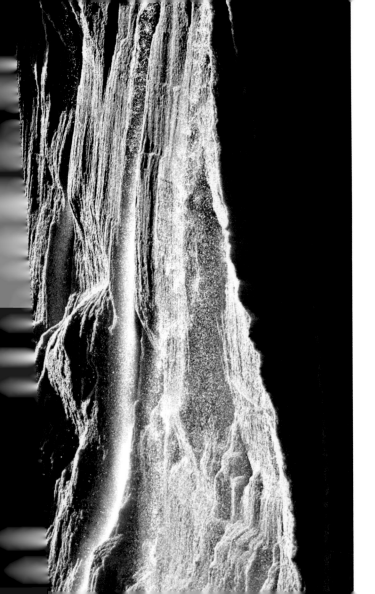

324-325 • Svalbard Islands (Norway) - Ice falls on the Austfonna Glacier.

326-327 • Churchill (Canada) - Polar bears tackle a deep crack in the ice.

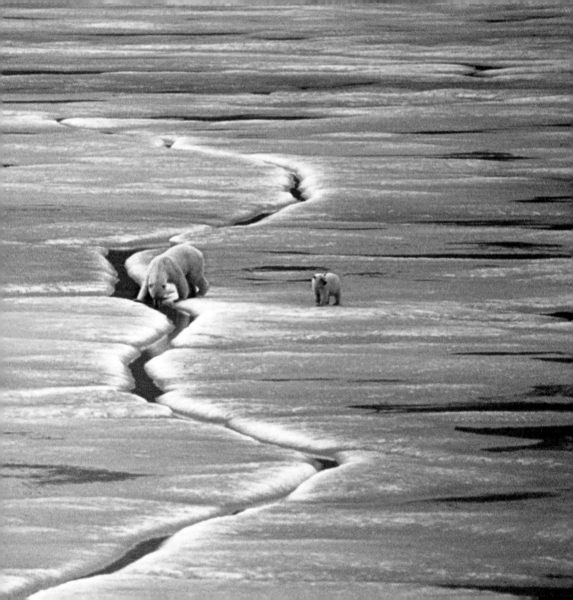

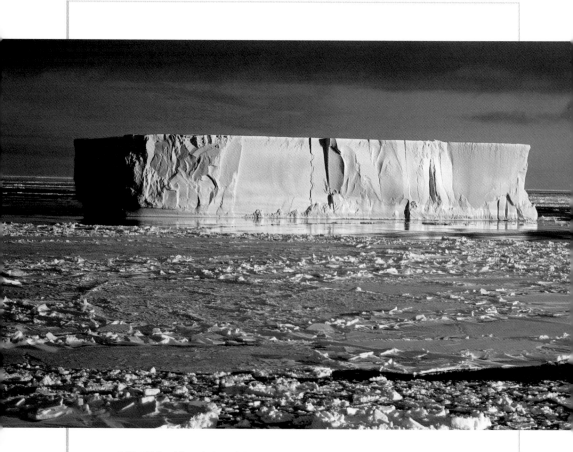

328-329 ● Victoria Land (Antarctica) - Iceberg off the Adare Peninsula.

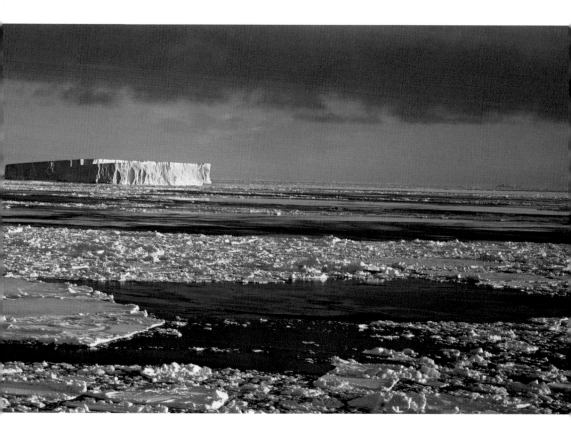

*330-331* ● Ross Sea (Antarctic) - Ross Ice Shelf.

*332-333* ● Greenland (Denmark) - Midnight sun over Disko Bay.

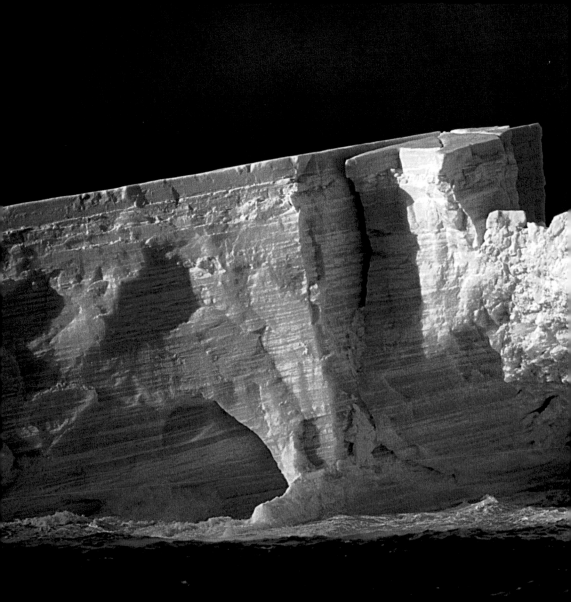

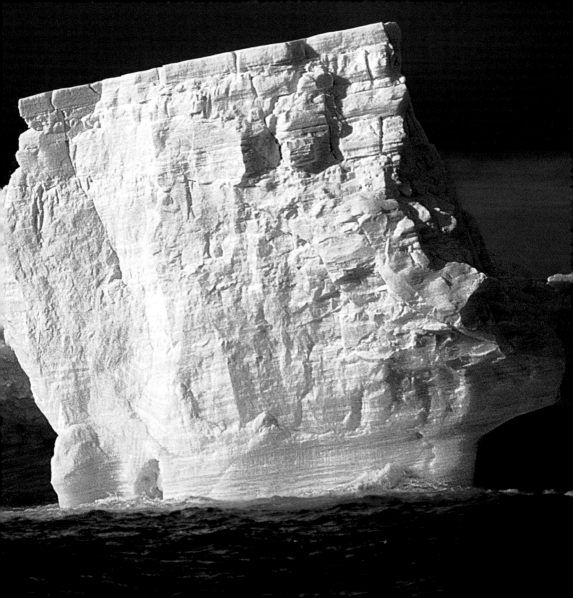

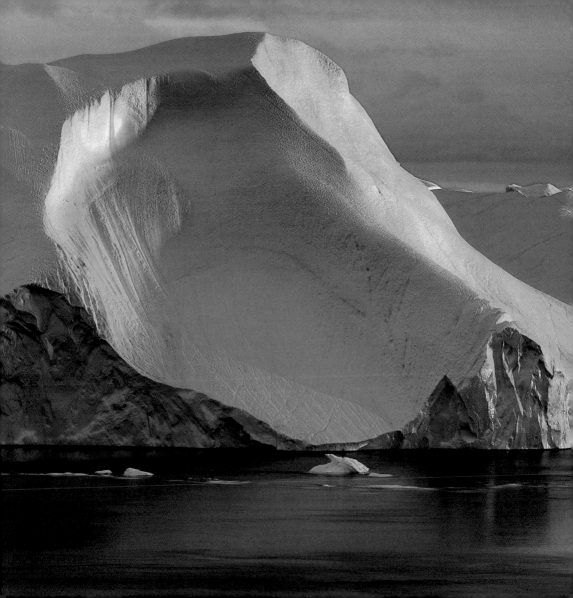

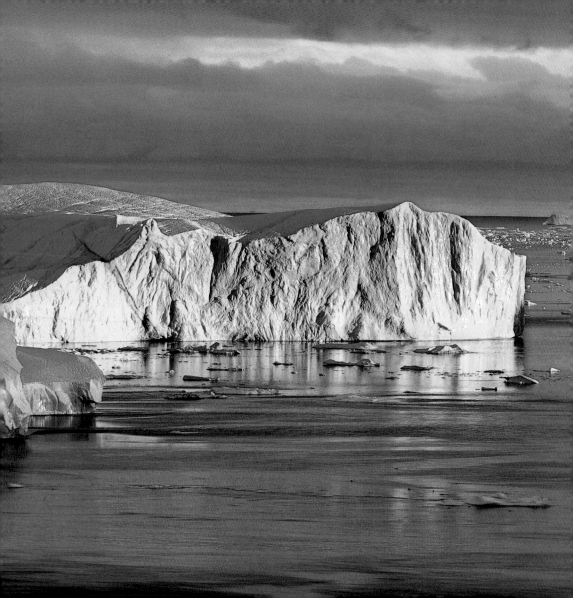

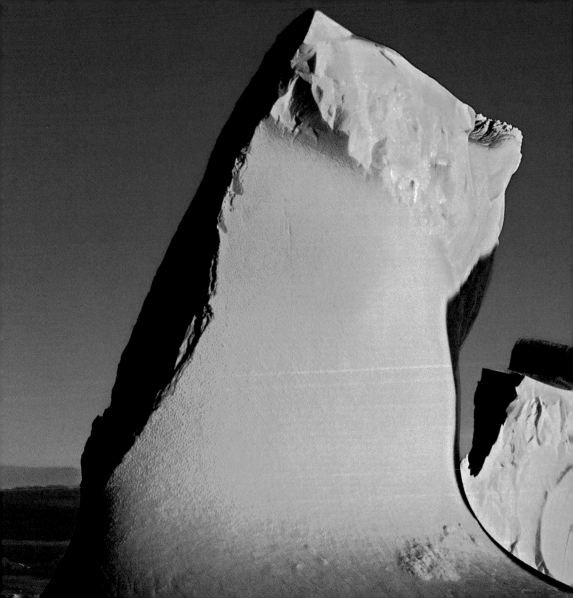

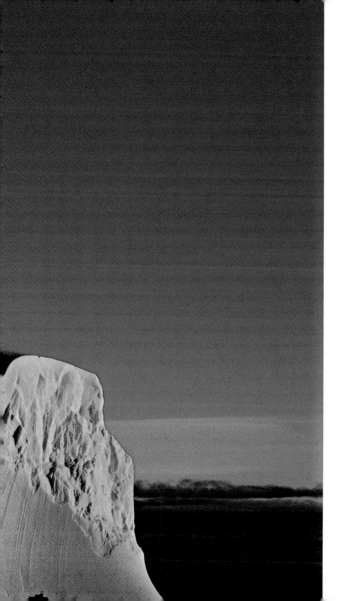

Antarctic Peninsula
(Antarctica) - Tower
iceberg near Anvers
Island.

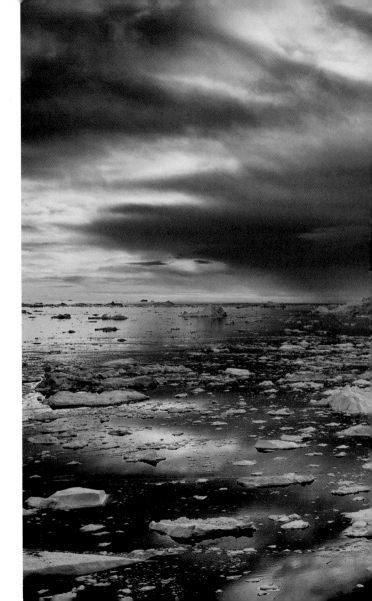

336-337 ● Greenland
(Denmark) - Disko Bay.

338-339 ● Falkland Islands
(United Kingdom) - Iceberg
off Saunders Island.

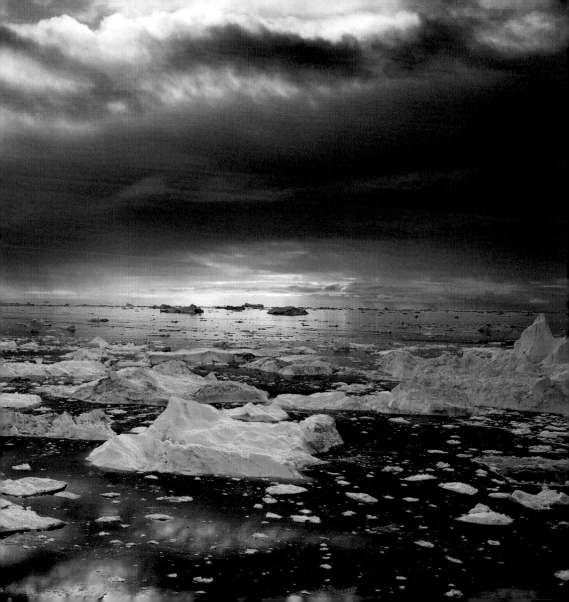

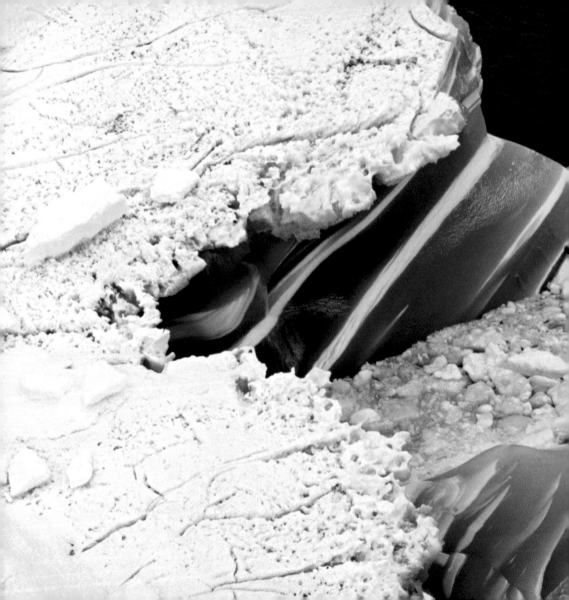

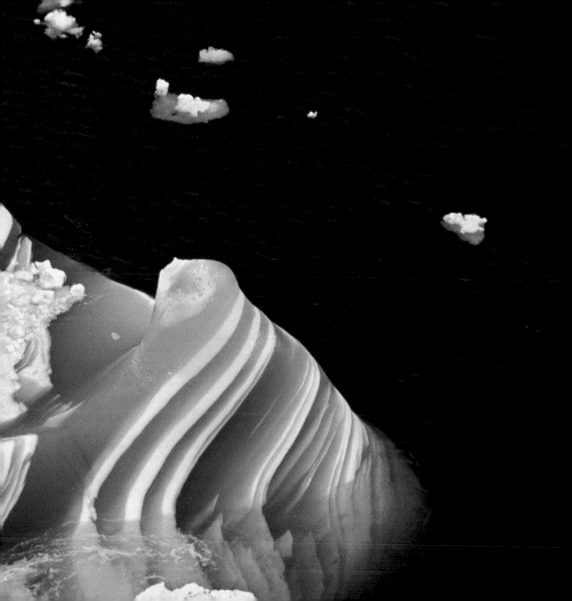

# The WORLD of STONE

Utah-Arizona (USA) - Monument Valley National Park.

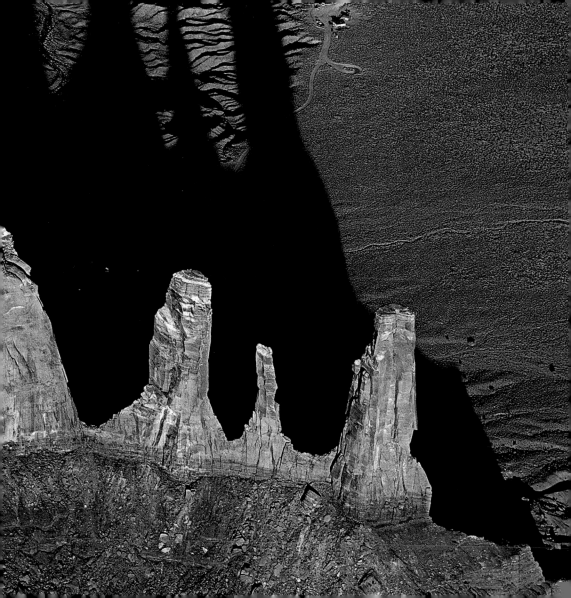

## INTRODUCTION The World of Stone

THE SUN RISES OVER THE VAST MESAS OF THE AMERICAN WEST LIKE AN OMNIPOTENT DEITY. AFTER A NIGHT OF BITTER COLD, THE FIRST RAYS REPRESENT THE REVIVAL OF LIFE, BLOOD THAT FLOWS AGAIN PAST THE LONG SHADOWS CREATED BY THE GIGANTIC STONES. AS IF WE WERE AT THE DAWN OF HUMAN EXISTENCE, IMMENSE STONE ARCHES, TALL AND STEEP WALLS, BIZARRE SHAPES, SHARP CRAGS, AND THIN STRIPS OF SANDSTONE, LIMESTONE, SCHIST AND GRANITE DESCRIBE A FANTASTIC SCENE INTERRUPTED BY RARE SIGNS OF MODERN LIFE: A DIRT ROAD, A SOLITARY ROAD SIGN, THE DUST FROM A CAR PASSING IN THE DISTANCE, THE WISPY TRAIL LEFT BY A JET PLANE IN THE SKY. A FEW INSECTS NUMBED BY THE NIGHT COLD LOOK FOR A HID-

• Sinai (Egypt) - Wadi Khudra.

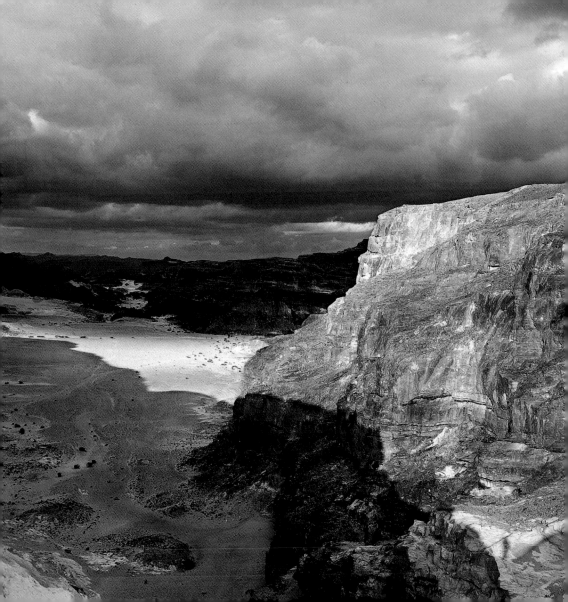

# INTRODUCTION The World of Stone

ING PLACE, ESCAPING THEIR FAMISHED PREDATORS. THE AIR IS CLEAR AND ALL THE COLORS SEEM TO BE KINDLED BY AN UNREAL LIGHT AND THE STREAKED ROCKS – BE THEY SMOOTH OR VARIEGATED, STRATIFIED OR SCULPT- ED, ERODED OR SLATEY – ARE FLAMING RED, PINK, OCHER AND YELLOW. THIS IS THE IRIDESCENT PALETTE THAT GENERATED THE EPICS OF THE NAVAHO AND HOPI, OF THE MYSTERIOUS ANASAZI CLIFF DWELLERS SUCH AS THE PUEBLO, AND OF THE PIONEERS AND COWBOYS. IN THE SOLITUDE OF THESE VAST EXPANSES, CONTEMPLAT- ING BARE CLIFFS BEARING CARVINGS TENS OF THOU- SANDS OF YEARS OLD, MAN CAN FIND HIMSELF OR, IF HE PREFERS, GOD. IT IS NO ACCIDENT THAT UPON VIEWING THE GRAND CANYON, THE NATURALIST DONALD CUL-

# INTRODUCTION The World of Stone

ROSS PEATTIE STATED HE HAD FELT "THE LORD'S WILL." OTHER HAVE DESCRIBED THE GORGES CARVED BY THE COLORADO RIVER AS THE "LAST JUDGMENT OF NATURE." BECAUSE OF THE GRANDIOSITY OF ITS SCENERY, THE AMERICAN SOUTHWEST IS THE "STONE GARDEN" *PAR EXCELLENCE.* OTHER CANYONS, DESERTS AND ROCK FORMATIONS IN DIFFERENT CORNERS OF THE EARTH BOAST FANTASTIC PANORAMAS. IN AUSTRALIA, CERTAIN GEOLOGICAL FORMATIONS, INCLUDING AYERS ROCK, HAVE ASTOUNDED THE WORLD AND PROMPTED LEADING ARTISTS TO GRAPPLE WITH THE MYSTERY AND FASCINATION OF THESE PHENOMENA. THE TROPICAL REGIONS OF AFRICA OFFER THE CRAGGY NEEDLES OF THE SAHARA RANGE, THE EXTRAORDINARY TASSILI ROCK PAINTINGS,

# The World of Stone
## Introduction

THE GRANITE TOWERS OF HOGGAR AND THE FALAISE DOGON, AN IMPRESSIVE CLIFF THAT CUTS THROUGH THE TROPICAL STEPPE IN MALI: ROCKS WITH FANTASTIC SHAPES, WILD VALLEYS AND RARE, PRECIOUS SPRINGS. IN THE MEDITERRANEAN REGION THE GORGES OF THE RHONE OR THE FABULOUS "FAIRIES' CHIMNEYS" IN CAP-PADOCIA LOOK LIKE MONUMENTS THAT NATURE BUILT FOR HERSELF, WITH THE SOLE AIM OF ASTONISHING HUMAN BEINGS. IN THESE PLACES, THE GEOLOGICAL ERAS AND THE HISTORY OF LIFE ITSELF ARE CARVED ON THE ROCKS LIKE PAGES OF A PRECIOUS ILLUMINATED MANUSCRIPT THAT BEARS CORALS, SHELLS AND FOSSILS MOUNTED LIKE JEWELS.

*347* ● New Mexico (USA) - Shiprock.

*348-349* ● Utah-Arizona (USA) - Monument Valley National Park.

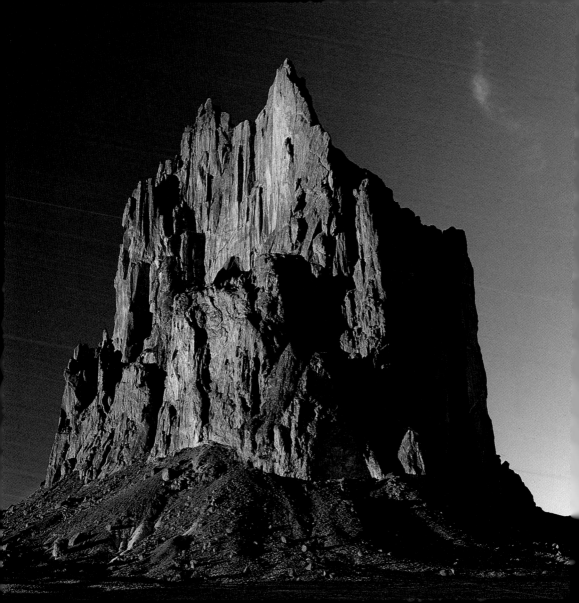

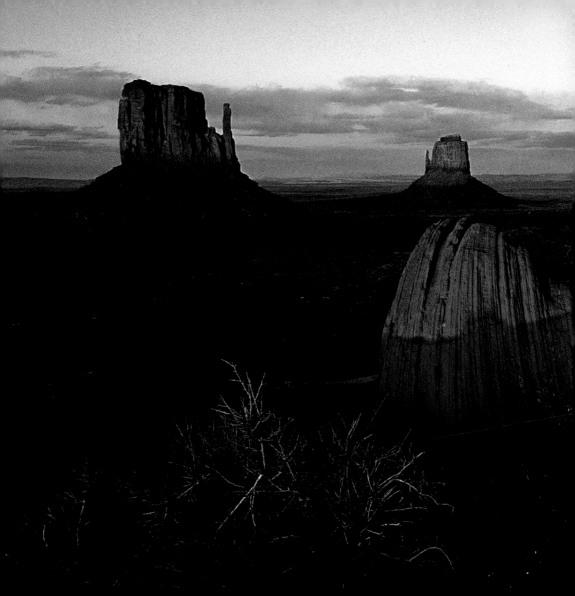

*350* ● Utah-Arizona (USA) - Monument Valley National Park, *mitten.*

*351* ● Utah (USA) - Arches National Park, Delicate Arch.

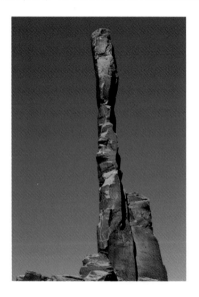

*352-353* ● Arizona (USA) - Grand Canyon, South Rim from Pima Point.

*354-355* ● Utah (USA) - Bryce Canyon.

*356-357* ● Utah (USA) - Castle Rock, La Sal Mountains.

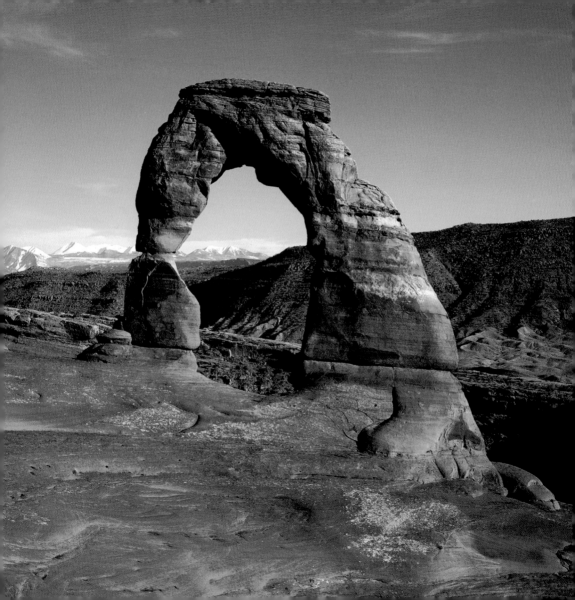

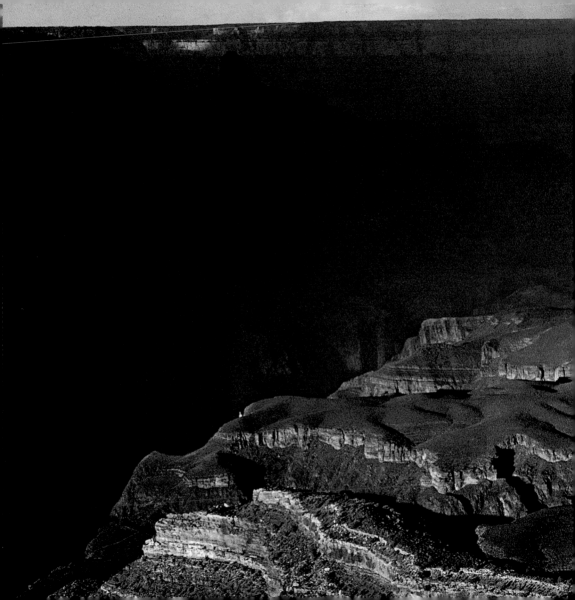

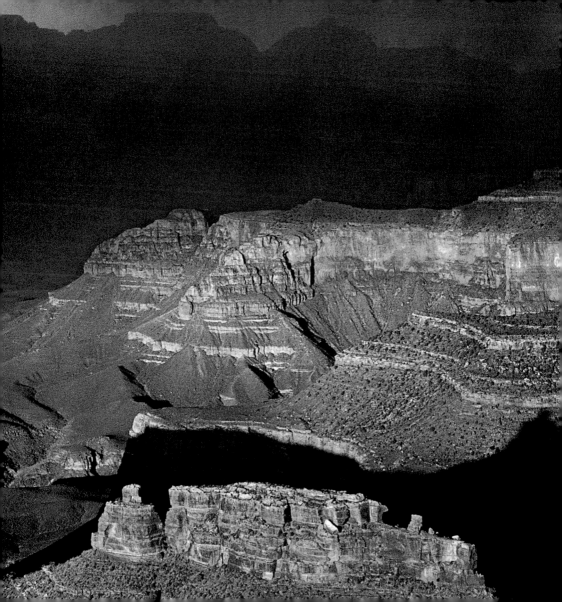

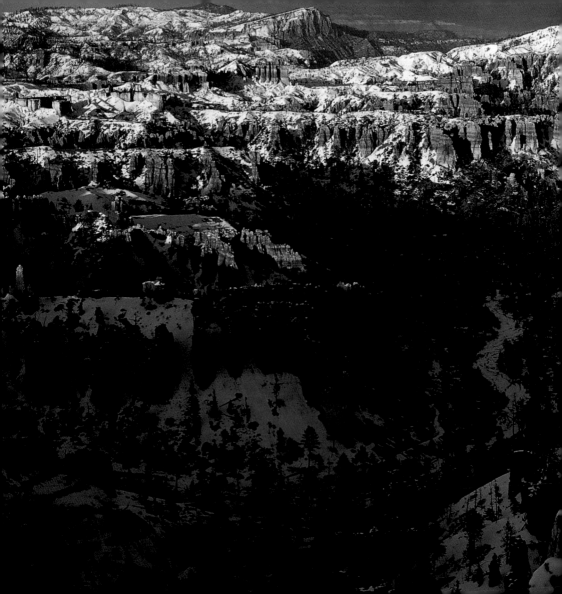

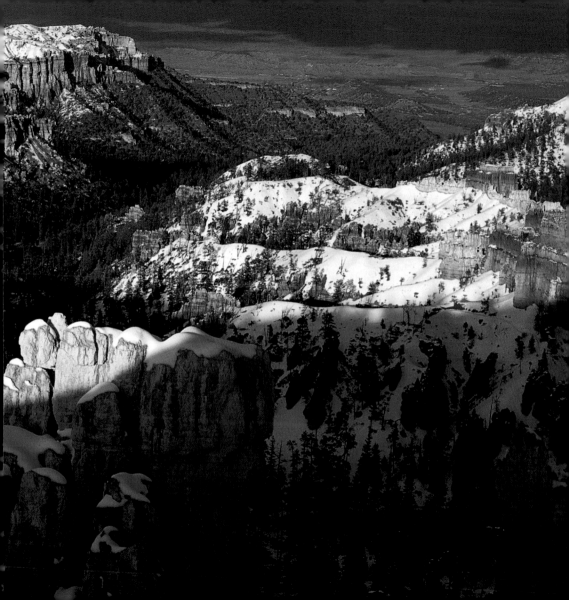

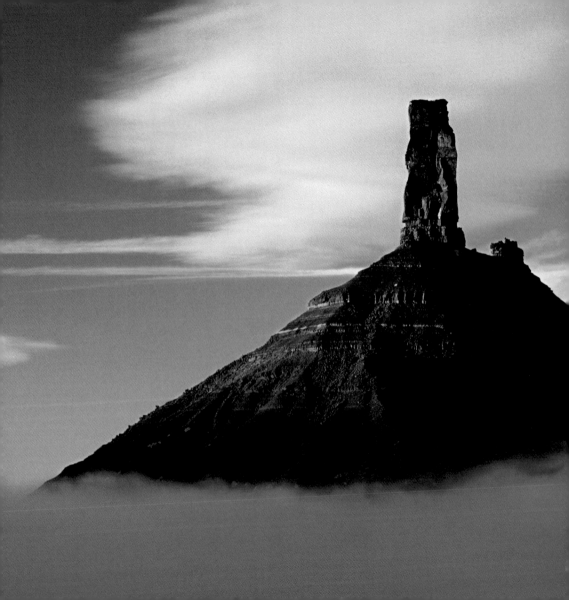

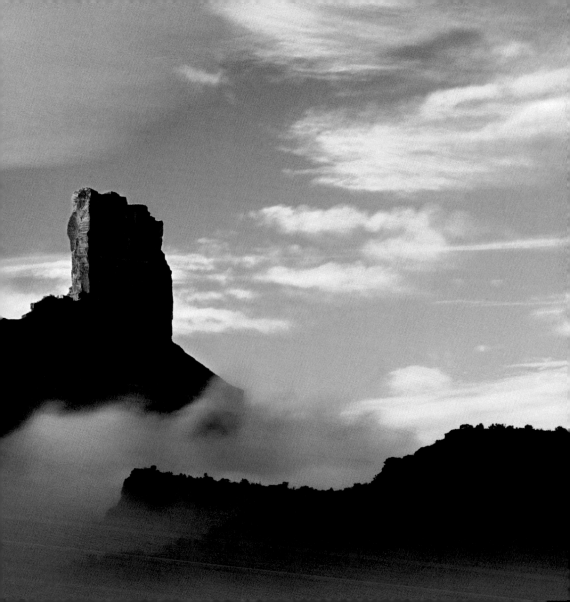

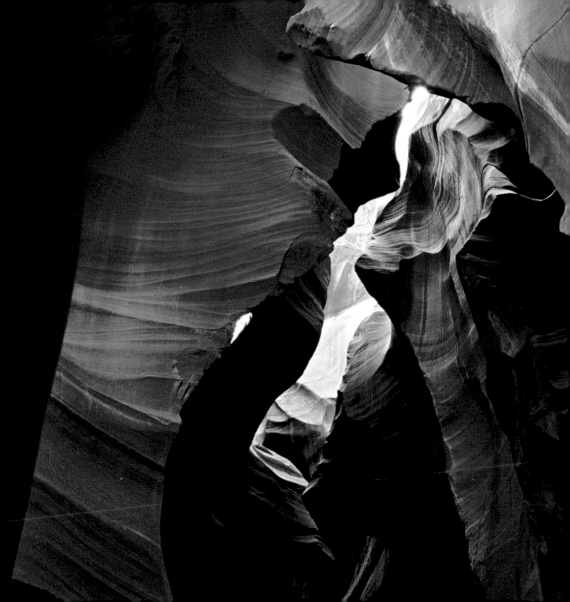

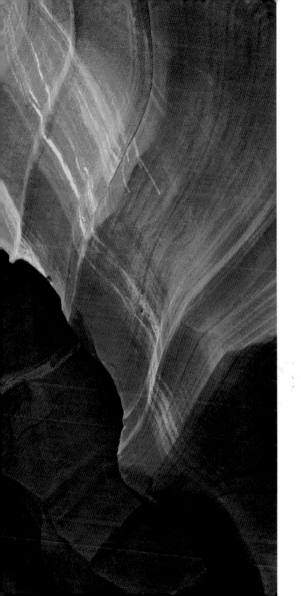

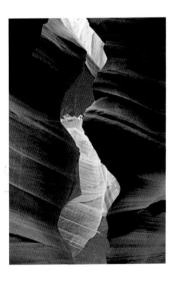

Arizona (USA) - Antelope Canyon, sandstone eroded by seasonal floods.

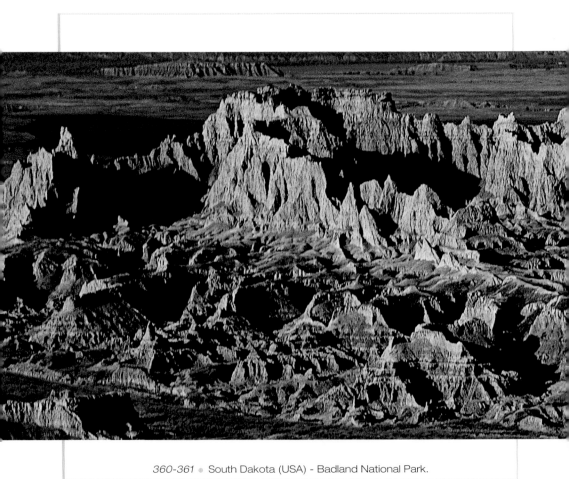

*360-361* ● South Dakota (USA) - Badland National Park.

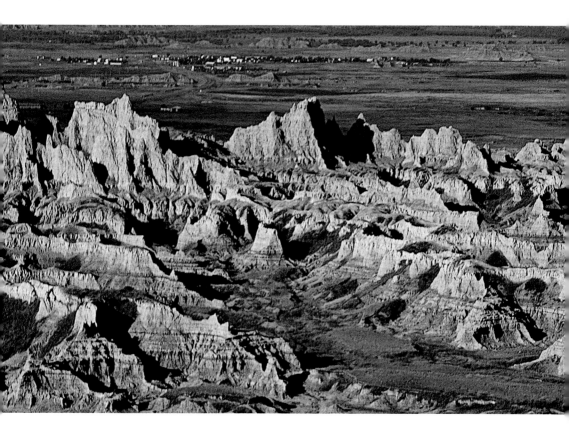

362-363 • Tanzania - Rift Valley.

364-365 • Region of Tamanrasset (Algeria) - Hoggar massif.

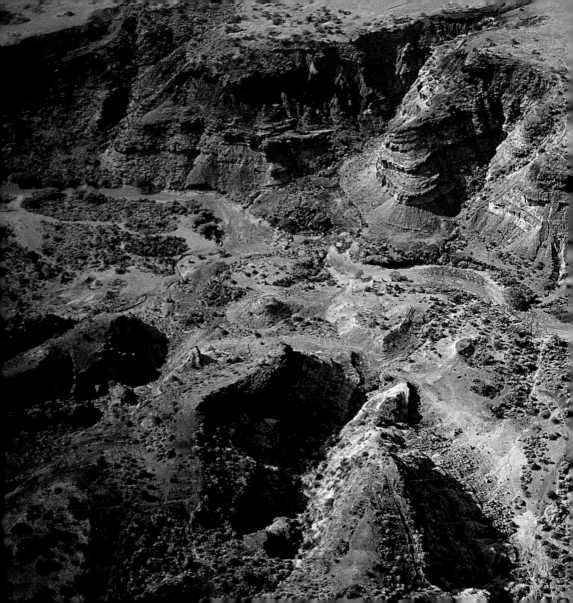

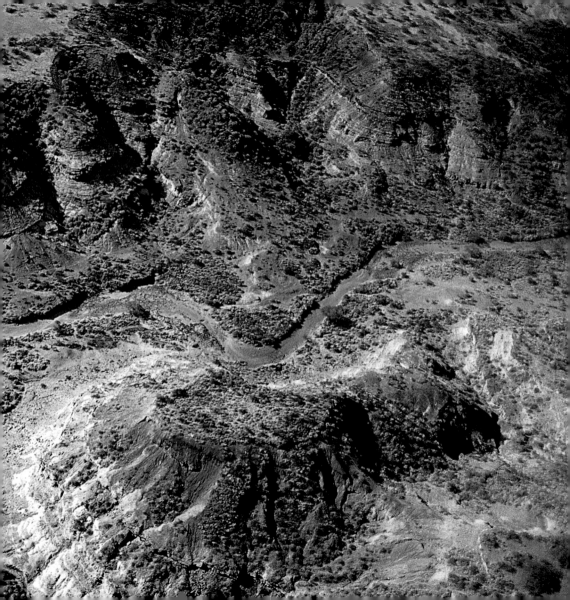

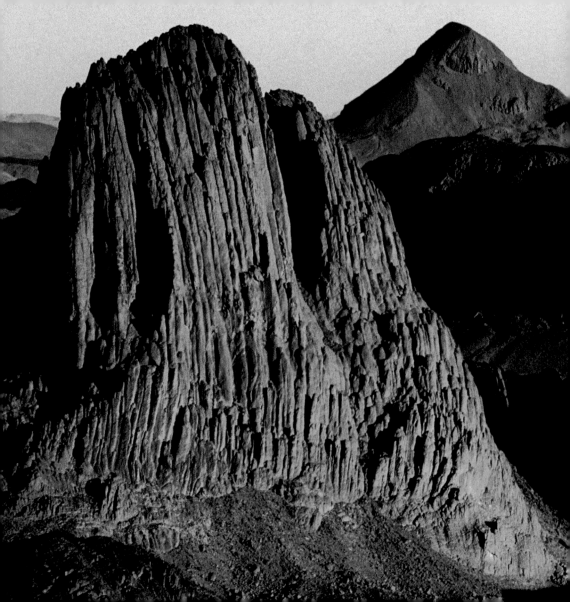

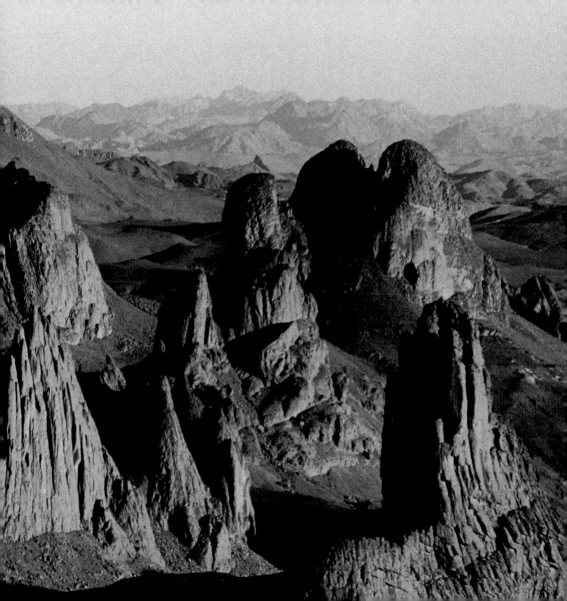

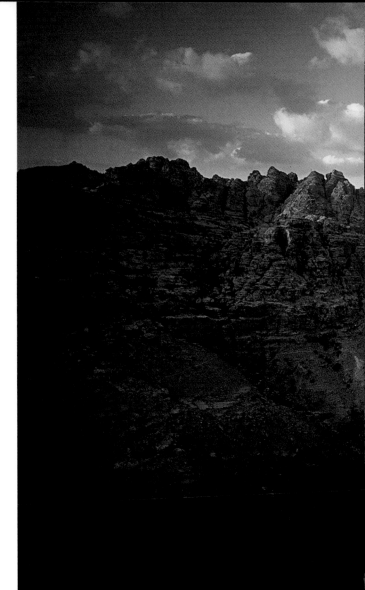

*366-367* ● Jordan -
Jebel Harun.

*368-369* ● Sinai (Egypt) -
Forest of Columns,
Jebel Fuga.

*370-371* ● Cappadocia
(Turkey) - Countryside
around Uchisar.

*372-373* ● Southern Gobi
(Mongolia) - The mountains
of Khermiyn-Tsau.

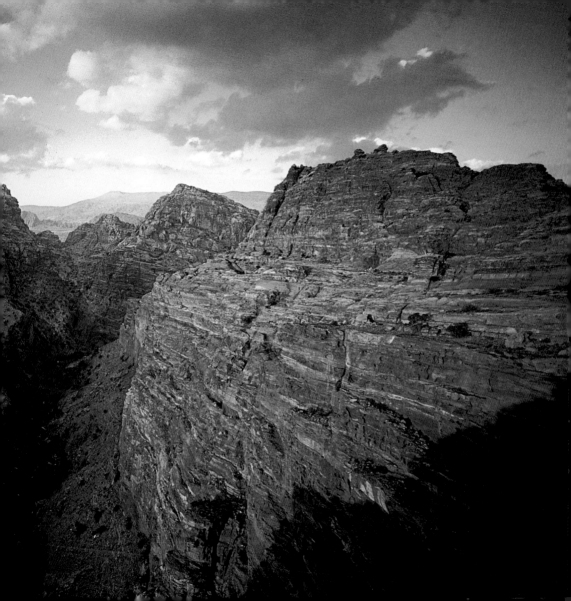

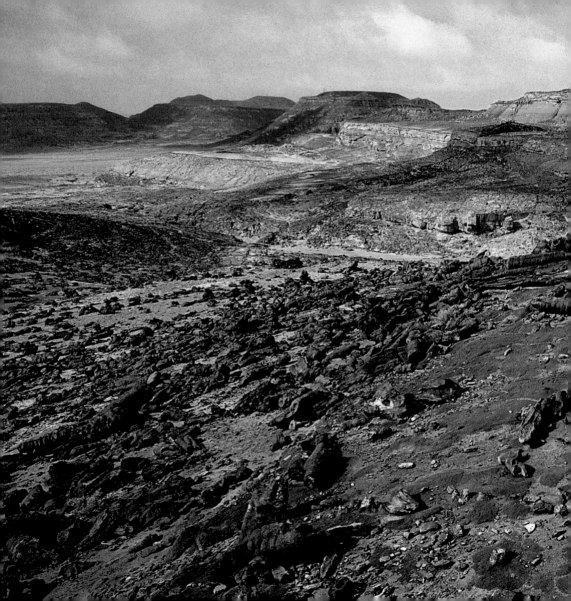

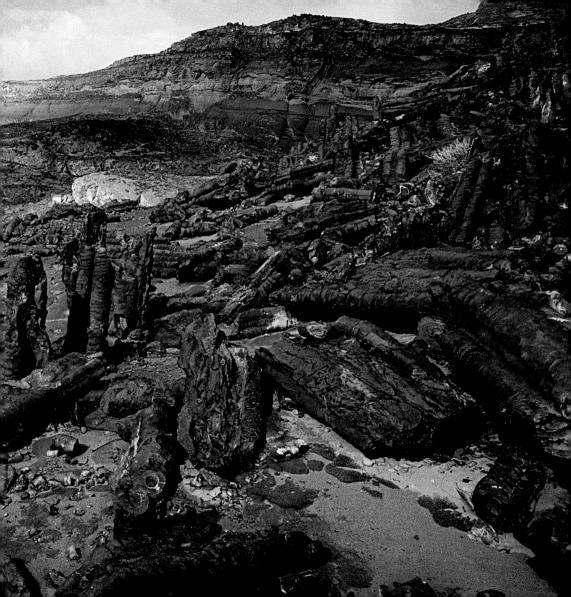

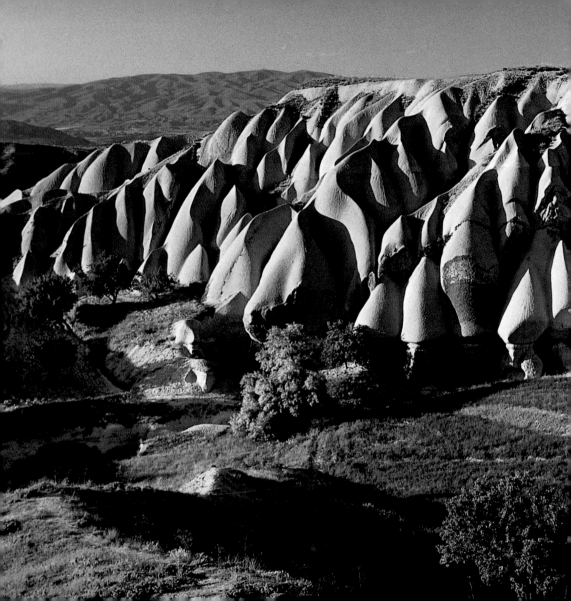

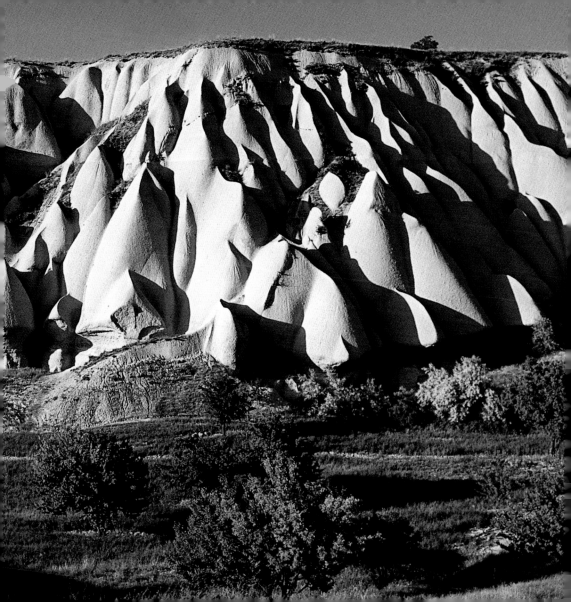

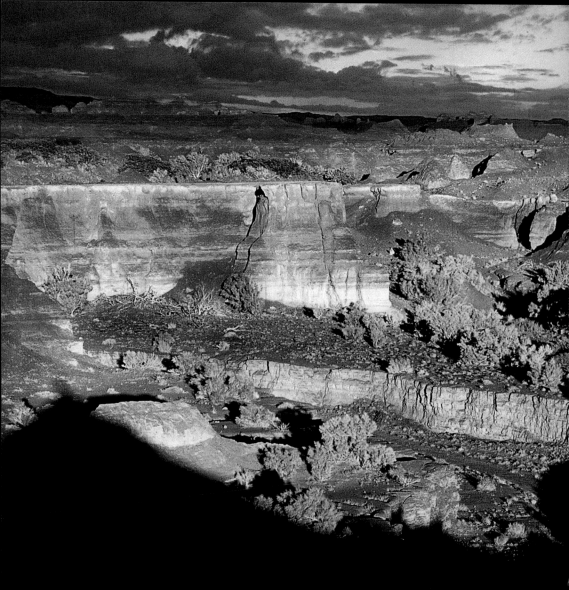

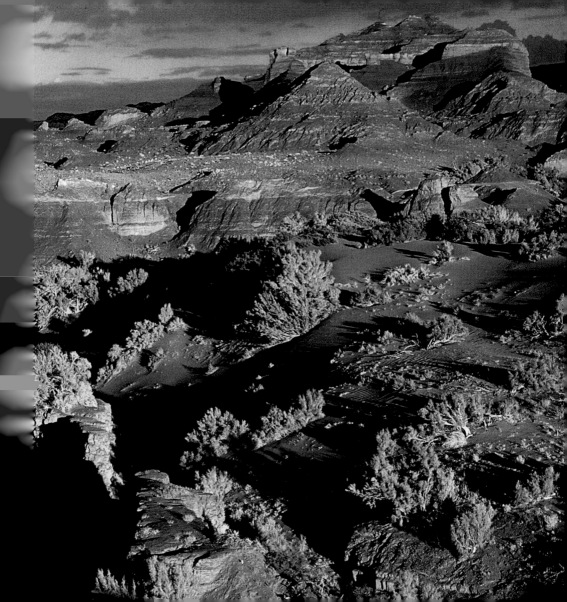

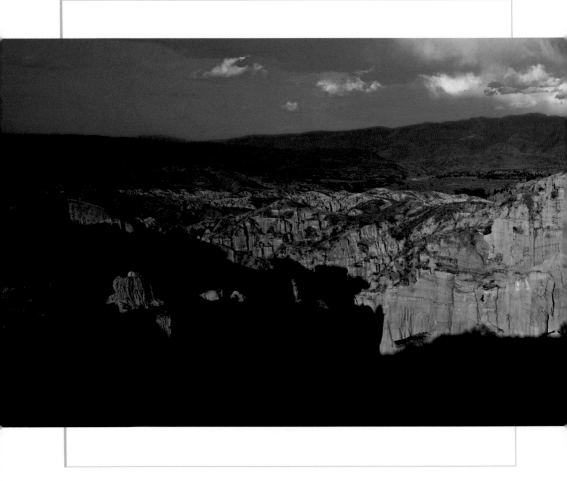

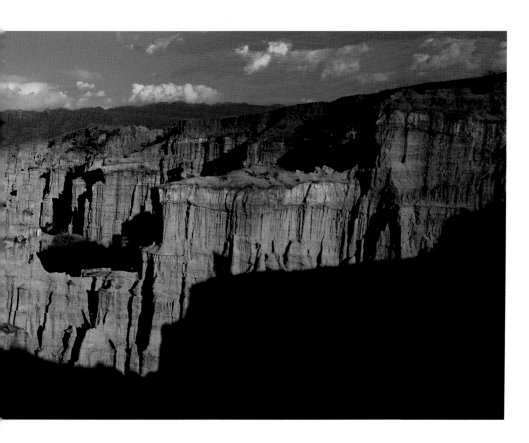

Yunnan (China) - Clay Forest near Yuanmou.

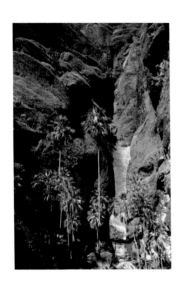

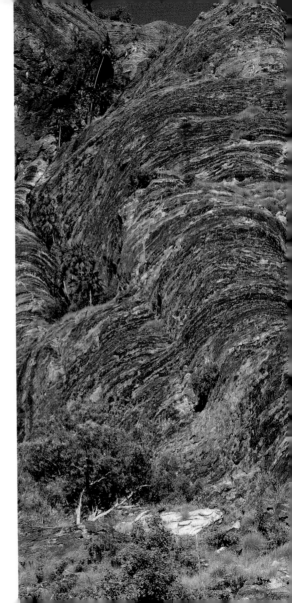

*376 and 376-377* ● Western Australia (Australia) - Bungle-Bungle Range, Purnululu National Park.

*378-379* ● Northern Territory (Australia) - Ayers Rock.

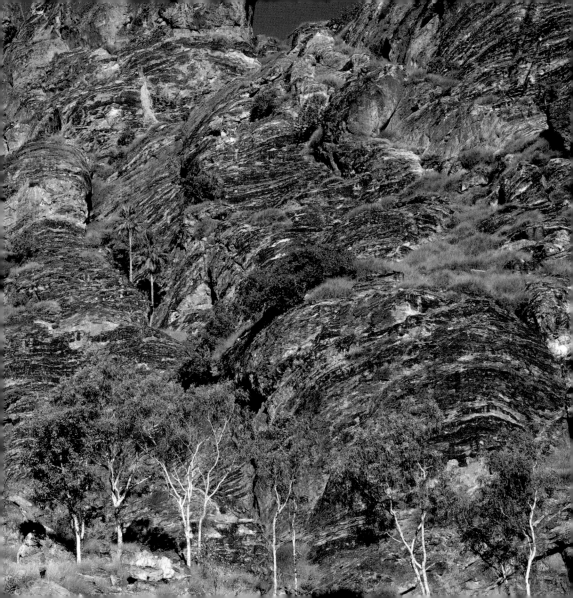

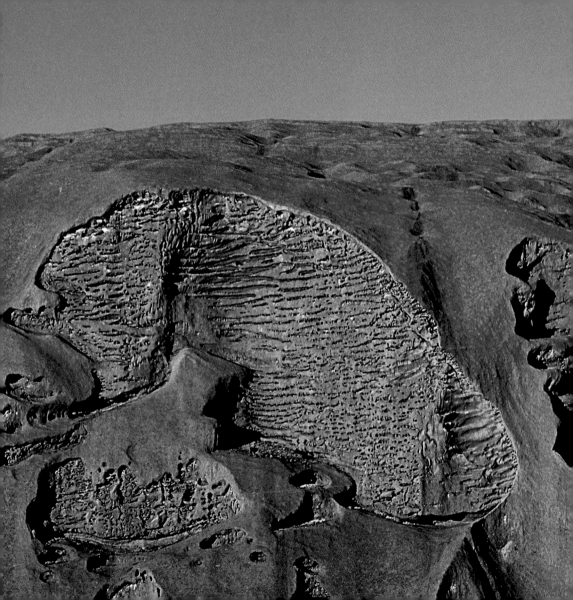

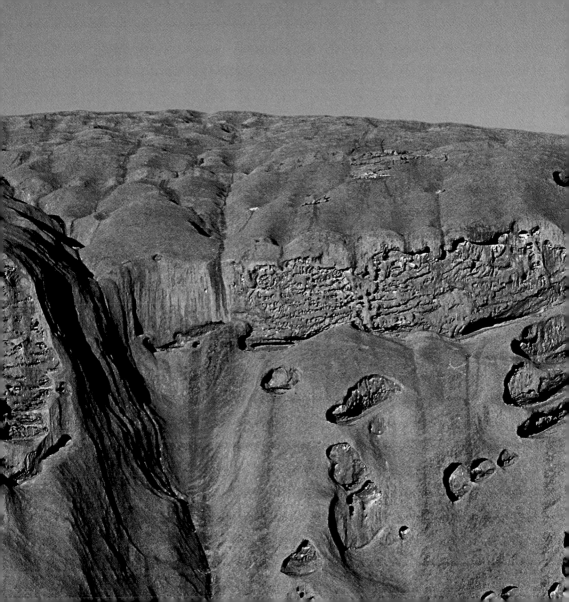

# The WORLD in BETWEEN

- Tanzania - Baobab in Tarangire National Park.

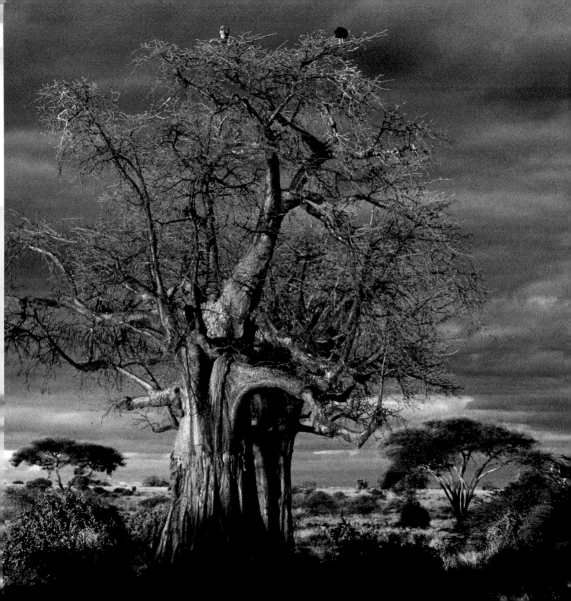

# The World in Between

THE ONLY PLANTS ABLE TO GROW AND SURVIVE IN THE TORRID HEAT ARE THORNY ACACIAS OR BAOBAB WITH THEIR TENTACULAR ROOTS. IN EVERY PART OF THE WORLD, SAVANNAS ARE THE LAND OF RUNNING ANIMALS. IN FACT, THEY ARE THE HOME OF SOME OF THE FASTEST CREATURES IN THE WORLD: CHEETAHS AND OSTRICHES IN AFRICA, NANDU IN SOUTH AMERICA, AND EMUS IN AUSTRALIA. A SWATHE OF THE LOST PARADISE, THE SAVANNAS HAVE INSPIRED ARTISTS AND WRITERS. BUT THEY ARE ABOVE ALL THE SYMBOLS OF NATURE AND THE MAIN CHARACTERS IN THE PLAY THAT IS PERFORMED EVERY DAY ON THIS STAGE, THE LIVING ICONS OF ECOLOGICAL CONSERVATION.

*385* • Australia - Patterns created by vegetation in the semi-desertic Uluru National Park.

*386-387* • Kenya - Column of migrating gnu in Masai Mara National Reserve.

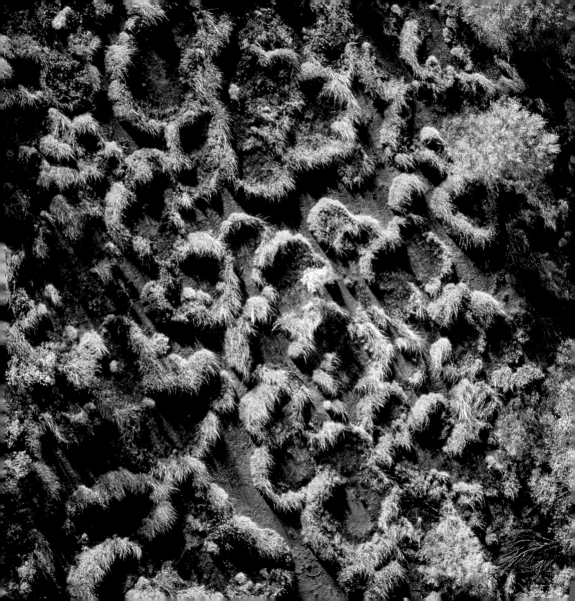

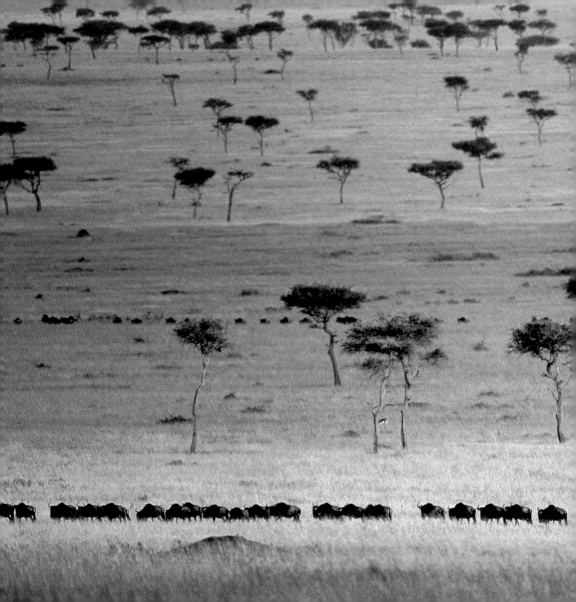

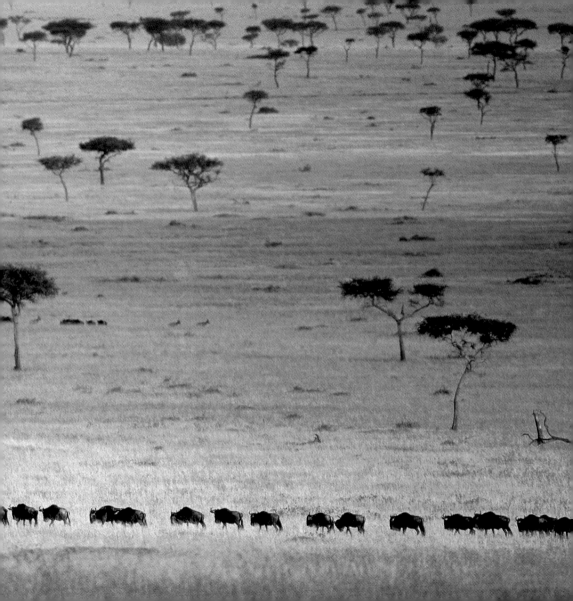

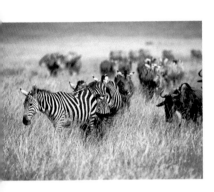

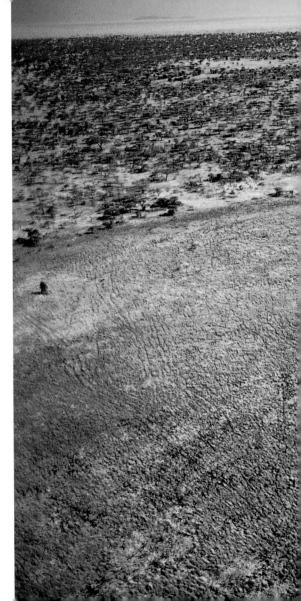

*388* ● Tanzania - Herds of zebra
and gnu in Ngorongoro
Conservation Area.

*388-389* ● Tanzania - Aerial view
of Serengeti National Park.

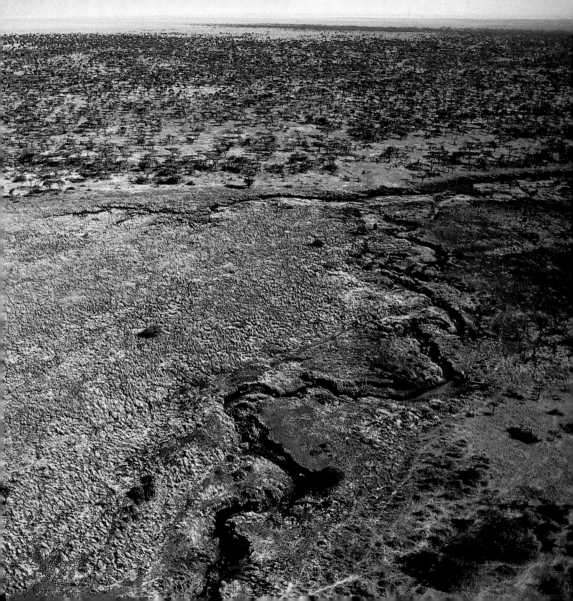

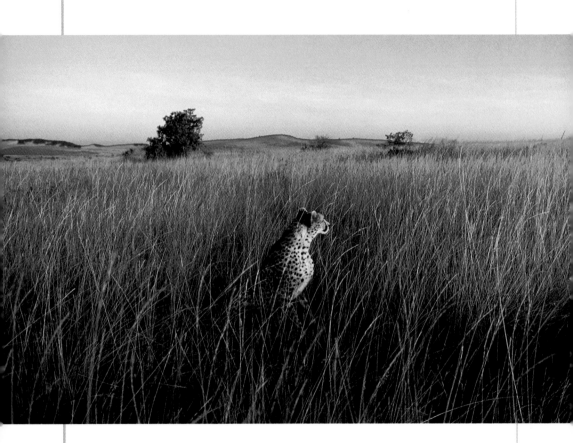

*390-391* ● Kenya - Cheetah lying in wait in the tall grass in Masai Mara National Reserve.

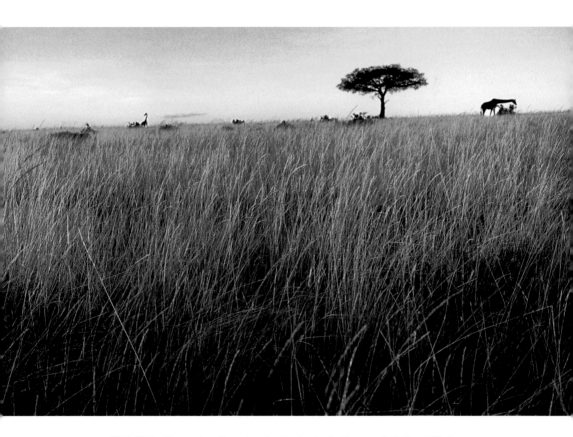

*392-393* ● Tanzania - Grassland with shrubs in Serengeti National Park.

*394-395* ● Tanzania - Acacia scrubland in Ngorongoro Conservation Area.

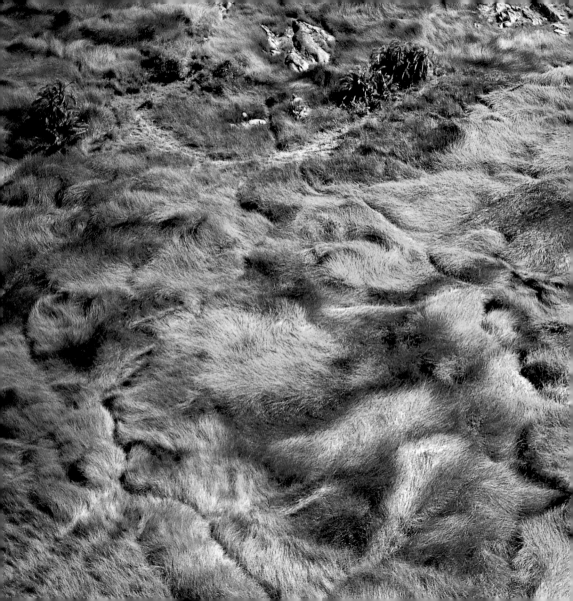

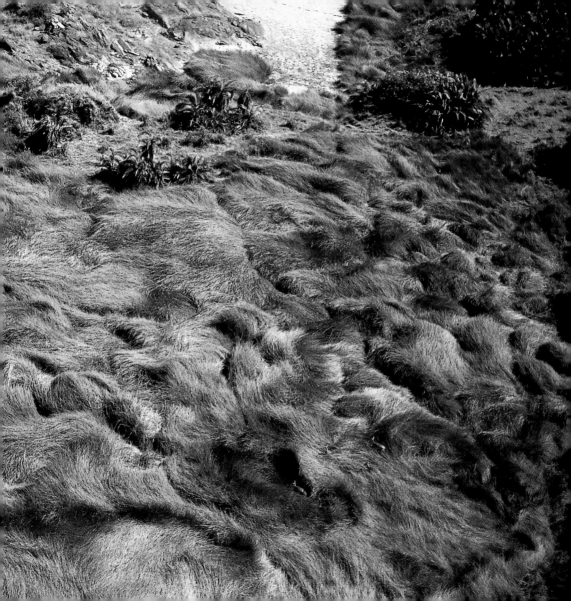

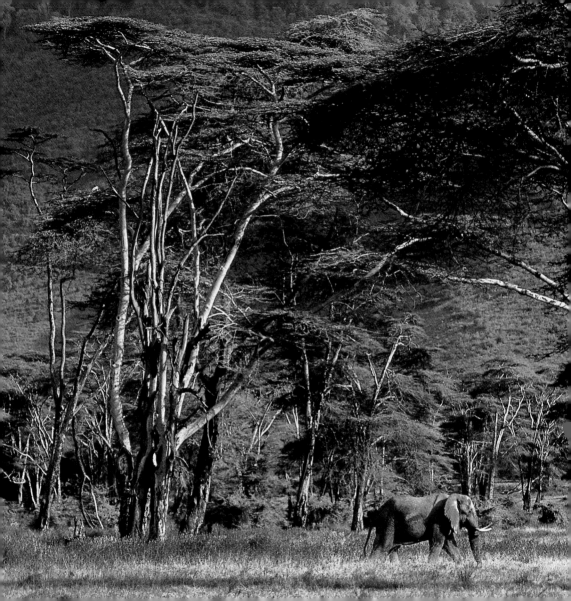

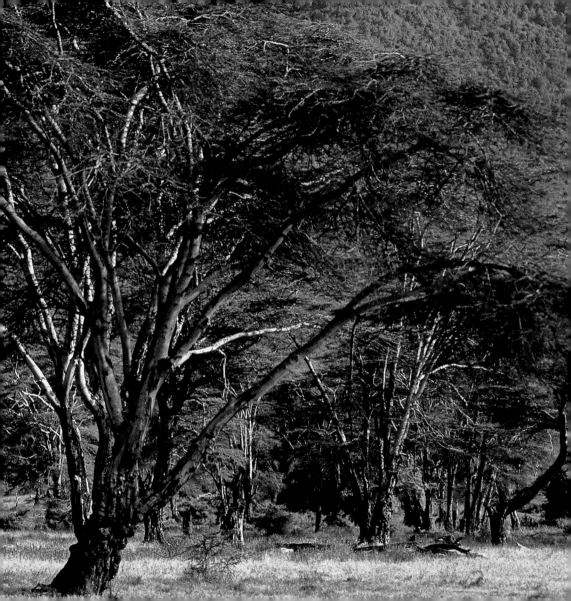

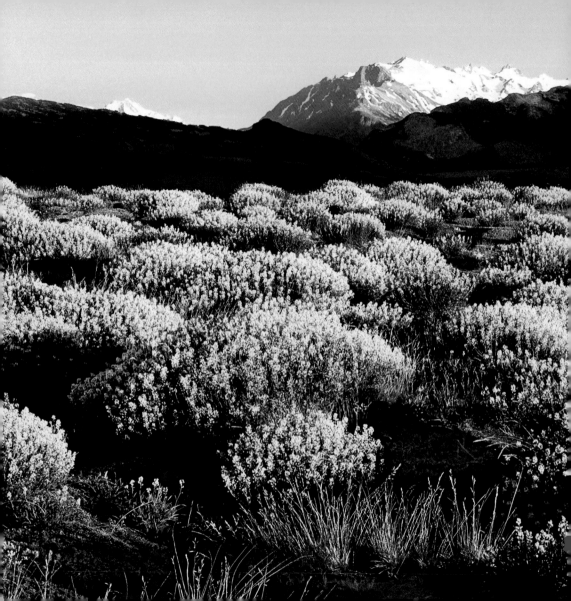

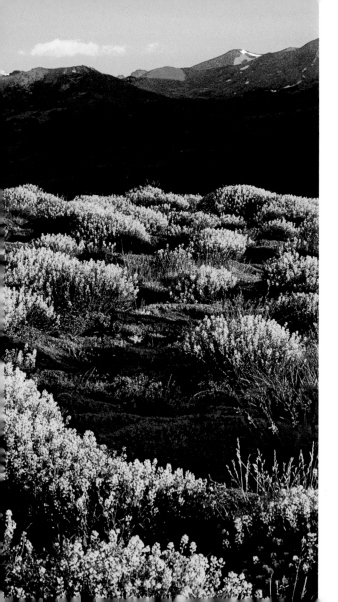

Argentina - Patagonian pampas and (in the background) the Andes, Los Glaciares National Park.

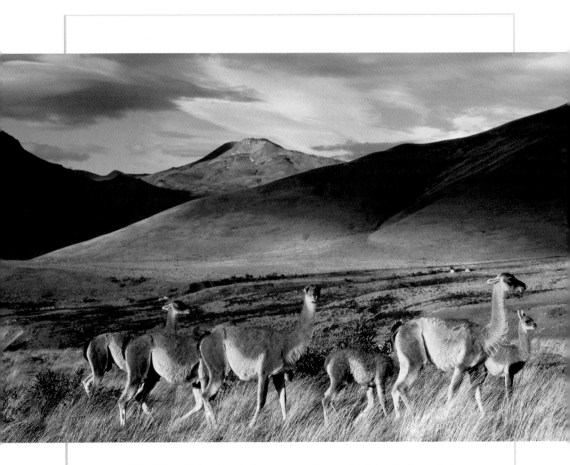

*398-399* ● Chile - Herd of guanacos, Torres del Paine National Park

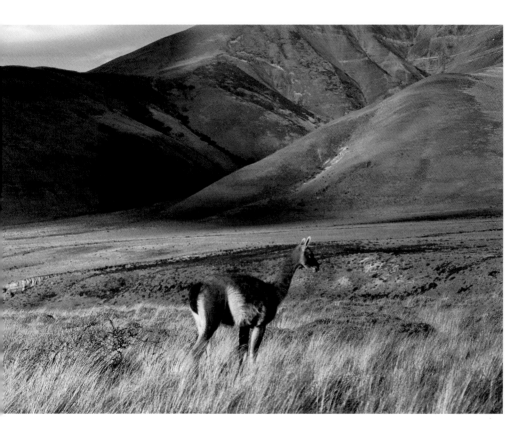

*400-401* ● Australia - Dunes with spiny bushes along the Canning Stock Route.

*402-403* ● Australia - Ayers Rock, Ayers Rock-Mount Olga National Park.

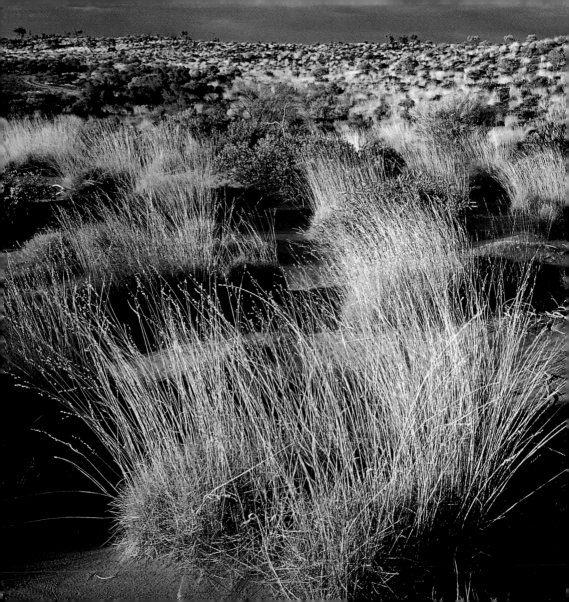

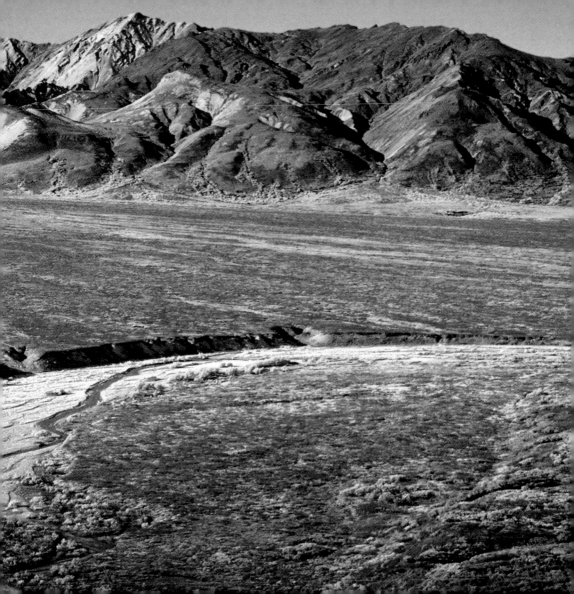

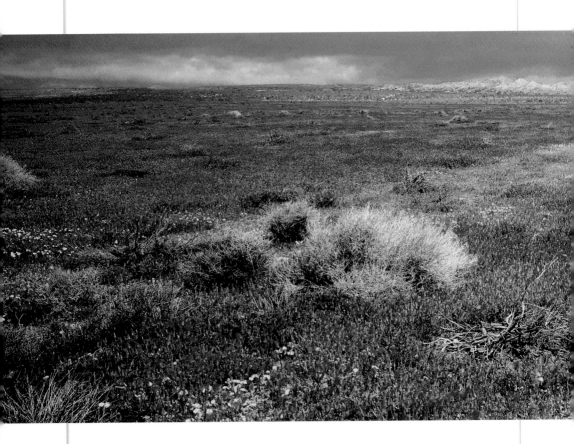

*418-419* • California (USA) - Antelope Valley, California Poppy Reserve.

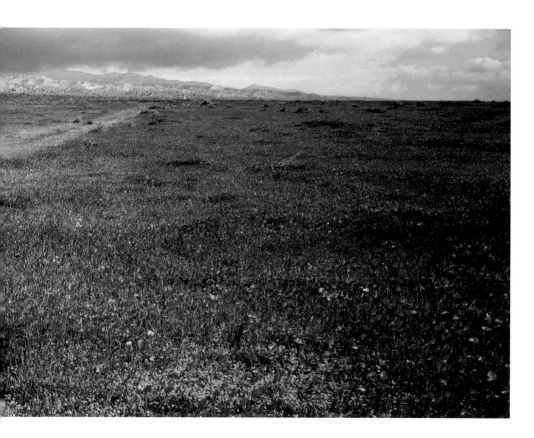

*420-421* ● Wyoming (USA) - Pitchstone Plateau, Yellowstone National Park.

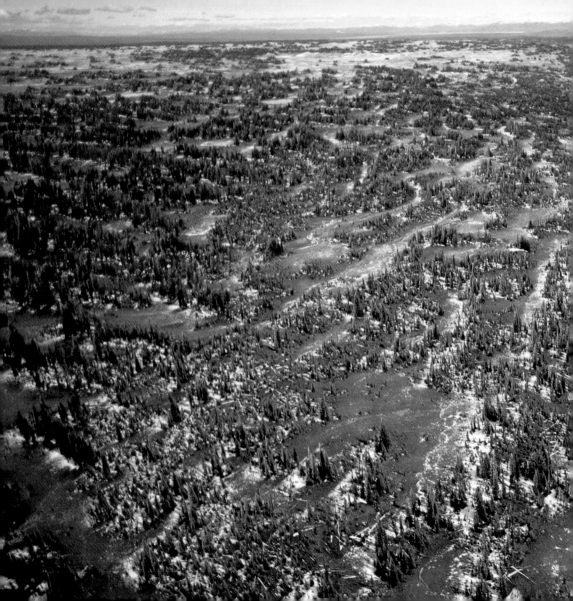

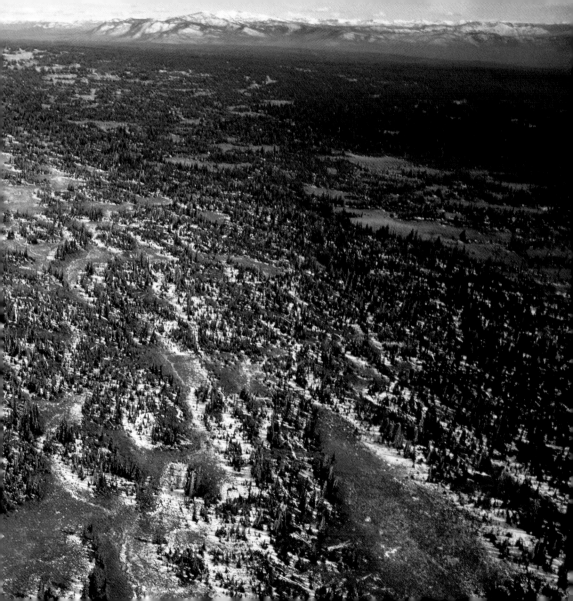

# ROLLING HILLS

Washington, (USA) - Palouse Hills seen from Steptoe Butte State Park.

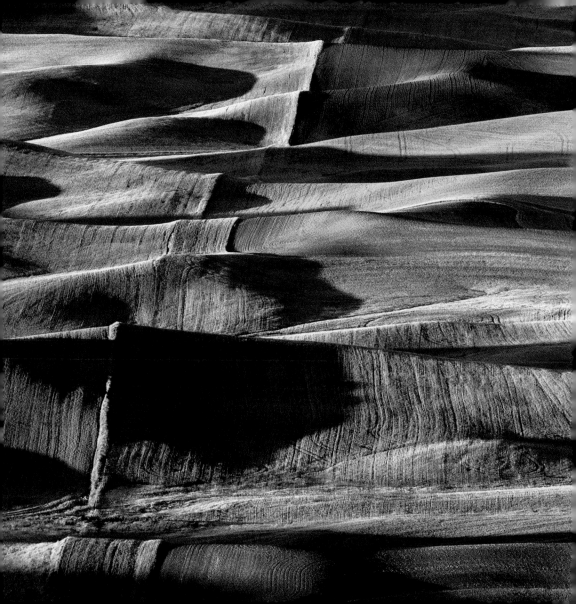

## INTRODUCTION Rolling Hills

A PAINTING BY LEONARDO DA VINCI, WHICH IS UNJUSTLY FAMOUS ONLY BECAUSE OF THE AMBIGUOUS EXPRESSION OF THE WOMAN PORTRAYED, CONVEYS ALL THE FASCINATION OF TUSCANY, WHICH IS EPITOMIZED IN THE SINUOUS LINES AND TENUOUS COLORS THE MASTER USED TO RENDER THE BACKGROUND. LEONARDO MAY HAVE CHOSEN THAT LANDSCAPE FOR "TECHNICAL" REASONS, SINCE ITS OUTLINES ENHANCE THE SOFT FORMS OF THE MONA LISA AND SOMEHOW ALSO EMBODY HER SUBTLY EROTIC OVERTONES. IN OTHER WORDS, THE TUSCAN HILLS HERE BECOME A SYMBOL OF FEMININITY. OR THE ARTIST MAY HAVE SIMPLY RECALLED THE HILLOCKS, THE ROWS OF CYPRESSES, THE SOLITARY OAKS AND THE OLIVE TREES HE HAD

## INTRODUCTION Rolling Hills

ALWAYS SEEN SINCE HE WAS A BOY AND RODE THROUGH THE COUNTRYSIDE ON A MULE. AGAIN, THERE MAY HAVE BEEN NO OTHER POSSIBLE SETTING FOR THE WORLD'S MOST FAMOUS PAINTING: WAVES OF REDDISH EARTH ALTERNATING WITH OTHER WAVES OF GREENERY AND, LIKE BUOYS LOST IN THE SEA, TREES, FARMSTEADS AND TOWNS WITH TURRETED WALLS. A LANDSCAPE THAT IN SPRING TAKES ON EVERY COLOR, THE PINK OF PEACHES, THE WHITE OF DAISIES, THE RED OF POPPIES, THE YELLOW OF SUNFLOWERS ....

THE HILLS OF NEW ENGLAND ARE QUITE DIFFERENT, WITH THEIR THICK, EVER-CHANGING WOODS AND THE INDIAN SUMMER THAT TRANSFORMS THEM INTO FIERY FORESTS. THE HILLS OF NEW ZEALAND ARE SO DISTANT

# Rolling Hills
## Introduction

YET SO NEAR, A MOONSCAPE, LIKE THE ENGLISH HILLS ON THE OTHER SIDE OF THE GLOBE, BUT WITH A GREEN SO RICH IT SEEMS TO HAVE BEEN PAINTED. THE BARREN HILLS BELOW THE ANDES THAT BEGIN IN PATAGONIA SEEM WILD, SILHOUETTED AGAINST THE LOW LIGHT THAT PENETRATES THE CRYSTAL-CLEAR AIR AT THAT LATITUDE. AND THE GREEN HILLS OF AFRICA SEEMED SO EXOTIC TO WESTERN WRITERS THAT THEY FELL IN LOVE WITH THE BLACK CONTINENT.... SO DIFFERENT AND YET SO ALIKE, IN EVERY PART OF THE WORLD, IN FORM AND COLOR, FROM THOSE THAT WERE PART OF OUR CHILDHOOD OR THAT WE WERE TAUGHT TO LOVE.

*427* ● Tibet (China) - The hills near Shigatse.

*428-429* ● Tuscany (Italy) - Val d'Orcia.

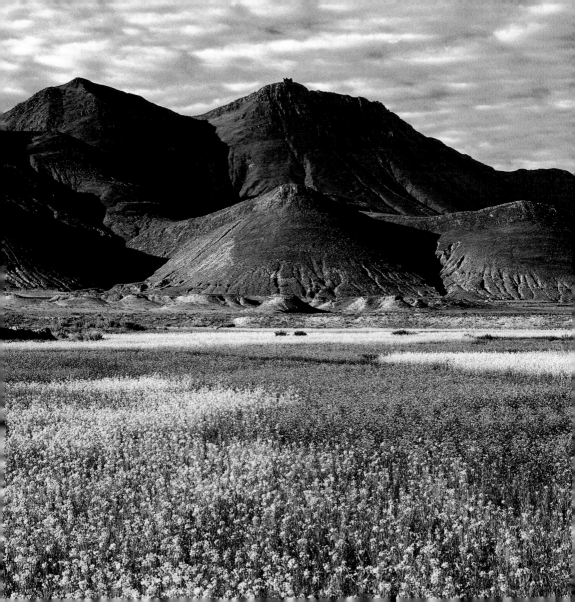

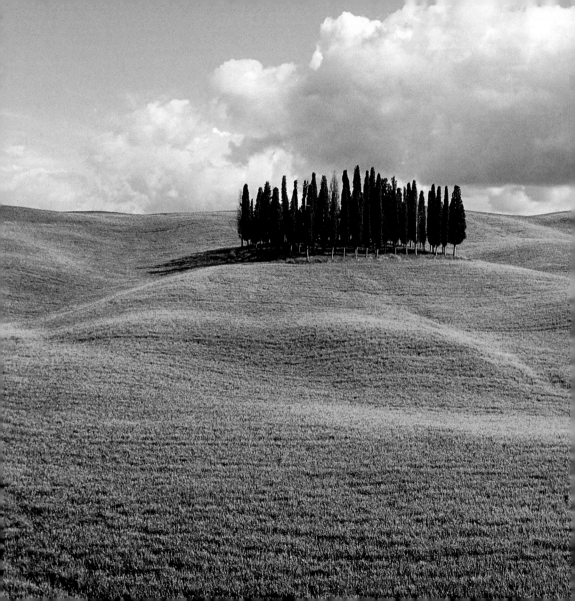

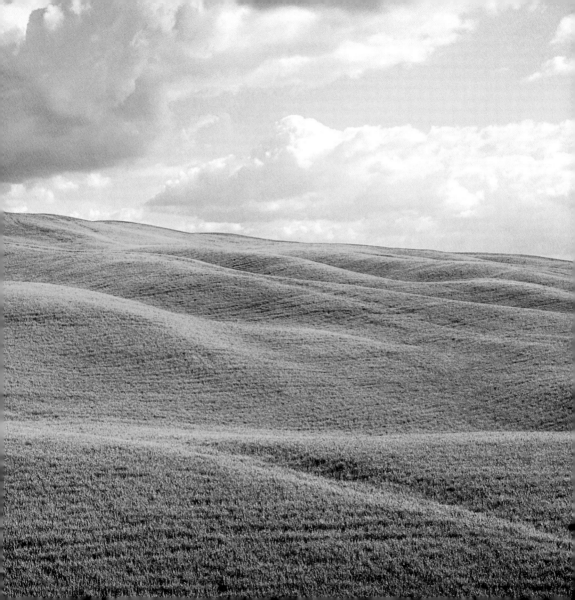

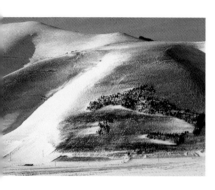

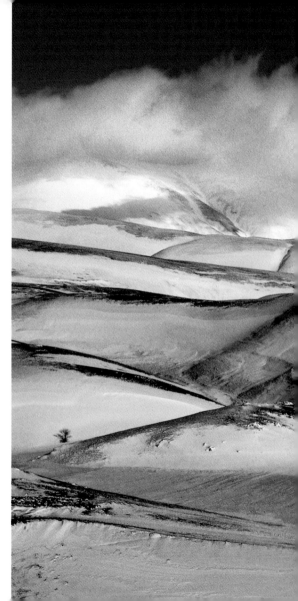

*430 and 430-431* ● Umbria (Italy) -
The Sybilline Mountains.

*432-433* ● Tuscany (Italy) -
The crags of Volterra.

*434-435* ● Marches (Italy) -
Apennine foothills in Umbria and the
Marches.

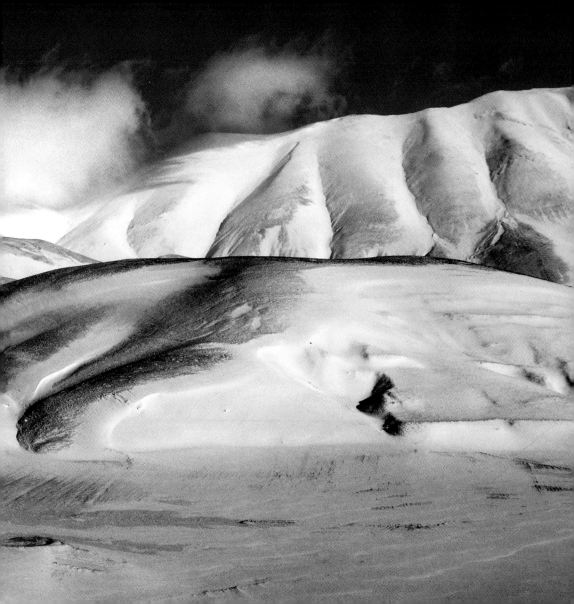

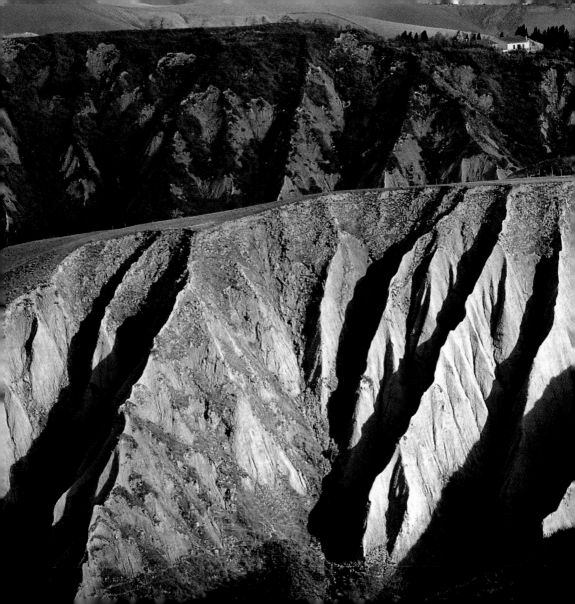

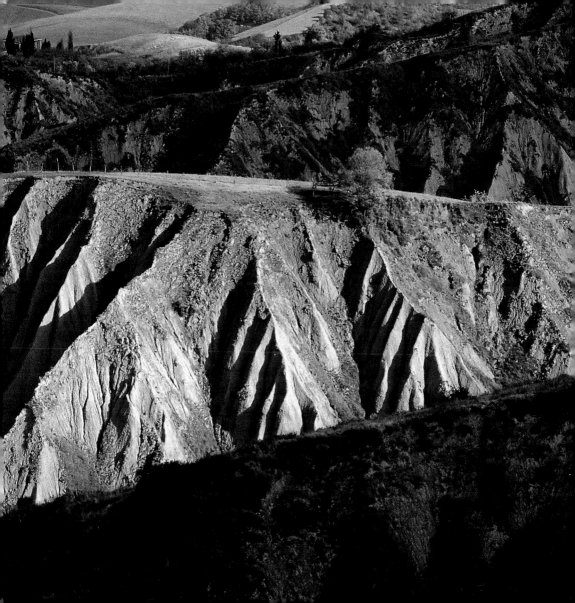

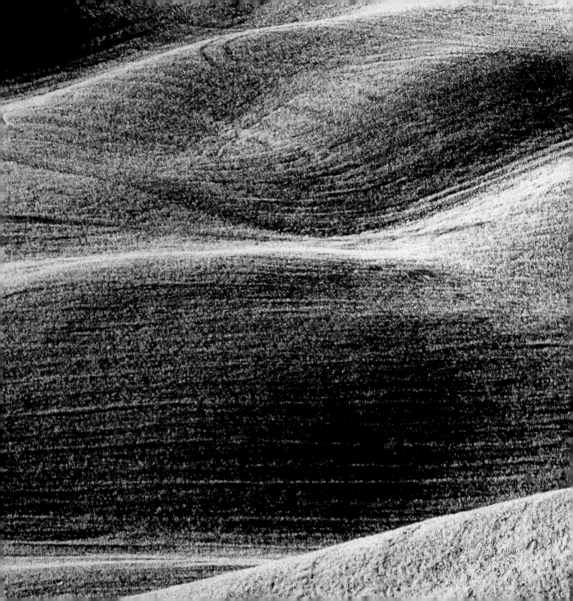

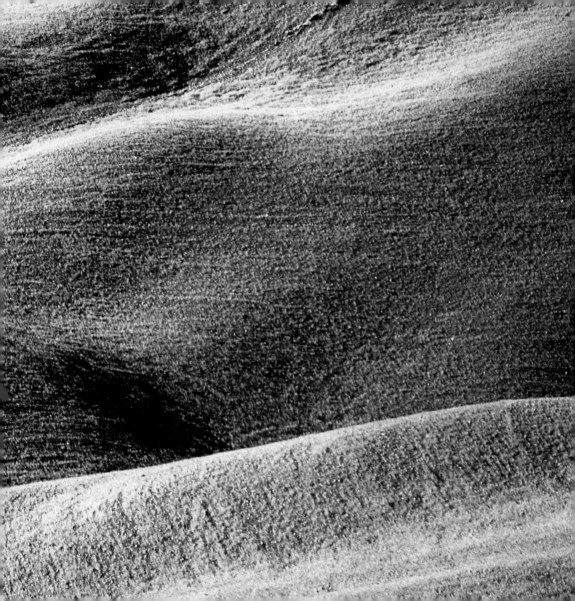

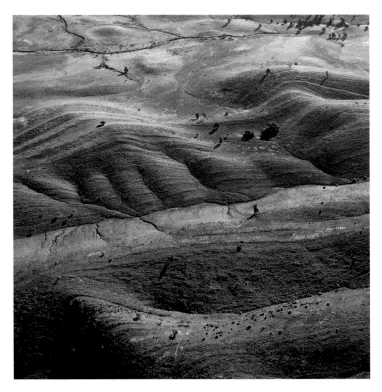

*436* ● South Australia (Australia) - North Flinders Ranges.

*437* ● Northern Territory (Australia) - Undulating hills in MacDonnel Ranges National Park.

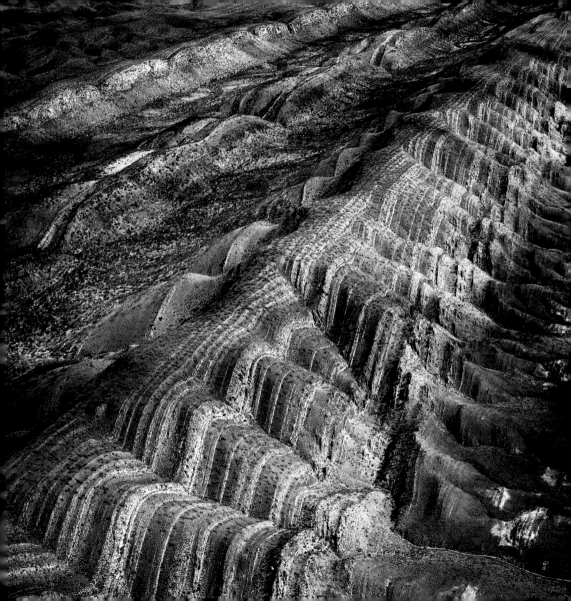

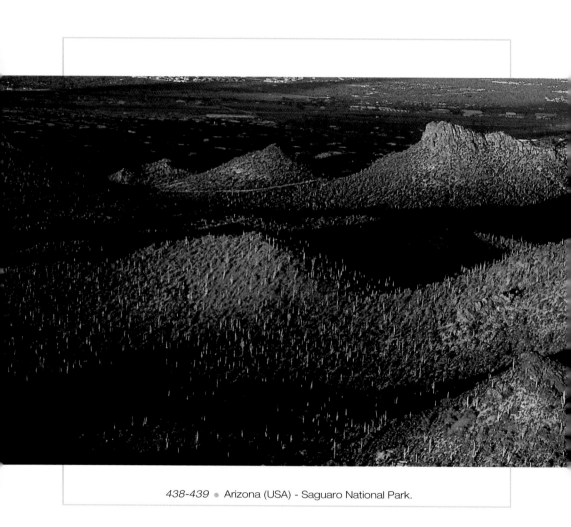

*438-439* ● Arizona (USA) - Saguaro National Park.

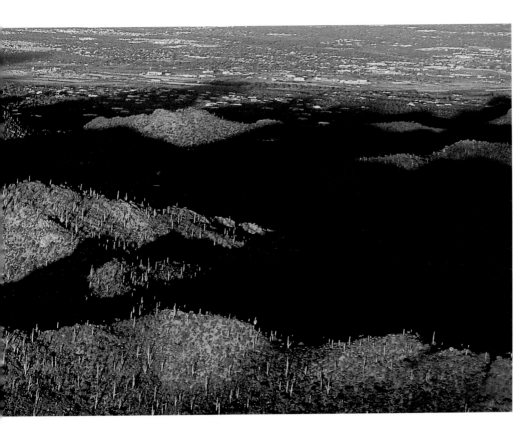

*440-441* ● Utah (USA) - Bryce Canyon National Park.

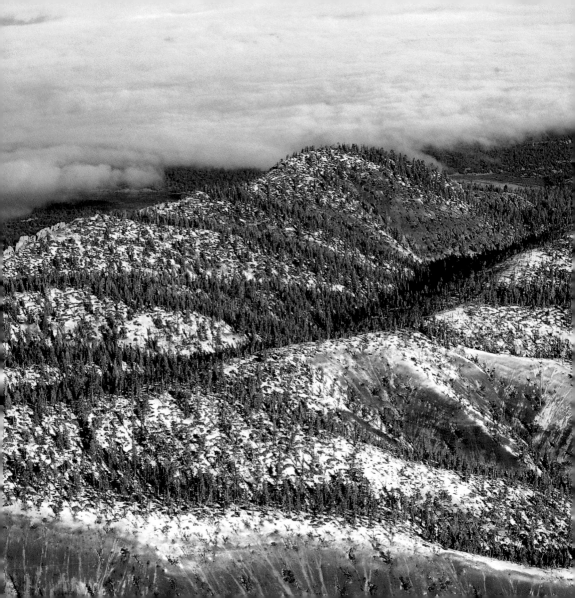

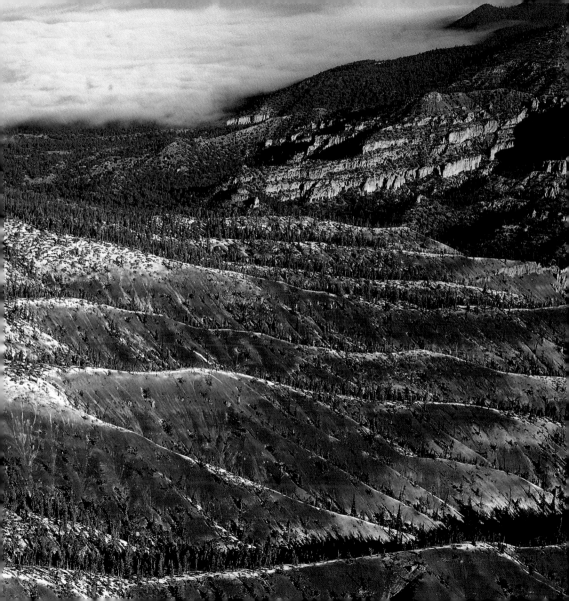

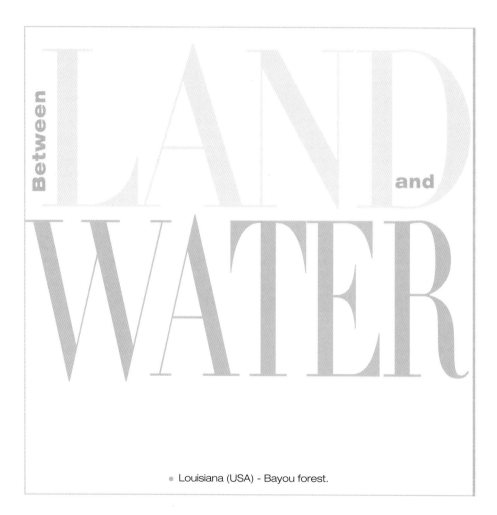

Between **LAND** and **WATER**

• Louisiana (USA) - Bayou forest.

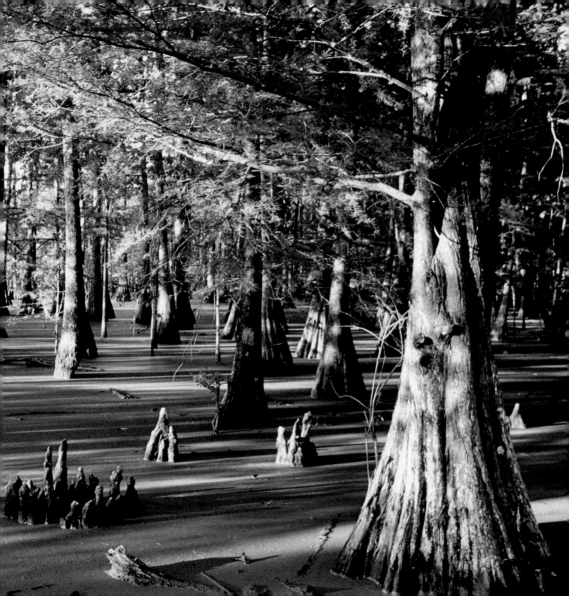

## INTRODUCTION Between Land and Water

The first man who ventured into a marsh must have thought he had entered hell: a gloomy underworld inhabited by fierce predators, infested by foul smells and by the continuous, unbearable hum of insects; an environment suffocated by overwhelming vegetation, monsters, quicksands and malaria. In fact, marshes have always triggered nightmarish fantasies in the soul of those who have had to traverse them, such as the first explorers of the Nile. In the heart of Africa, these hardy men were seeking the fabulous mountains of the moon, where they believed the wellsprings of the divine water rose, but their search came to an abrupt halt when they arrived

# INTRODUCTION Between Land and Water

AT IMPASSABLE SWAMPS BEYOND LAY ONLY MYSTERY. AND YET, SWAMPS HAVE ALSO BEEN GENEROUS TO MAN, PROVIDING WATER, EDIBLE FRUITS, WOOD, CANE AND RUSHES, FISH AND GAME BIRDS. THE RELATIONSHIP BETWEEN MAN AND MARSHLAND IS MARKED BY THE FOLLOWING CONTRADICTION: THE UNHEALTHIEST ENVIRONMENT IS ALSO THE WEALTHIEST IN OFFERING THE FRUIT OF VARIED FORMS OF LIFE TO THOSE WHO KNOW HOW TO EXPLOIT THEM. AND THIS IS NOT A QUESTION ONLY OF MATERIAL GOODS RESULTING FROM RECLAMATION, AS THESE MARSHY AREAS ARE ALSO A TREASURE TROVE OF MARVELOUS SCENERY AND A BIOLOGICAL PARADISE FOR THOUSANDS OF LIVING SPECIES. IN THOSE ZONES WHERE RECLAMATION HAS FAILED OR HAS NOT

# Between Land and Water
## Introduction

BEEN ATTEMPTED, THE MARSHLAND HAS PRESERVED THAT AURA OF MYSTERY AND FASCINATION REPRESENTED IN MANY WORKS OF LITERATURE, ART AND FILM: FOG PASSING OVER THE STAGNANT WATER OF THE SCOTTISH PEAT-BOGS; WILD HORSES GALLOPING ALONG THE CAMARGUE SWAMPS; THE FLAMINGOES ALIGHTING REGALLY AFTER A SHORT FLIGHT AMONG THE TROPICAL REEDS; THE SNAPPING OF THE ALLIGATORS, LORDS OF THE EVERGLADES; THE CRY OF THE BLUE HERON THAT RESOUNDS IN THE BOGS OF CANADA. IN THESE PLACES THE MARRIAGE OF LAND AND WATER HAS GENERATED A FABULOUS REALM, AS OPAQUE AS AN UNCUT DIAMOND AND AS PRECIOUS AS A PEARL IN ITS SHELL....

447 ● New Caledonia (French Overseas Territories) - A 'heart' created by a mangrove swamp.

448-449 ● South Carolina (USA) - Sea Islands.

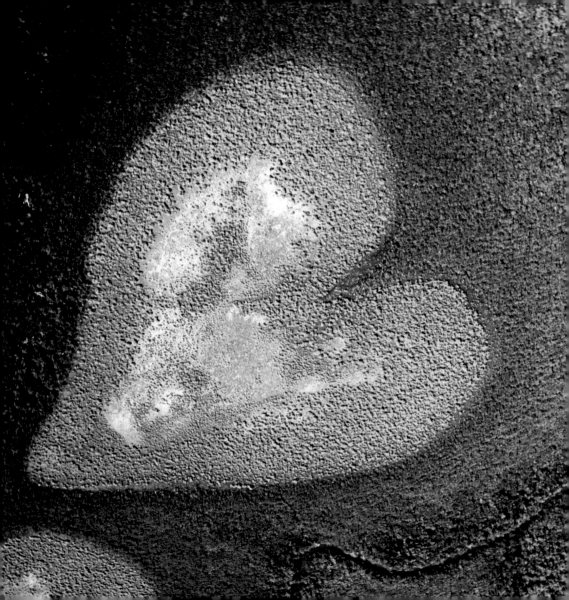

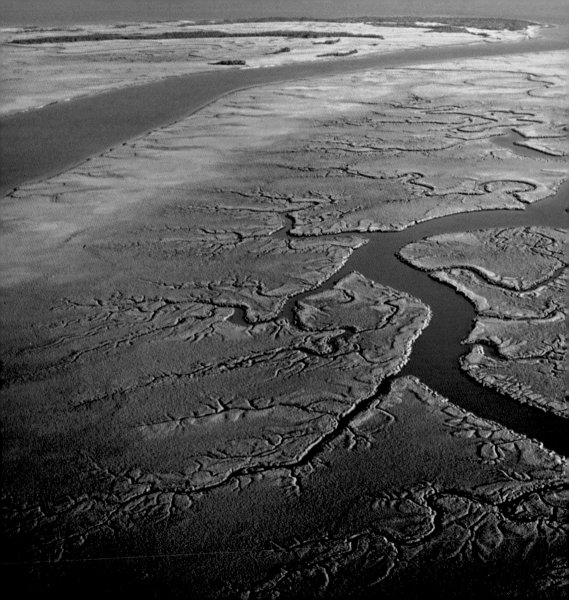

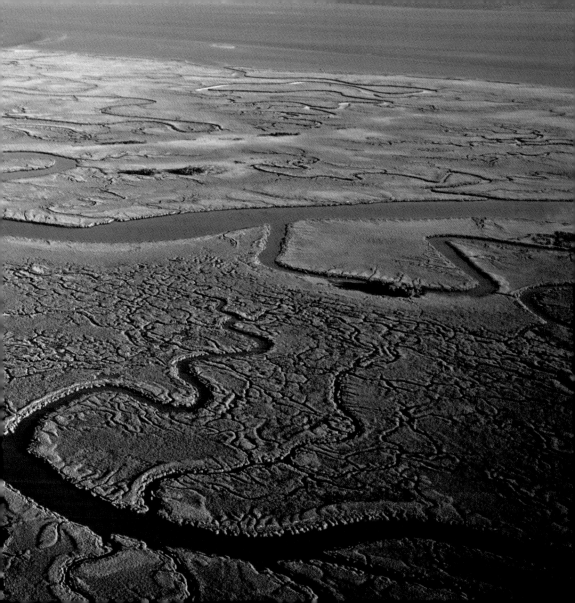

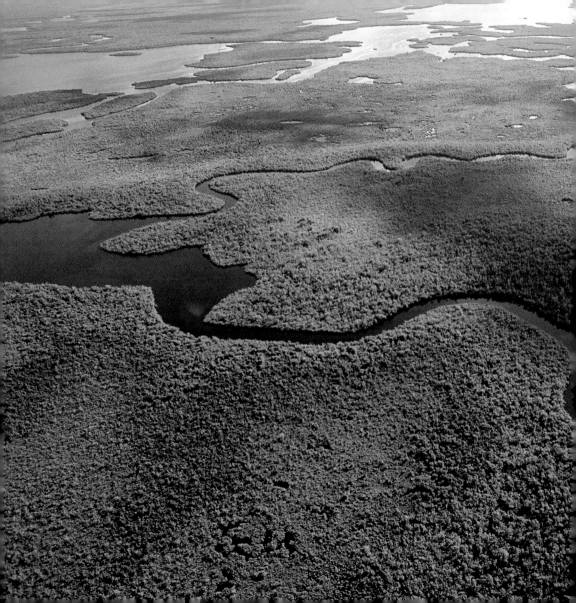

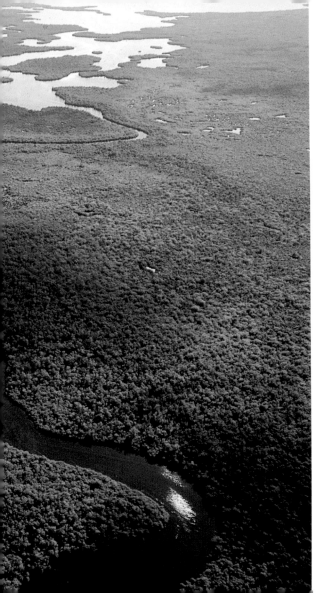

450-451 ● Florida (USA) - Everglades National Park.

452-453 ● Northwest Territories (Canada) - Northwest shore of the Great Slave Lake.

454-455 ● Northwest Territories (Canada) - Cape Bathurst.

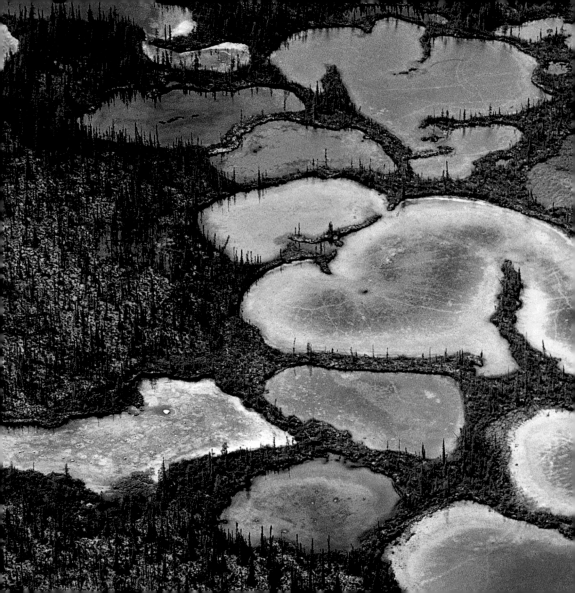

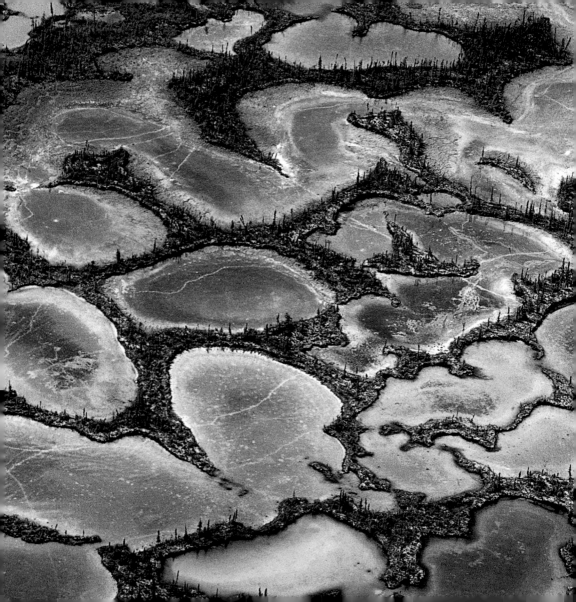

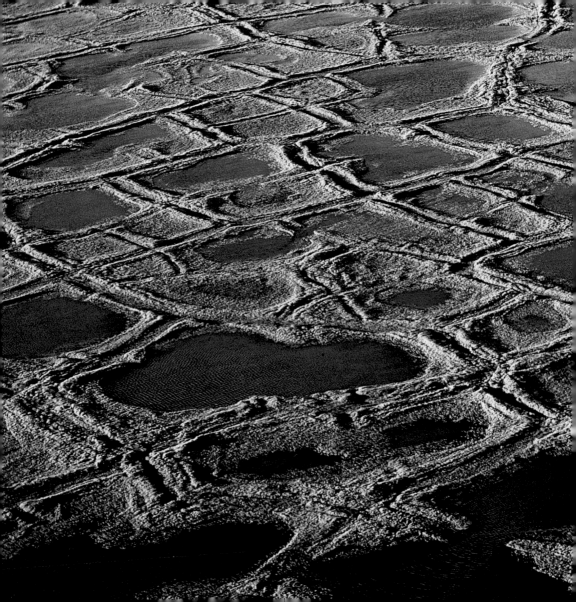

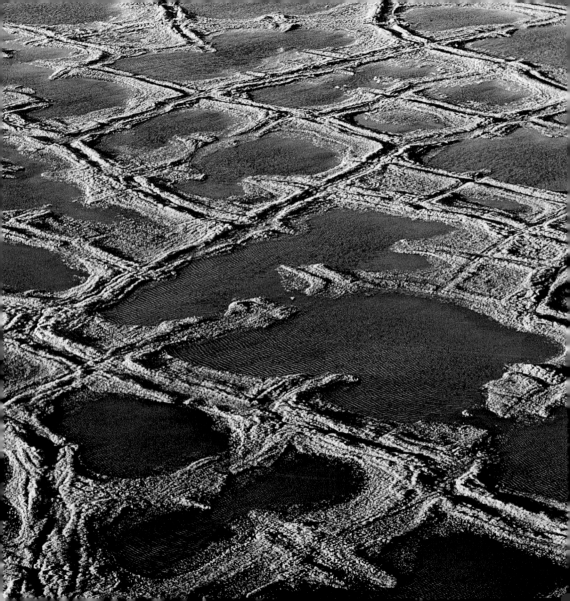

*456* ● Northern Territory (Australia) - Swamps in Magela Creek, Kakadu National Park.

*457* ● Northern Territory (Australia) - Malaleuca forest, Kakadu National Park.

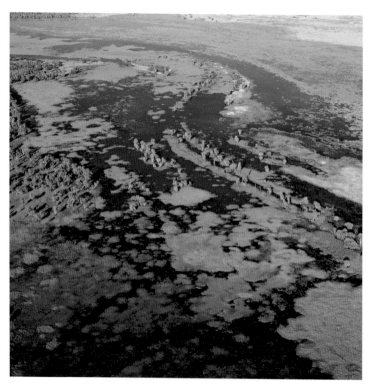

*458-459* ● Northern Territory (Australia) - Aerial view of Djarr Djarr Wetlands, Kakadu National Park.

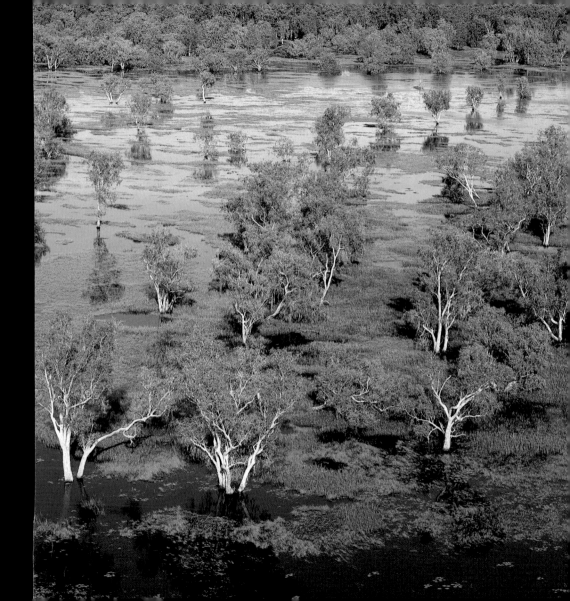

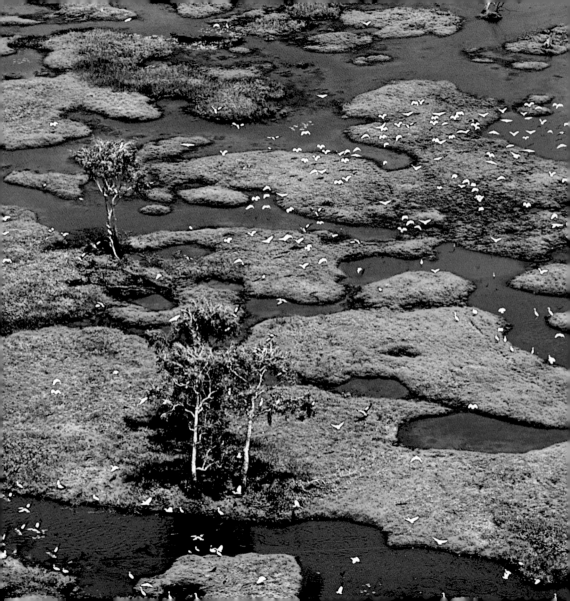

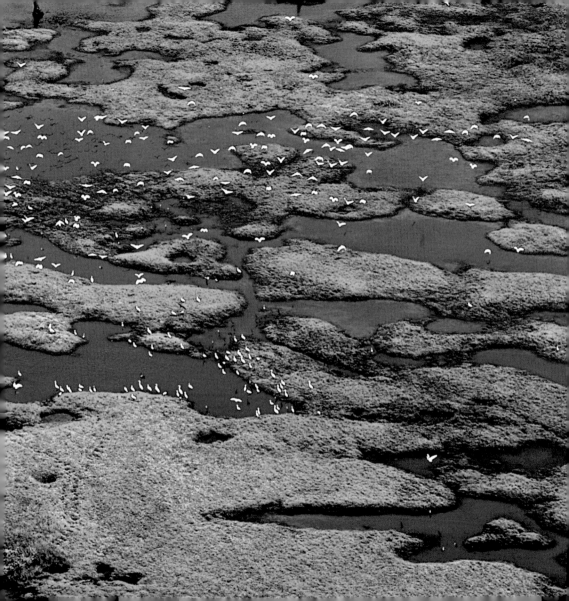

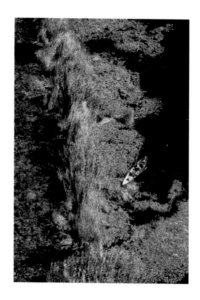

*460, 461 and 462-463* ● Egypt - Marshland around Lake Manzala, in the Nile Delta.

*464-465* ● Ireland - Pools in County Mayo.

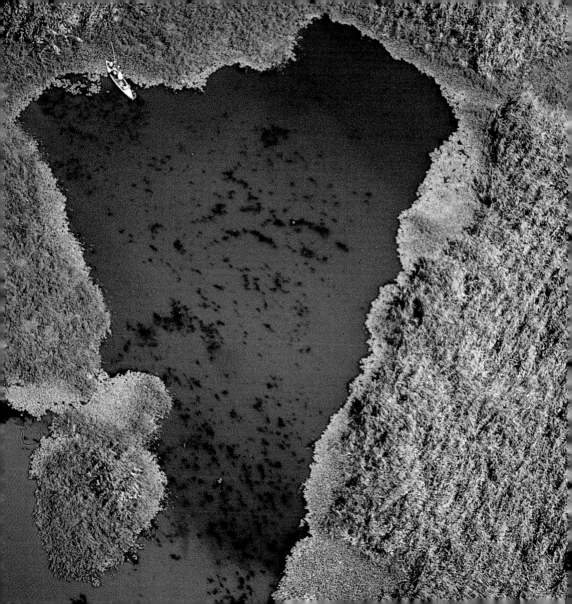

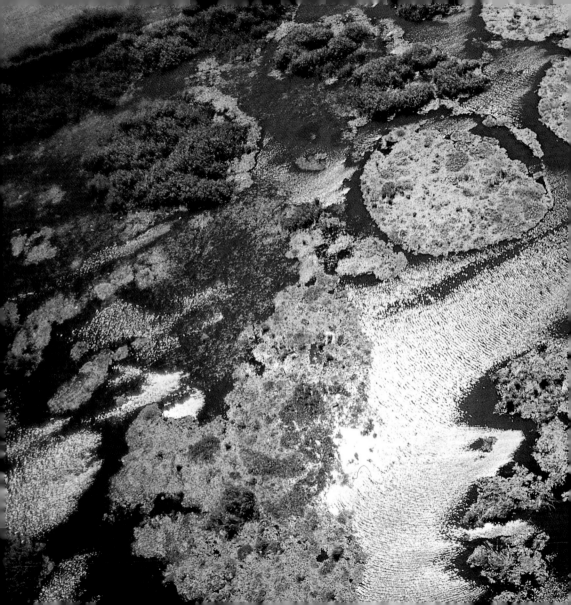

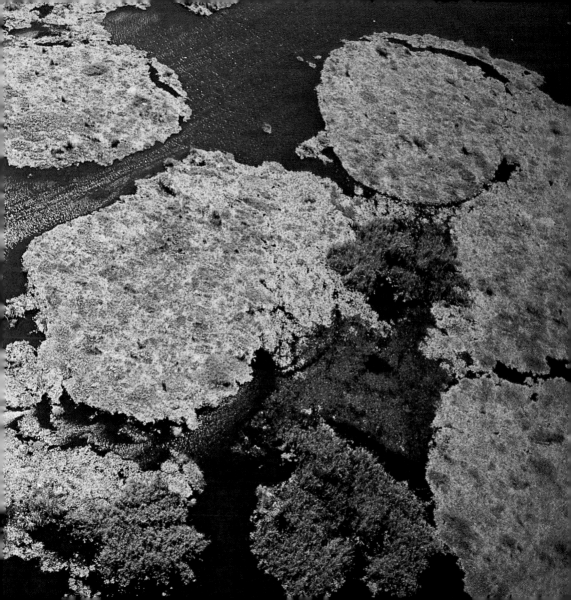

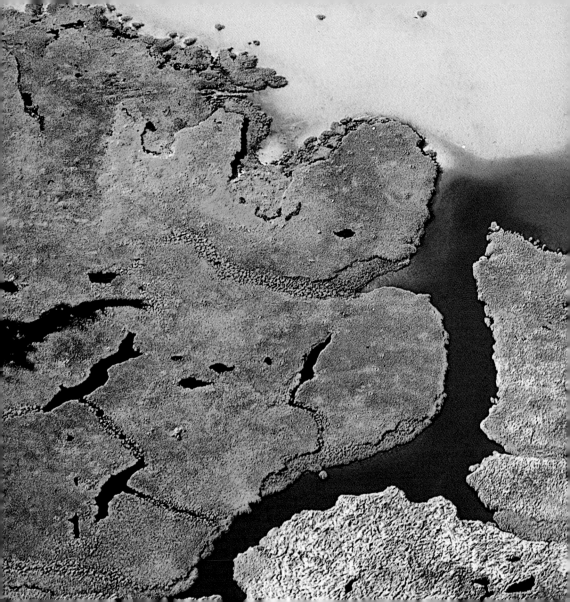

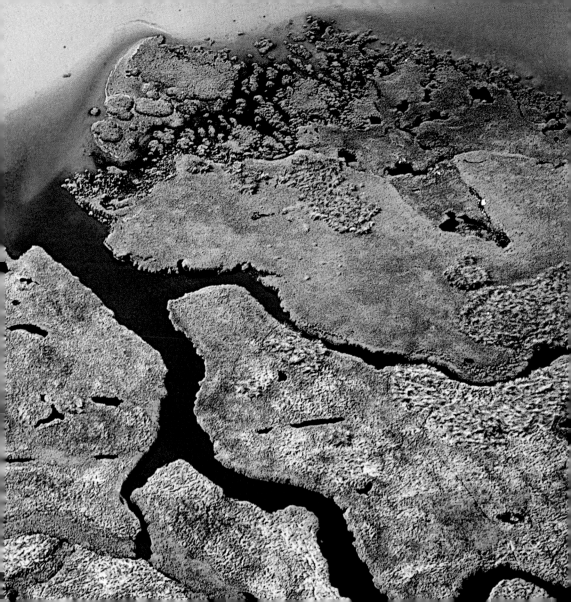

" WHITE HORSES GALLOP THROUGH THE SPRAY. GRAY HERONS AND GIANT PELICANS GLIDE BETWEEN THE RUSHES. AN ALLIGATOR STRETCHES OUT AMONG THE AQUATIC PLANTS. THE MARSHES ARE WHERE LAND AND WATER MEET, THEY ARE THE WET UNDERBELLY OF THE PLANET AND TEEM WITH LIFE. "

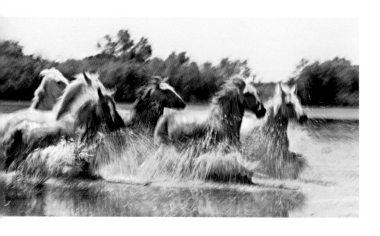

466 and 467 ● Provence (France) - Horses in the Camargue.

468-469 ● Provence (France) - Marshes along the Rhone.

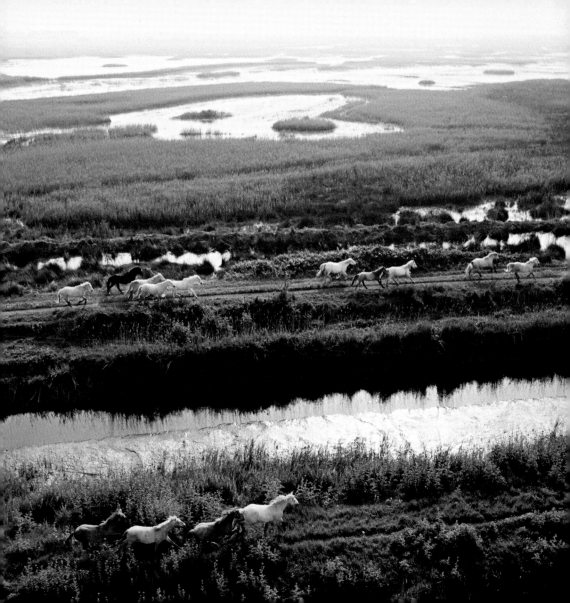

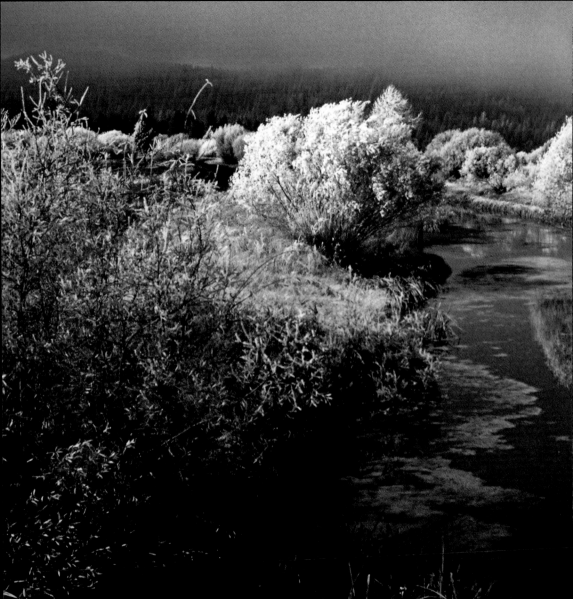

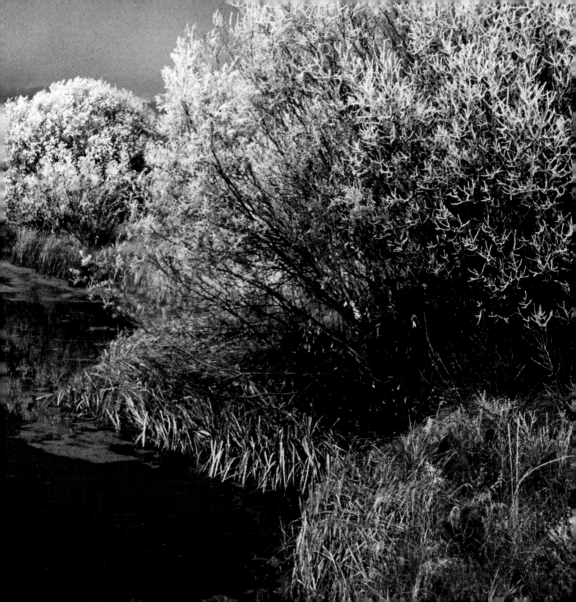

# The RAINBOW PLANET

● Utah (USA) - Waterfalls in Lower Calf Creek.

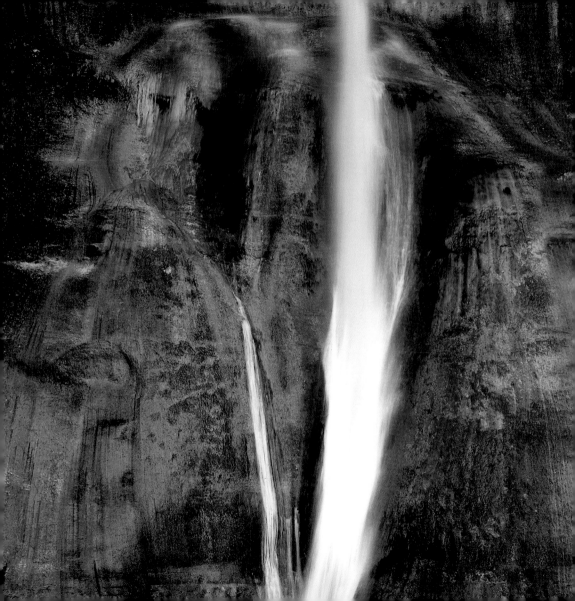

## INTRODUCTION The Rainbow Planet

MILLIONS OF YEARS AGO, MAGICAL VIBRATIONS BEGAN TO COLOR THE TIMELESS DAYS OF SPACE. NOW THE COSMOS IS A SHIMMERING KALEIDOSCOPE OF STARS, PLANETS AND GASSES WITH MYRIAD NUANCES. FROM ITS WOMB THE EARTH WAS BORN, A MAGICAL SPHERE IN WHICH ONE CAN READ THE PAST, PRESENT AND FUTURE OF THE UNIVERSE, THE CRADLE OF LIFE AS WE KNOW IT AND THE PLACE WHERE BEAUTY WAS FIRST CONSCIOUSLY CONTEMPLATED. THE WELLSPRINGS OF LIFE HAVE IRRIGATED THE INERT MINERALS OF A PLANET LOST AMID BILLIONS OF OTHER PLANETS AND STARS, TRANSFORMING IT INTO AN IRIDESCENT GLOBE, MUCH LIKE A CHILD'S TOY. UNIQUE AND EXTRAORDINARY, THIS EARTH IS A THREE-DIMENSIONAL CANVAS TRAVERSED BY

## INTRODUCTION The Rainbow Planet

THE BRUSHSTROKES OF A GREAT ARTIST. THE THOUSANDS OF NUANCES OF WHITE ON THE GLACIERS THAT ENFOLD THE POLAR REGIONS, CROWN THE HIGHEST PEAKS, AND SLIDE SILENTLY INTO THE OCEANS; THE WHITE OF THE CLOUDS AND SEAGULLS THAT STAND OUT AGAINST THE SKY; THE WHITE OF CORAL SAND AND OF THE BLINDING REFLECTIONS OF THE SUN. THE INFINITELY VARIED HUES OF BLUE: THE SKY-BLUE OF THE AIR AT ANY LATITUDE, THE TURQUOISE IN TROPICAL SEAS, THE SAPPHIRE OF ALPINE LAKES, THE COBALT BLUE IN DEEP WATER .... THEN THERE ARE THE REDS AND ORANGES OF BLISTERING SAND, OF MAPLE LEAVES IN AUTUMN, OF THE PLUMAGE OF CERTAIN EQUATORIAL BIRDS, OF SUNSETS ILLUMINATED BY THE LAST RAYS OF THE SUN, OF THE

# The Rainbow Planet

Introduction

MAGMA THAT FLOWS MENACINGLY FROM A VOLCANO. THE EVANESCENT GREEN OF THE AFRICAN FORESTS IMMERSED IN VELVETY CLOUDS, THE BRIGHT GREEN OF IRISH MEADOWS AND IN CULTIVATED FIELDS IN MAY, THE RICH GREEN OF LIZARDS IN THE SUNLIGHT AND DARK GREEN OF PINE GROVES IN WINTER. NEXT COME THE YELLOWS, FROM THE OCHER OF THE HILLS AROUND SIENA TO THE RUSTY HUES OF FERRUGINOUS MOUNTAINS, THE GOLD IN RIPE WHEAT AND THE BLOND SHADES IN THE COATS OF LARGE FELINES. LASTLY, THERE IS THE DARK BLACK IN THE OCEAN ABYSSES, IN MOONLESS NIGHTS, IN THE INFINITE SPACE THAT ENFOLDS OUR PLANET.

*475* ● Iceland - Kirkjubaejarklaustur Delta.

*476-477* ● Ethiopia - Lichens, Bale Mountains National Park.

*478-479* ● Alberta (Canada) - Salt flats in Wood Buffalo National Park.

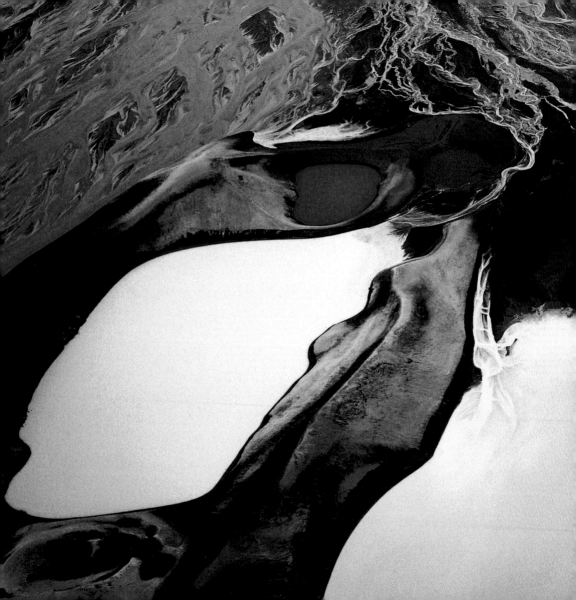

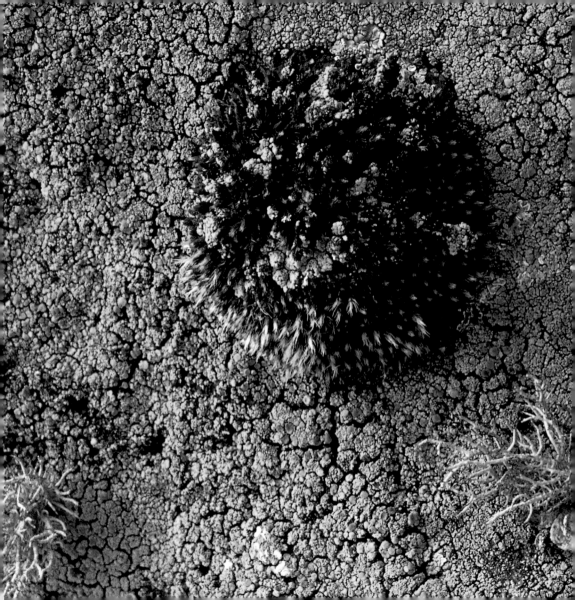

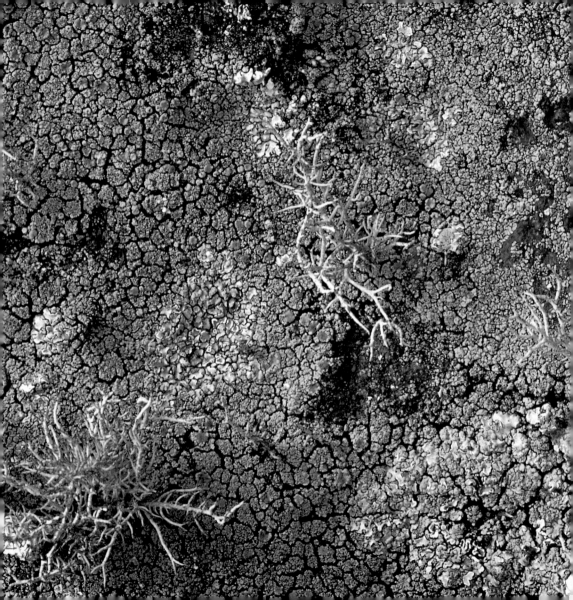

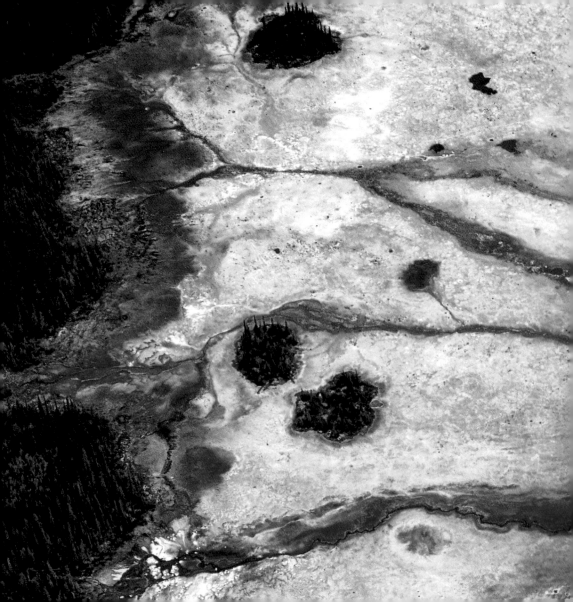

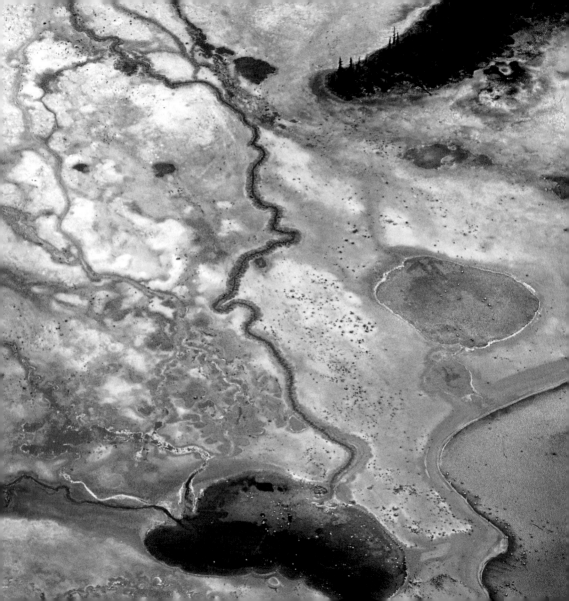

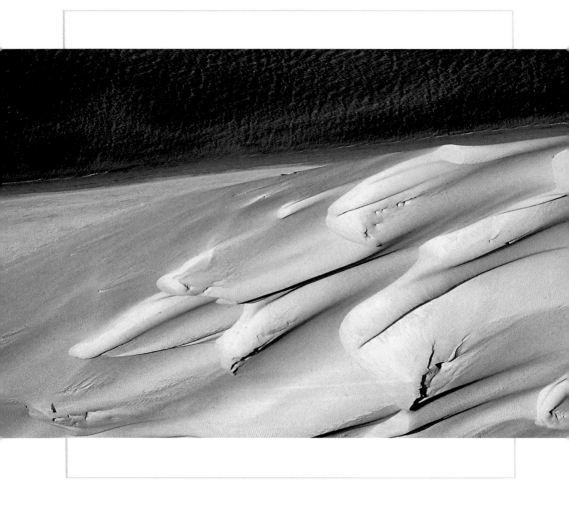

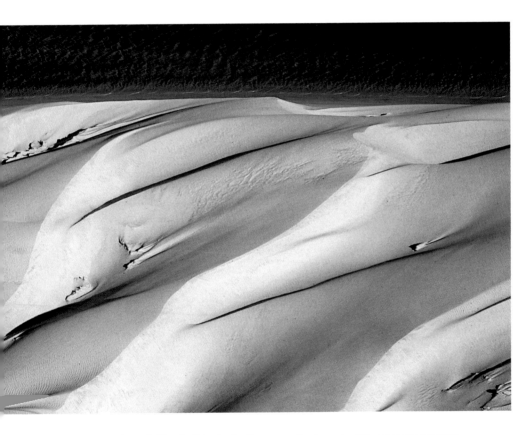

Baja California (Mexico) - Dunes on the beach of Scammons Lagoon.

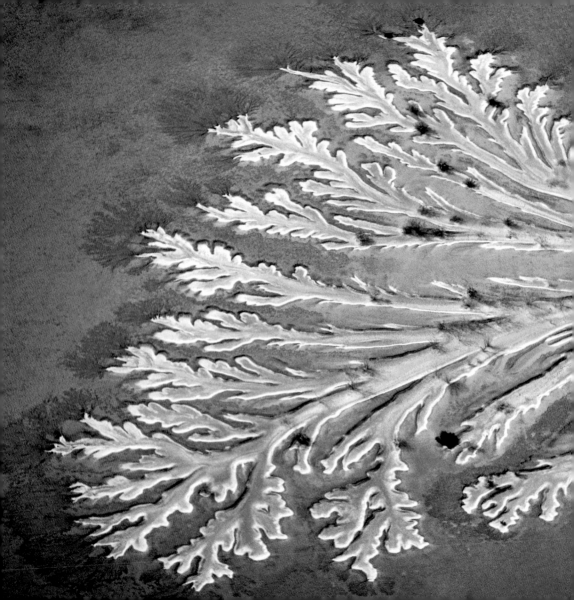

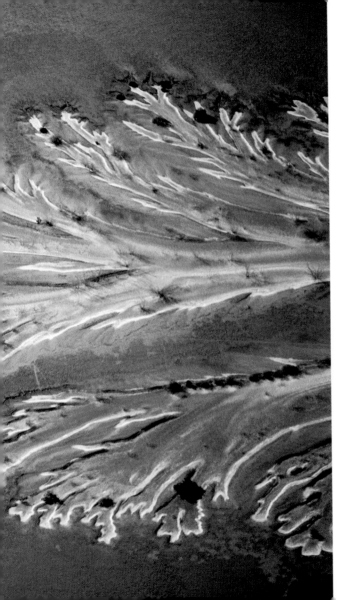

● Sonora (Mexico) - Erosion produced in the desert sand by ancient water flows.

*484 and 485* ● Umbria (Italy) - Fields at Castelluccio, near Norcia.

*486-487* ● Lazio (Italy) - Fields of poppies, sunflowers and alfalfa on the Sybilline Mountains.

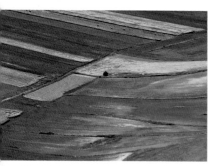 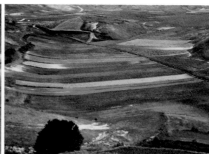

66 FIELDS LIKE FORMS IN CONTINUAL MOVEMENT, LIKE PATCHES OF COLOR ON A PALETTE: HERE THE WHITE OF THE DAISIES, THERE THE RED OF THE POPPIES, IN BETWEEN THE VIOLET OF THE LAVENDER AND THE YELLOW OF THE SUNFLOWERS. ALL AROUND, GREEN IN ALL ITS HUES SPREADS LIKE A WATERCOLOR OR IS CLUMPED IN THICKETS LIKE A MODERN PAINTING. 99

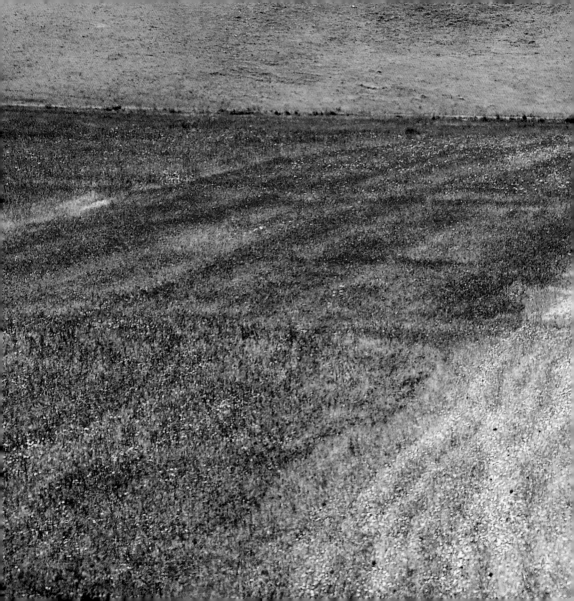

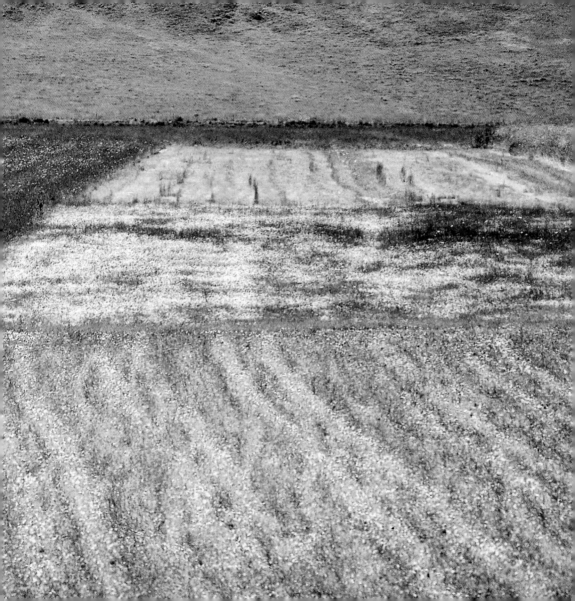

*488-489* ● Landeyjar (Iceland) - Iron deposits along a river Delta.

*490-491* ● Tuamotu Islands (French Polynesia) - Rangiroa.

*492-493* ● Iceland - Water plays among the springs.

*494-495* ● Oregon (USA) - Basalt columns in the ravine formed by the River Umpqua.

*496-497* ● California (USA) - Salt formations in San Francisco Bay.

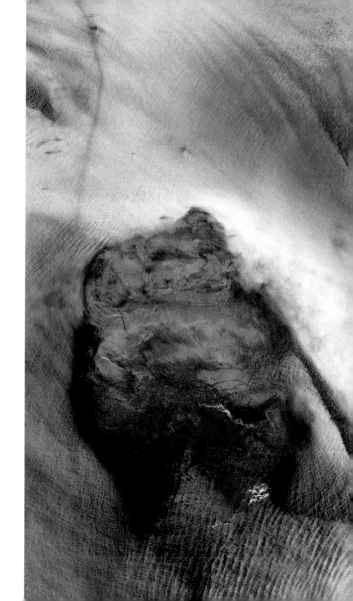

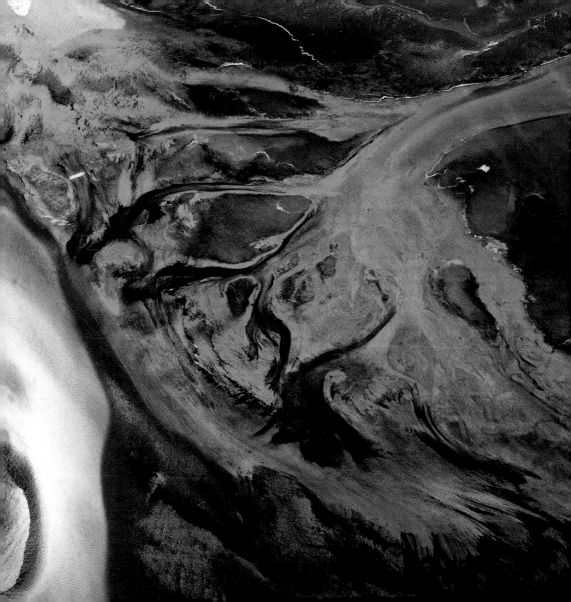

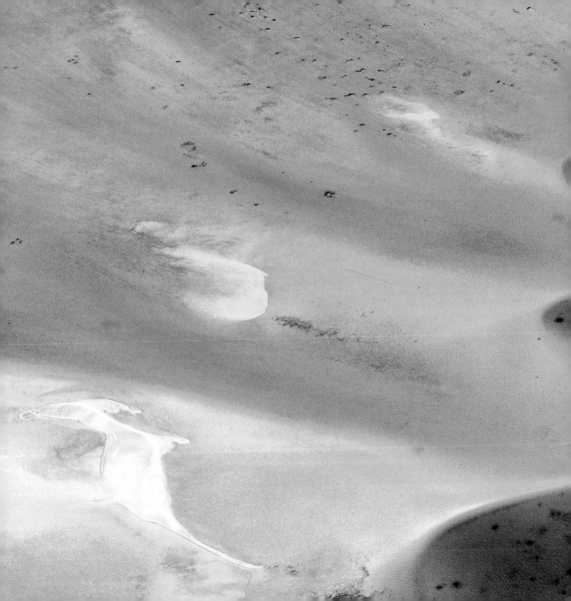

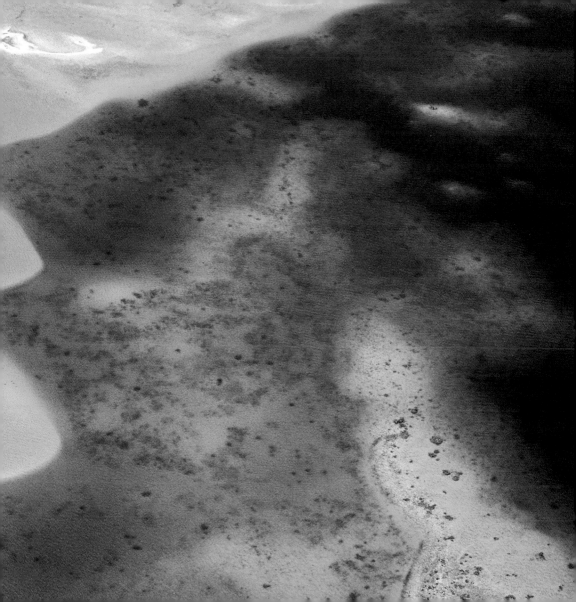

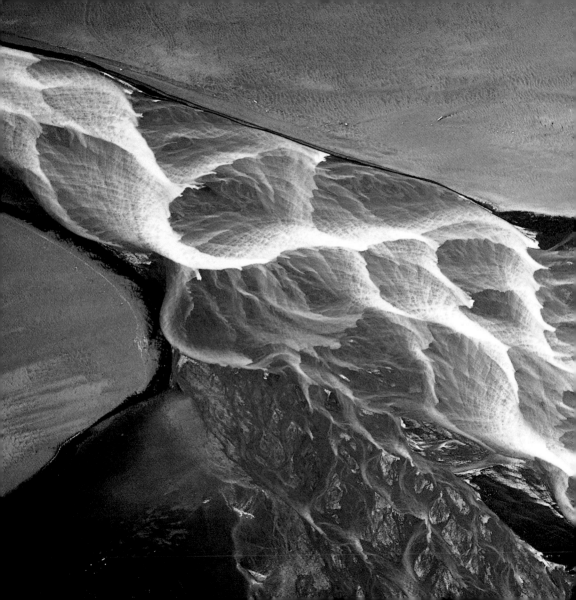

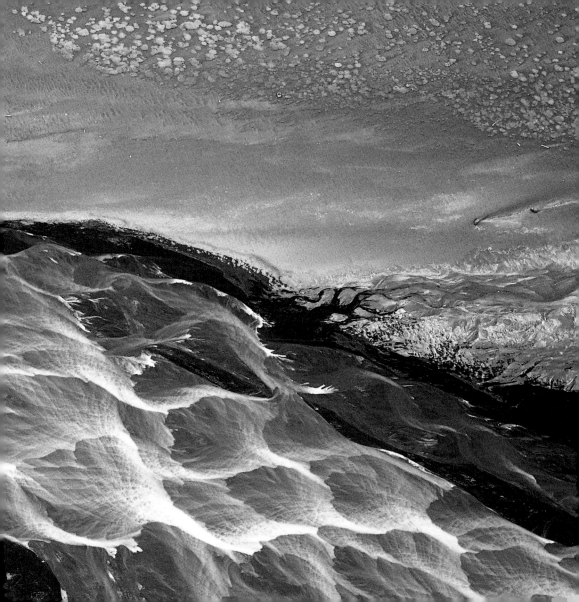

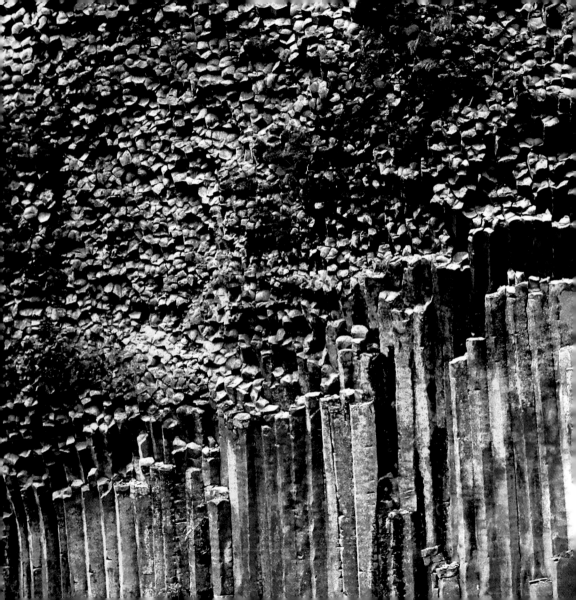

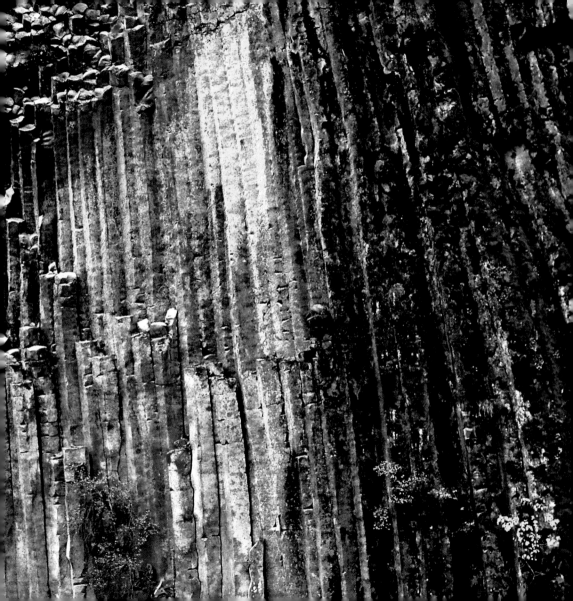

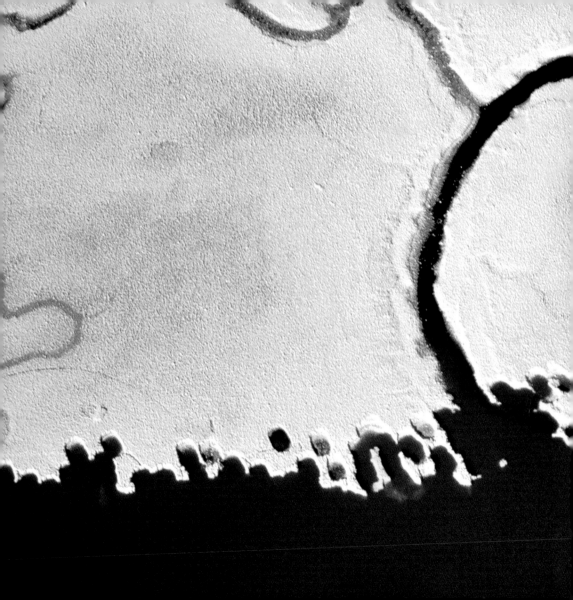

# AUTHORS Biographies

## INDEX

### VALERIA MANFERTO DE FABIANIS

She is the editor of the series. Valeria Manferto De Fabianis was born in Vercelli, Italy, and studied arts at the Università Cattolica del Sacro Cuore in Milan, graduating with a degree in philosophy. She is an enthusiastic traveler and nature lover. She has collaborated on the production of television documentaries and articles for the most prestigious Italian specialty magazines and has also written the text for many photography books. She co-founded Edizioni White Star in 1984 with Marcello Bertinetti and is the editorial director.

### ALBERTO BERTOLAZZI

Born in 1961, Alberto Bertolazzi studied Philosophy at the University of Pavia. He is an enthusiastic traveler and naturalist who, following a brief period as a teacher, began writing for various Italian newspapers, including *La Repubblica, La Stampa, Il Giornale Nuovo, Il Piccolo di Trieste* and *Il Giorno*, and the periodicals *Meridiani, Sestante* and *Panorama*. For White Star Publications he has written the volumes *Lisbon* (1997) and *Portugal* (1998) and has contributed to the editing of many other books dedicated to the natural world.

**AFGHANISTAN**
Band i Amir Lakes, 277c

**ALGERIA**
Hoggar Massif, 361c

**ANTARCTICA**
Adare Peninsula, 310c
Anvers Island, 335c
Fief Mountains, 88c
Ross Ice Shelf, 329c
Weddel Sea, 320c
Wiencke Island, 88c

**ARGENTINA**
Fitz Roy, 80c
Parque Nac. Los Glaciares, 80c
Patagonian pampas, 397c
Perito Moreno, 320c

**AUSTRALIA**
Ayers Rock, 345, 376c, 399c
Bungle-Bungle Range, 376c
Canning Stock Route, 399c
Djarr Djarr Kreek, 456c
East Gippsland Errinundra National Park, 208c
Everard Ranges, 170c
Great Ocean Road, 96c
Kakadu National Park, 456c
Lake Boomanjin, 274c
Lake McKenzie, 274c
MacDonnel Ranges, 436c
Mt. Field Nat. Park, 211c
North Flinders Ranges, 436c
Pelorus River Scenic Res., 211c
Strzelecki Desert, 170c
The Pinnacles, 170c
Uluru National Park, 384c
Wall of China, 142c
Whitsunday Island, 106c

**BAHAMAS**
Exuma Keys, 128c

**BRAZIL**
Anavilhanas Archipelago, 245c
Iguazú Falls, 24c, 245.
Rio Negro, 245c

**CANADA**
Cape Bathurst, 451c
Kluane Lake, 262c
Moraine Lake, 268c
Mount Kidd, 264c
Niagara Falls, 214, 237c
O'Hara Lake, 268c
Peace River, 238c
Rampart Range Peaks, 73c
Slave River, 238c
St. Elias Mountains, 67c
Wedge Pond, 264c
Wood Buffalo National Park, 474c

**CHILE**
Lake Pehoe 268c
Torres del Paine, 80c, 398c

**CHINA**
Brahmaputra, 255c

Everest, 51c, 59c
Huanglong, 24c
Kailash, 60c
Lake Shuzheng, 291c
Lake Yamdruk, 277c
Shigatse, 426c
Siguniang, 51c
Silk Road, 163c
Yuanmou Clay Forest, 375c

**CONGO**
Gorges de Diosso, Pointe Noire, 183c
Loufoulakari Falls, 232c
Mayombe Forest, 12c

**COSTA RICA**
Foresta di Monteverde, 196

**CUBA**
Cayo Coco, 128c

**DENMARK**
Disko Bay (Greenland), 329c, 336c
Nordskoven Forest, 183c

**EGYPT**
Ain Um Ahkmed Oasis, 138c
Bahariya, 150c
Farafra, 150c
Forest of Columns, Jebel Fuga, 366c
Jebel Bayda, 283c
Jebel Musa, 156c
Lake Manzala, 460c
Lake Nasser, 283c
Lake Siwa, 283c

Nile, 232c, 444, 460c
Ras Gharib, 12c
Shali, 156c
Siwa Oasis, 156c
Tiran Island, 106c
Wadi Khudra, 342c

**ETHIOPIA**
Bale Mountains National Park, 474c

**FINLAND**
Oulanka Joki River, 221c
Oulanka National Park, 221c

**FRANCE**
Camargue, 446, 466c
Corsica, 123c
Ètretat Bay, 126c
Finistère, 123c
Gironde, 222c
Mont Blanc, 41c
Pays de Caux, 126c
Petit Langoustier, 123c
Porquerolles, 123c

**FRENCH OVERSEAS TERRITORIES**
Blue Lagoon 12c
Bora Bora, 96c
Huahiné, 96c, 201c
New Caledonia, 446c
Rangiroa 12c, 488c
Society Islands, 92c, 96c, 201c

**GERMANY**
Bavaria, 51c
Little Watzmann, 51c
Watzmann, 51c

**INDIA**
Bagirathi Peaks, 64c
Shivling Peak, 64c

**INDONESIA**
Gunung Leuser National Park, 201c

**IRELAND**
County Kildare, 409c
County Mayo, 460c
County Sligo, 128c
Gweebarra River, 225c
Sligo Bay, 128c

**ICELAND**
Kirkjubaejarklaustur, 474c
Landeyjar, 488c

**ISRAEL**
Negev, 156c

**ITALY**
Brenta Dolomites, 12c
Brenta Group, 34c
Budelli, 92c
Castelluccio di Norcia, 484c
Catinaccio, 34c
Chiaia di Luna, 119c
Cima Madonna, 38c
Dolomites, 34c, 38c
Etna, 296c, 308c
Fusine River, 217c
Giant's Tooth, 41c
Island of Vulcano, 119c
Lampedusa, 106c
Mattherom, 41c
Mont Blanc, 41c
Monte Rosa, 41c

Laghi di Fusine National Park, 292c
Piedmont, 404c
Pink Beach, 92c
Ponza, 119c
Rabbit Beach, 106c
Sass Maor, 38c
Val d'Orcia, 426c
Valsesia, 178c

**JORDAN**
Jebel Harun, 366c
Wadi Rum, 163c

**KENYA**
Lake Nakuru, 12c
Masai Mara Nat. Reserve, 384c, 390c

**LIBYA**
Akakus zoomorphic rocks, 147c
Fezzan, 24c, 147c
Libyan Desert, 142c
Sebha Oasis, 147c

**MALAYSIA**
Kinabalu National Park, 201c
Sabah Forest, 201c

**MEXICO**
Scammons Lagoon, 481c
Sonora, 483c

**MICRONESIA**
Lekes Sandspit, 96c
Palau, 96c

**MONGOLIA**
Khermiyn-Tsau, 366c

# INDEX

Southern Gobi Desert,
   366c

**NAMIBIA**
Gamsberg Pass,
   150c
Skeleton Coast, 106c
Sussusvlei, 150c

**NEPAL**
Ama Dablam, 18c
Annapurna, 63c
Everest, 51c, 59c
Gangapurna, 60c
Machapuchare, 63c

**NEW ZEALAND**
Bowen Falls, 252c
Mount Cook, 88c
Sutherlands Falls,
   252

**NIGERIA**
Niger River, 174c

**NORWAY**
Austfonna Glacier,
   325c

**PAKISTAN**
Gasherbrun IV, 63c
K2, 30c, 67c

**PERU**
Cordillera Blanca, 86c
Monte Huandoy, 86c

**PORTUGAL**
Praia da Rocha, 121c
Sagres (Algarve),
   121c

**RUANDA**
Kagera River, 227c

**SEYCHELLES**
La Digue, 106c

**SPAIN**
Gallocanta, Plain of,
   413c

**SRI LANKA**
Udowattakele Forest
   Reserve, 201c

**SWEDEN**
Lapland, 182c

**SWITZERLAND**
Eiger, 51c
Jungfrau, 51c
Mönch, 51c

**TANZANIA**
Kilimanjaro, 305c
Lake Natron, 12c, 291c
Lake Victoria, 208c, 286c
Ngorongoro
   Conservation Area,
   388c, 391c
Oldonyo Lengai,
   307c
Rift Valley, 361c
Rufiji River, 229
Serengeti National Park,
   286c, 383, 388c,
   391c, 413c
Tarangire National Park,
   380c

**THAILAND**
Rai Lai Beach, 106c

**TURKEY**
Uchisar, 366c

**UNITED KINGDOM**
Lake District of Cumbria,
   262c
Saunders Island, 336c

**USA**
Alaska Range, 67c
Antelope Canyon,
   359c
Antelope Valley, 418c
Aspen, 193c
Bayou Forest, 442c
Big Sur, 128c
Bryce Canyon, 350c,
   439c
Castle Rock, 350c
Colorado River, 163c,
   345
Copper River Valley, 12c
Delicate Arch, 350c
Denali National Park,
   413c
Everglades National Park,
   451c
Grand Prismatic Spring,
   504c
Half Dome, 80c
Kalaupapa Nat. Historical
   Park, 245c
Kilauea, 300, 308c, 313c,
   315c
Lake Powell, 258c,
   268c
Lake Woodruff Nat.
   Wildlife Refuge, 196c
Lower Calf Creek,
   470c
Mauna Ulu, 315c

Monument Valley, 12c,
   340c, 346c, 350c,
   361c
Moosehead Lake, 264c
Mt. Rainier, 78c
Mt. St. Helens, 300c
Olympic Nat. Park,
   78c
Palouse Hills, 422c
Pitchstone Plateau,
   419c
Redwood Natural Park,
   194c
Saguaro National Park,
   438c
San Francisco Bay,
   488c
Sea Islands, 446c
Shiprock, 346c
South Rim, 350c
Umpqua River, 488c
Waialeale, Kauai,
   245c
Waipio Bay 137c
Wrangell-St. Elias
   National Park, 73c
Yavapai Point, 242c
Yellowstone National
   Park, 11c, 20c
Yellowstone River,
   241c
Yosemite National Park,
   80c
Zabriskie Point, 163c

**VENEZUELA**
Angel Falls, 212c
Orinoco River, 245c

**ZIMBABWE**
Victoria Falls, 229

# PHOTO CREDITS

# PHOTO CREDITS

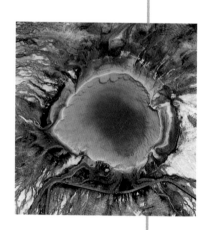

● Wyoming (USA) - Grand Prismatic Spring, Yellowstone National Park.

*Cover* ● Antonio Attini/Archivio White Star

*Back cover* ● Antonio Attini/Archivio White Star